MW01014085

War in International Thought

As scholars and citizens, we are predisposed to think of war as a profoundly destructive activity that ideally should be abolished altogether. Yet before the twentieth century, war was widely understood as a productive force in human affairs that should be harnessed for the purposes of creating peace and order. Analyzing how the concept of war has been used in different contexts from the seventeenth to the late nineteenth century, Jens Bartelson addresses this transition by inquiring into the underlying and often unspoken assumptions about the nature of war, and how these have shaped our understanding of the modern political world and the role of war within it. He explores its functions in the process of state making and in the creation of the modern international system to bring the argument up to date to the present day, where war is now on the center stage of world politics.

JENS BARTELSON is Professor of Political Science at Lund University. He is the author of *Visions of World Community* (Cambridge, 2009), *The Critique of the State* (Cambridge, 2001), *A Genealogy of Sovereignty* (Cambridge, 1995), as well as of articles in leading journals in international relations, international law, political theory, and sociology.

War in International Thought

JENS BARTELSON
Lund University, Sweden

CAMBRIDGE
UNIVERSITY PRESS

CAMBRIDGE
UNIVERSITY PRESS

University Printing House, Cambridge CB2 8BS, United Kingdom

One Liberty Plaza, 20th Floor, New York, NY 10006, USA

477 Williamstown Road, Port Melbourne, VIC 3207, Australia

314–321, 3rd Floor, Plot 3, Splendor Forum, Jasola District Centre, New Delhi – 110025, India

79 Anson Road, #06–04/06, Singapore 079906

Cambridge University Press is part of the University of Cambridge.

It furthers the University's mission by disseminating knowledge in the pursuit of education, learning, and research at the highest international levels of excellence.

www.cambridge.org
Information on this title: www.cambridge.org/9781108419352
DOI: 10.1017/9781108297707

© Jens Bartelson 2018

This publication is in copyright. Subject to statutory exception and to the provisions of relevant collective licensing agreements no reproduction of any part may take place without the written permission of Cambridge University Press.

First published 2018

Printed in the United Kingdom by Clays, St Ives plc

A catalogue record for this publication is available from the British Library.

ISBN 978-1-108-41935-2 Hardback
ISBN 978-1-108-41049-6 Paperback

Cambridge University Press has no responsibility for the persistence or accuracy of URLs for external or third-party Internet websites referred to in this publication and does not guarantee that any content on such websites is, or will remain, accurate or appropriate.

To Caspian

Contents

Preface and Acknowledgments

I am certainly not the first to write a book on war in international thought. Yet most of what has been written that tries to capture the meaning of war remains forgetful of the fact that war also is that which makes the modern world meaningful by virtue of having been consistently invoked in its making. Hence this book tries not only to make sense of war in international thought but also to explore the role of war in the shaping of that very body of thought from the early modern period onward.

The topic of war has a curious propensity to generate cognitive arousal even among pacifists, something that I discovered during the many conversations I had with colleagues and friends in the process of writing this book. This process started and ended at the Swedish Defence University, where Jan Willem Honig graciously commented on a draft chapter many years ago. Several years later, I returned to the same place with a more finished product that Kjell Engelbrekt and Jan Ångström then dissected with great acumen. In the meantime, Judith Butler and Wendy Brown had invited me to a seminar at Berkeley, an immensely rewarding experience that provided me with fresh feedback during a critical phase of writing. Something similar happened later in Cambridge, where Duncan Bell and Ayşe Zarakol had invited me for a talk. The response I received was intellectually overwhelming and compelled me to rethink parts of the argument in light of sharp interventions by John Dunn and many others. Another great source of positive influence has been my colleagues within the research program Time, Memory, and Representation. Generously funded by the Bank of Sweden Tercentenary Foundation and gracefully led by my friend Hans Ruin, this program gathered together some of the brightest scholars in the humanities in Sweden for a period of six years. I am very grateful for the funding received and for the constructive engagement of the participants with my work during these years. Many colleagues in Lund and elsewhere have also provided inspiration and helpful suggestions over the years either by reading parts of the book or by responding to oral presentations: Matilda Arvidsson, Andreas Behnke, Chris Bickerton, Leila Brännström, Agustín Goenaga, Markus Gunneflo, Alexander von Hagen-Jamar, Peter Haldén, Martin Hall, Caroline Jonsäter, Sara Kalm, Oliver Kessler, Johannes Lindvall, Debbie Lisle, Tom Lundborg, Gregor Noll, Mikkel Vedby Rasmussen, Nisha Shah, Jayne Svennungsson, Jan Teorell, Sven Tägil, Rob Walker, Pål Wrange, Dan Öberg, and Eva Österberg have all made thoughtful contributions to my work. Still other colleagues went far beyond the call of duty. Nick Onuf read most chapters with his usual enthusiasm and provided me with invaluable suggestions for improvement. Casper Sylvest read the entire manuscript with great attention to the many missing parts of the story. In the end, Pia Lonnakko was kind enough to compile a bibliography out of what had become a heap of disorganized notes. I am also grateful to my wife, Mia, who for several years patiently suffered the consequences of having a husband obsessed with war. My deepest gratitude goes to John Haslam at Cambridge University Press for his unwavering support of my work for more than twenty years. Lastly, I am grateful to Oxford University Press for granting me permission to republish parts of Chapters 1, 2, and 3 that were published in "Blasts from the Past: War and Fracture in the International System," *International Political Sociology* 10, No. 4 (2016): 252–368.

1 | *Toward a Historical Ontology of War*

Introduction

This is a book about the meaning of war in international thought from the early seventeenth to the late nineteenth century. Such a topic lends itself to many approaches, with many possible results. One rather conventional way to approach this topic would be to investigate how the concept of war has been used by different authors in different historical contexts and for what kinds of ideological and political purposes. From such an inquiry we would hopefully be able to make inferences about the changing functions of the concept of war across time and space and from these perhaps distill more general insights about the meaning of war in international thought.

My approach is different, however. Instead of inquiring into how the concept of war has been used by different authors across multiple historical contexts, this book inquires into how the underlying and unspoken assumptions about the nature of war have shaped our understanding of the modern political world and the role of war within it. As such, this book is not so much a conceptual history of war as it is an analysis of the historical ontology of war – of the world that war made. Although conceptual history and historical ontology reflect a similar ambition to better understand the present in terms of the past, they raise different questions and focus on different objects of inquiry. Whereas a conceptual history of war would remain content to describe how different authors have used the concept of war in different contexts to accomplish different things, a historical ontology of war cuts deeper than that by focusing on what different conceptions of war have *presupposed* in order to be used by interlocutors in a meaningful and coherent way, as well as on what the usages of this concept in turn have done to the range of phenomena it purports to describe and render meaningful.[1] This book tries to uncover these presuppositions, how they have shaped the meaning of war in international thought, as well as how those meanings in turn have shaped the way we understand the nature of war.

But is the concept of war really amenable to historical inquiry at all? Judging from the ways in which war is understood in the social sciences today, the answer seems to be no. To many philosophers and political scientists, war itself is a timeless and immutable category, albeit one with a great variety of instantiations. As Coker has recently argued, "we tend to believe that, unlike the character of war which is indefinable because it is always changing, the nature of war can be defined because it does not ... war has a nature which is eternal but which at the same time takes a finite form." From this it would follow that "the nature of war is not transformed through history, its nature is made manifest in time, but time does not substantially affect the eternal; the character of war is the actualization of its nature."[2] Since the quest for the essence of war has been going on at least since Clausewitz, the denial of its historicity is quite common among modern scholars of military thought and strategy. For example, as Gat has stated, "[W]hile the forms of war may change with time, its spirit, or essence, remains unchanged."[3] As we shall notice later in this chapter, among those who have studied the causes of war, their practices of definition point in a similar direction. Even though the precise definition of this concept has been and still is much contested – such as the nature of the belligerents and the number of causalities required for any given outburst of violence to qualify as war proper – there is a general agreement to the effect that at least *some* definition is necessary for all further

---

[1] For this contrast, compare Ian Hacking, *Historical Ontology* (Cambridge, MA: Harvard University Press, 2002), 1–26; Reinhart Koselleck, *Futures Past: On the Semantics of Historical Time* (Cambridge, MA: MIT Press, 1985); Reinhart Koselleck, *The Practice of Conceptual History: Timing History, Spacing Concepts* (Redwood City, CA: Stanford University Press, 2002).

[2] Christopher Coker, *Barbarous Philosophers: Reflections on the Nature of War from Heraclitus to Heisenberg* (New York: Columbia University Press, 2010), 12–13.

[3] Azar Gat, *Military Thought in the Nineteenth Century* (Oxford: Oxford University Press. 1992), 67. For the quest for the essence of war, see Beatrice Heuser, *The Evolution of Strategy: Thinking War from Antiquity to the Present* (Cambridge: Cambridge University Press, 2010), 100ff.

theoretical and empirical inquiry into the phenomenon of war and its causes.

On this view, studying the historical ontology of war would be a rather pointless exercise because such an inquiry would only lead us back to and affirm those meanings that were at its starting point. We can certainly write histories of war and warfare, but only by virtue of the fact that the concept of war is unchanging enough to allow such histories to be written in the first place and distinguished from histories of other things in the second. This points to an important fact that I will elaborate on in the Chapter 2. One reason why war seems to lack a history of its own is the fact that it has been allowed to structure historical narratives of the emergence and consolidation of the modern state and the international system; war seems to lack a history of its own simply because it has long been a condition of possible history, especially when it comes to telling stories of how individual states once emerged out of a dark past of civil or international strife.

Yet I suspect that there is another and more important reason why the historicity of war has been downplayed or denied by so much modern scholarship. To say that the meaning of war is historically contingent could be taken to imply that war is a social construct, and to say that war is a social construct could by some be taken to imply that the human suffering it brings is somehow less real. Yet I think these objections rest on a misunderstanding of the upshot of conceptual history in general and perhaps that of historical ontology in particular. A historical inquiry into the ontological presuppositions of war does not imply that human experiences of war are unreal: rather, it is a matter of showing how these experiences became real in the first place and how some of these presuppositions still condition experiences and expectations of war in the present day. It is a matter of bringing war back within the scope of human volition and responsibility.[4]

Although many other political concepts have been subjected to detailed historical analysis during the past decades, war has not yet received much systematic treatment by historians of political thought,

---

[4] For suggestions in this direction, see Jan-Werner Müller, "On Conceptual History," in Darrin M. McMahon and Samuel Moyn (eds.), *Rethinking Modern European Intellectual History* (Oxford: Oxford University Press, 2014), 74–93.

and the few exceptions in this regard still leave much to be desired in terms of their empirical scope. While an otherwise impressive article in *Geschichtliche Grundbegriffe* deals with the history of this concept within a German-speaking context only, a recent book by Armitage focuses exclusively on the concept of civil war and how civil wars have shaped historical and political experience from Roman to modern times.[5] By contrast, this book takes the notion of international war as the starting point of inquiry and then traces its genealogy backward in time across a series of historical contexts and intellectual fields over roughly three centuries. By focusing on international rather than civil war, this book aims to explain how the modern concept of international war came into being, how war came to be understood as a contest between two or more identifiable actors of which sovereign states became the paradigmatic case, and how recent and profound challenges to this conception of international war have contributed to changes in the ways in which wars are waged in the contemporary world.

Yet the fact that the concept of international war has not received any systematic treatment by historians of political thought does not mean that there is no scholarship of potential value to such inquiry, once we come to terms with some of its presentist tendencies. For example, and as noted earlier, while historians of military thought have contributed immensely to the historical understanding of war, many of them have assumed that war has some kind of timeless meaning or essence and have thereby failed to note the many changes that the concept of war in fact has undergone in the wider context of political and legal thought.[6] And although recent efforts to align the traditional concerns of military history with those of the cultural turn in the human sciences have produced fresh and valuable insights into the specific contexts in which ways of thinking about war have evolved, it has not made any direct contribution to a conceptual history of war, let alone to its

---

[5] Wilhelm Janssen, "Krieg," in *Geschichtliche Grundbegriffe: Historisches Lexikon zur politisch-sozialen Sprache in Deutschland*, vol. III (Stuttgart: Klett-Cotta, 1982): 567–615; David Armitage, *Civil Wars: A History in Ideas* (New York: Knopf, 2017).

[6] See, for example, Azar Gat, *A History of Military Thought: From the Enlightenment to the Cold War* (Oxford: Oxford University Press, 2001); Azar Gat, *War in Human Civilization* (Oxford: Oxford University Press, 2006); Heuser, *Evolution of Strategy*, passim.

historical ontology.[7] Furthermore, although the changing legal and moral justifications of war have attracted much attention from historians of political thought, even otherwise historically sensitive accounts of the rights of war and peace seem to assume that the meaning of war has remained relatively stable over time and across different contexts, perhaps in order to facilitate comparison between different authors from different traditions.[8] Finally, while recent efforts have been made by sociologists to study the role of war in social thought from the early modern period onward, their account is primarily geared toward understanding its role in modern social theory rather than with the meanings and functions attributed to war within international thought.[9]

In this book, I try to amend this situation by inquiring into the changes that the understanding of war has undergone from the early seventeenth to the late nineteenth century. This focus is motivated by my conviction that this period marks a series of important changes in the understanding of war, changes that have profoundly influenced our view of the modern state and the role of war in the modern international system. Yet the story I will tell is slightly at odds with two views widespread among historians of international law. According the first of these, the history of international war is a history of how warfare among European states gradually became subjected to legal restraints from the early modern period onward. As Schmitt famously argued, the decisive step from medieval to modern international law lies in the separation of questions of just cause grounded in moral arguments from the idea of the legal equality of belligerents.[10] This paved the way for the subsequent creation of a legal framework that effectively limited the use of force among European states. In a similar vein, Neff has described how the meaning of war changed from the Middle Ages to the early modern period. Although consistently used to refer to conflict

---

[7] Jeremy Black, *War and the Cultural Turn* (Cambridge: Polity Press, 2012), esp. 1–43.

[8] See, for example, Richard Tuck, *Rights of War and Peace: Political Thought and International Order from Grotius to Kant* (Oxford: Oxford University Press, 1999).

[9] Hans Joas and Wolfgang Knöbl, *War in Social Thought: Hobbes to the Present* (Princeton, NJ: Princeton University Press, 2013).

[10] Carl Schmitt, *The Nomos of the Earth in the International Law of the Jus Publicum Europaeum* (New York: Telos Press, 2006), 110.

between distinct political communities rather than between domestic authorities and their internal opponents, war has mainly been conceived as an instrument of justice in the Western legal tradition. In his account, war as means of law enforcement was eventually replaced by an understanding of war as a contest between sovereign equals, which was then opened to regulation through a gradual codification of the principles of balance of power in international law from the seventeenth century onward.[11]

Second, it has been maintained that these restraints on war were made possible by a European expansion and the appropriation of land on other continents. Beyond the lines of demarcation that separated the European system from the rest of the world, no such legal restraints were considered valid or applicable. As Schmitt argued, beyond these lines was a zone "in which, for want of any legal limits to war, only the law of the stronger applied ... this freedom meant that the line set aside an area where force could be used freely and ruthlessly ... everything that occurred beyond the line remained outside the legal, moral and political values recognized on this side of the line."[12] As he went on to explain, "the designation of a zone of ruthless conflict was a logical consequence of the fact that there was neither a recognized principle nor a common arbitrational authority to govern the division and allocation of lands." But, simultaneously, "a rationalization, humanization, and legalization – a bracketing – of war was achieved against this background of global lines."[13] Hence the increased regulation of warfare between European states during the early modern period was premised on the unleashing of unprecedented violence against non-European peoples and a much less restrictive use of force between imperial powers competing for territory on foreign shores. Somewhat curiously, similar views are today common among postcolonial theorists of international law, who argue that the outward projection of violence was justified with reference to ideologies that

---

[11] Stephen C. Neff, *War and the Law of Nations: A General History* (Cambridge: Cambridge University Press, 2005); Stephen C. Neff, *Justice among Nations* (Cambridge, MA: Harvard University Press, 2014), 148–78.

[12] Carl Schmitt, *The Nomos of The Earth*, 93–4. For an interesting commentary, see Martti Koskenniemi, "International Law as Political Theology: How to Read *Nomos der Erde?*," *Constellations* 11 (2004): 492–511.

[13] Schmitt, *The Nomos of the Earth*, 100.

assumed non-European peoples to be stuck in an uncivilized and stateless condition, therefore being fair game for conquest and colonization by European powers.[14] Although the rise and spread of such ideologies have received considerable attention by historians during the past decades, this has not led to any sustained attempt to study the functions of war and violence in creating and upholding the distinction between civilized and uncivilized peoples that lies at the heart of these ideologies.[15]

In this book, I shall contest the above-mentioned views on both historical and philosophical grounds. First, as I will maintain, there was never any clean break between war as punishment of evildoers or law enforcement, on the one hand, and war as an armed contest between moral and legal equals, on the other. In fact, the idea that war was a way of punishing wrongdoers and enforcing the law remained important precisely in order to produce the kind of legal equality between states that since then has become a foundational assumption of modern international law. The integrity and cohesion of the nascent international system in Europe required its internal enemies to be punished or even eliminated, and this, in turn, motivated recourse to forms of violence that were ruled out in the intercourse between sovereigns. Yet, simultaneously, the notion of war as law enforcement presupposes that there already is an

---

[14] See, for example, Antony Anghie, *Imperialism, Sovereignty and the Making of International Law* (Cambridge: Cambridge University Press, 2007); Brett Bowden, "The Colonial Origins of International Law: European Expansion and the Classical Standard of Civilization," *Journal of the History of International Law* 7, no. 1 (2005): 1–23; Edward Keene, *Beyond the Anarchical Society, Grotius, Colonialism, and Order in World Politics* (Cambridge: Cambridge University Press, 2002); Anne Orford, *International Law and Its Others* (Cambridge: Cambridge University Press, 2006).

[15] See, for example, Anthony Pagden, *Lords of All the World: Ideologies of Empire in Spain, Britain and France c. 1500–c. 1850* (New Haven: Yale University Press; 1995); Uday Singh Mehta, *Liberalism and Empire: A Study in Nineteenth-Century British Liberal Thought* (Chicago: University of Chicago Press, 1999); David Armitage, *The Ideological Origins of the British Empire* (Cambridge: Cambridge University Press, 2002); Jennifer Pitts, *A Turn to Empire: The Rise of Imperial Liberalism in Britain and France* (Princeton, NJ: Princeton University Press, 2005); Duncan Bell (ed.), *Victorian Visions of Global Order: Empire and International Relations in Nineteenth-Century Political Thought* (Cambridge: Cambridge University Press, 2007). For an excellent overview, see Duncan S. A. Bell, "Empire and International Relations in Victorian Political Thought," *The History Journal* 49 (2006): 281–98.

established jurisdiction within which law enforcement is possible and thus that there has been a successful claim to a political authority of a corresponding scope. As I intend to show, for much of the early modern period, irregular warfare was the preferred means of carving such jurisdictions out and backing such authority claims up.

Second, although wars waged against non-European peoples were often justified on grounds different from those waged among European states – such as ideas of a Christian empire – they were not legitimized with reference to ideologies premised on the superiority of the Europeans, or at least not initially. Rather, it seems to have been the other way around. The dissemination of ideas of natural hostility and enmity coincided in time with the proliferation of cultural prejudices inside Europe, which were often convenient pretexts for waging war among European states. Assumptions of natural hostility and enmity had been first introduced in order to legitimize secular political authority in Europe and only later were projected onto non-European peoples, and then only after many of them had been conquered and subjected to colonial rule. The main source of the many prejudices at play in this process of political exorcism was rather the dark past of barbarism that had been invented to legitimize the transition from a stateless past to what in the minds of Protestant elites now was in the process of becoming secular states. It was not until the late nineteenth century that these undesirable traits were projected outward to justify the indiscriminate use of force against non-European peoples, a process greatly facilitated by the uptake of doctrines of evolution and natural selection across different intellectual fields. Yet all the preceding raises the more basic question of how such assumptions of natural hostility found their way into the foundations of early modern political thought in the first place. As we shall see, answering this question compels us to revisit views of war that have long been marginalized or even forgotten by students of international thought.

My main reason for undertaking this inquiry into the historical ontology of war is the intellectual confusion that surrounds this concept in the present day. Much of this confusion is the result of recent debates about the changing role of war in a globalized world. The first of these debates started almost immediately after the end of the Cold War, when some authors optimistically predicted the declining relevance of international war as an instrument of state policy and started to focus on those low-intensity conflicts in the Third World that appeared to bring many already fragile states to the brink of collapse.[16] As Hassner remarked, although still possible, international war "has already lost its justification, or its meaning, and it may become less and less frequent and less and less central for political life."[17] Since the study of international relations had long been preoccupied with international war and its many causes, the declining incidence of international wars brought a shift in focus to the proliferation of domestic conflicts that soon followed.[18] Since then, it has become common to study violent conflicts without presupposing the existence of a specific kind of actor or any definite level of hostilities between them because both of these requirements are deemed contingent on the context at hand rather than on stipulative definitions.[19] Consequently, many scholars agreed that the modern concept of war has lost much of its analytical purchase in a world in which sovereign states no longer are the main belligerents and in which the distinction between international and domestic conflicts has ceased to make much empirical sense. And what had ceased to make empirical sense had already ceased to make legal sense. As Greenwood had pointed out, "it is doubtful ... whether it is still meaningful to talk of war [as] a legal concept or institution at all. If no direct legal consequences flow from the creation of a state of war, the state of war

[16] John Mueller, *Retreat from Doomsday: The Obsolescence of Major War* (New York: Basic Books, 1990); Martin Van Creveld, *Transformation of War* (New York: Free Press, 1991).

[17] Pierre Hassner, "Beyond the Three Traditions: The Philosophy of War and Peace in Historical Perspective," *International Affairs* 70, no. 4 (1994): 737–56, at 754.

[18] See, among others, Kalevi J. Holsti, *The State, War, and the State of War* (Cambridge: Cambridge University Press, 1996); James D. Fearon, and David D. Laitin, "Ethnicity, Insurgency, and Civil War," *American Political Science Review* 97, no. 1 (2003): 75–90.

[19] See, among others, Mary Kaldor, *New and Old Wars: Organized Violence in a Global Era* (Oxford: Polity, 1999); Christopher Coker, *The Future of War: The Re-enchantment of War in the Twenty-First Century* (Oxford: Blackwell, 2004); Mikkel Vedby Rasmussen, *Risk Society at War* (Cambridge: Cambridge University Press, 2006). For a critique of the newness of "new" forms of war, see Stathis Kalyvas, "New and Old Civil Wars," *World Politics* 54, no. 1 (2001): 99–118.

has become an empty shell which international law has already discarded in all but name."[20] Responding to this predicament, students of armed conflict faced a hard choice between stretching the meaning of the modern concept of war to fit new circumstances or to abandon this concept altogether in favor of concepts that carry fewer commitments as to the identity of the belligerents and the level of hostilities required for any outburst of violence to qualify as war proper. Yet, as a result of the blurring of the distinction between international and civil wars, the once seemingly solid distinction between peace and war also began to crumble. From having referred to two states of affairs incapable of coexisting within the same portion of time and space, war and peace now occupy extreme points of a continuum with many shades of gray in between.[21]

Hence those distinctions that made the concept of war analytically useful have been blurred, if not altogether dissolved, by contemporary efforts to come to terms with changing practices of warfare, making analysts opt for concepts such as "violent conflict" in the hope of avoiding the ambiguities and theoretical difficulties that ensue when the meaning of war is stretched too far. But quite regardless of our choice of terminology, the same underlying problem will reappear in new guises because understanding violent conflict presupposes some prior account of the belligerents and their identity. Since even the most minimalistic definition of war or violent conflict presupposes that it takes at least two to tango, this requires that the belligerents are identifiable if not to the analyst, so at least to each other. And such identification of belligerents presupposes that they are distinct and bounded and that there is some determinate locus of political authority that can account for their inner cohesion and capacity to act. But if such a locus cannot be pinpointed with sufficient precision, then the actors involved cannot be properly identified either. And if actors cannot be properly identified, it is hard to make sense of any outburst of violence between them in conventional terms because there is no one there to

---

[20] Christopher Greenwood, "The Concept of War in Modern International Law," *International and Comparative Law Quarterly* 36, no. 2 (1987): 283–306, at 305.

[21] For a sophisticated statement of this view, see Jairus Victor Grove, "Becoming War: Ecology, Ethics, and the Globalization of Violence," Ph.D. dissertation, Johns Hopkins University, Baltimore, 2011.

whom we can attribute motives, causal powers, or moral responsibility. Hence, in the absence of a determinate locus of political authority and firm boundaries between belligerent entities, not only does the distinction between international and civil war collapse, but so does our ability to explain the incidence of war with reference to the interests and identities of actors.[22] Since the distinction between war and peace is contingent on the presence of political authority within actors and the existence of boundaries between them, this distinction becomes equally difficult to uphold whenever these requirements are not fulfilled.[23]

What goes for the terms of explanation goes for the terms of justification. The next debate was less concerned with ontological issues and more with legal and moral justifications of war and their ideological implications. Many of the wars that have been waged during the last decades have been justified with reference to the threats to the international system posed by failed states and terrorist groups, which made the former legitimate targets of military interventions and the latter fair game for exceptional measures and the extralegal use of force.[24] But in order for us to be able to pass moral or legal judgments on the use of force, some things must be known in advance and taken for granted. As Butler has pointed out, however contingent their form and content, definitions of war are never innocent semantic exercises. From definitions of war follow normative principles, and from those principles follow rules that make it possible to promote or restrict the violent

---

[22] See Stathis Kalyvas, "The Ontology of 'Political Violence': Action and Identity in Civil Wars," *Perspectives on Politics* 1, no. 3 (2003): 475–94.

[23] See Jens Bartelson, "Double Binds: Sovereignty and the Just War Tradition," in Hent Kalmo and Quentin Skinner (eds.), *Sovereignty in Fragments: The Past, Present, and Future of a Contested Concept* (Cambridge: Cambridge University Press, 2010), 81–95.

[24] Ayşe Zarakol, "What Makes Terrorism Modern? Terrorism, Legitimacy, and the International System," *Review of International Studies* 37, no. 5 (2011): 2311–36; Frédéric Mégret, "From 'Savages' to 'Unlawful Combatants': A Postcolonial Look at International Humanitarian Law's Other," in Anne Orford (ed.), *International Law and Its Others* (Cambridge: Cambridge University Press, 2006), 265–317; Oliver Kessler and Wouter G. Werner, "Extrajudicial Killing as Risk Management," *Security Dialogue* 39, nos. 2–3 (2008): 289–308; Wouter G. Werner, "From Justus Hostis to Rogue State: The Concept of the Enemy in International Legal Thinking," *International Journal for the Semiotics of Law* 17, no. 2 (2004): 155–68.

practices thus defined: our moral and legal responses to war are always already conditioned by practices of definition and classification.[25] From the debate that ensued, it seems clear that some of the new ways of conceptualizing violent conflict that had evolved after the end of the Cold War actually went some way toward justifying global or imperial wars simply by nullifying many of the restrictions that were coeval with the modern distinction between civil and international wars. And since these wars were justified with reference to universal values and rights, they either implied claims to boundless political authority or presupposed the imminent possibility of a community of all humankind.[26]

Taken together, these contemporary reconceptualizations of war have brought a change away from the modern notion of war as a contest between moral and legal equals back to signifying a contest of unequal parties that by definition cannot be just on both sides. This could be taken to indicate that the modern meaning of the concept of war has been dissolved in favor of a swift return to older conceptions of war as law enforcement or as the punishment of evildoers.[27] In a dystopian version of this argument, even the element of law enforcement and punishment is gone from contemporary warfare. What we are facing is nothing but a return to premodern and primitive forms of warfare between actors of different kinds, unhampered by any moral or legal constraints.[28]

[25] Judith Butler, *Frames of War: When Is Life Grievable?* (London: Verso, 2009), 1–32. Also Etienne Balibar, "What's in a War? (Politics as War, War as Politics)," *Ratio Juris* 21, no. 3 (2008): 365–86.

[26] See, for example, Michael Hardt and Antonio Negri, *Multitude: War and Democracy in the End of Empire* (New York: Penguin, 2004); Rens Van Munster, "The War on Terrorism: When the Exception Becomes the Rule," *International Journal for the Semiotics of Law* 17, no. 2 (2004): 141–53; Hauke Brunkhorst, "The Right to War: Hegemonic Geopolitics or Civic Constitutionalism?," *Constellations* 11, no. 4 (2004): 512–26; Vivienne Jabri, "War, Security and the Liberal State," *Security Dialogue* 37, no. 1 (2006): 47–64.

[27] Carl Schmitt, "The Turn to the Discriminating Concept of War" [1937], in Carl Schmitt (ed.), *Writings on War*, trans. Timothy Nunan (Cambridge: Polity Press, 2011), 30–74.

[28] Loretta Napoleoni, *The Islamist Phoenix* (New York: Seven Stories Press, 2014).

Ontogenetic War

Reflecting the traumatic experiences of two world wars, we have become accustomed to thinking of war as profoundly destructive of political order and therefore morally undesirable. From this conviction has followed a long and arduous search for the causes of war in the hope of preventing future wars. As Andrew Carnegie stated in his letter to the trustees of what was to become the Carnegie Endowment for International Peace, the purpose was "to hasten the abolition of international war, the foulest blot upon our civilization. Although we no longer eat our fellowmen, nor torture prisoners, nor sack cities killing their inhabitants, we still kill each other in war like barbarians."[29] The horrors of the First World War seemed to confirm this view and contributed greatly to push the public attitude toward war in a more pacifist direction. War became seen as something to be abolished, avoided, or at least limited in the interest of minimizing human suffering.[30] Even if the impact of interwar idealism may have been exaggerated by historians of international relations, it seems clear that the first efforts to establish international relations as an autonomous scholarly field were guided by a widespread desire to abolish war.[31] Alfred Zimmern, who became the first professor of international relations in 1919, advocated the creation of a global commonwealth of nations to this end. War will be preventable only "when the world has a common will, and has created a common government to express and enforce that will."[32] Similar sensibilities animated the study of international relations in the United States, which to a

[29] Andrew Carnegie, "Letter to the Trustees," December 14, 1910, spelling modified. For the context in which this letter was written, see David S. Patterson, "Andrew Carnegie's Quest for World Peace," *Proceedings of the American Philosophical Society* (1970): 371–83.

[30] See, for example, John Mueller, "Changing Attitudes towards War: The Impact of the First World War," *British Journal of Political Science* 21, no. 1 (1991): 1–28.

[31] See Lucian M. Ashworth, "Where Are the Idealists in Interwar International Relations?," *Review of International Studies* 32, no. 2 (2006): 291–308; Casper Sylvest, "Interwar Internationalism, the British Labour Party, and the Historiography of International Relations," *International Studies Quarterly* 48, no. 2 (2004): 409–32; Andreas Osiander, "Rereading Early Twentieth-Century IR Theory: Idealism Revisited," *International Studies Quarterly* 42, no. 3 (1998): 409–32.

[32] See Alfred Zimmern, "German Culture and the British Commonwealth," in *Nationality and Government with Other War-Time Essays* (London: Chatto & Windus, 1918), 1–31, at 22. For a critical analysis of his ideas, see Jeanne

large extent was devoted to understanding the causes of war with the aim
of minimizing the likelihood of future war.[33] This ambition was certainly
not confined to liberal idealists. As Morgenthau stated in his *Politics
among Nations* (1948), "the abolition of war is obviously the fundamental problem confronting international thought."[34] The invention and use
of nuclear weapons had further reinforced the awareness of the destructive character of war to the point of institutionalizing that awareness in
the doctrine of nuclear deterrence after the Second World War. As
Brodie then argued, "[t]hus far, the chief purpose of our military
establishment has been to win wars. From now on its chief purpose
must be to avert them. It can have almost no other useful purpose."[35]
And as he added a few years later, "[o]ur problem is now to develop
the habit of living with the atomic bomb, and the very incomprehen-
sibility of the potential catastrophe inherent in it may well make that
task easier."[36] Living with the prospect of nuclear disaster indeed
changed the meaning of life itself. As Morgenthau later was to
remark, "[t]he significance of the possibility of nuclear death is that
it radically affects the meaning of death, of immortality, of life itself
... [i]t destroys the meaning of immortality by making both society
and history impossible. It destroys the meaning of life by throwing
life back upon itself."[37] Thus the atomic age made nuclear deterrence
the great equalizer of nations and the great stabilizer of the international system. Since then, very few people have been prepared to
argue that war is morally desirable, and even fewer are likely to
celebrate the virtues of war in fostering individual character or patriotic

      Morefield, *Covenants without Swords: Liberal Idealism and the Spirit of
      Empire* (Princeton, NJ: Princeton University Press, 2005).
[33]   See, for example, Brian C. Schmidt, *The Political Discourse of Anarchy: A
      Disciplinary History of International Relations* (Albany, NY: SUNY Press,
      1998), 157–65; Brian C. Schmidt, "On the History and Historiography of
      International Relations," in Walter Calsnaes, Thomas Risse, and Beth Simmons
      (eds.), *Handbook of International Relations* (London: SAGE, 2002), 3–22.
[34]   Hans J. Morgenthau, *Politics among Nations: The Struggle for Power and Peace*
      (New York: Knopf, 1985), 47.
[35]   Bernard Brodie (ed.), *The Absolute Weapon: Atomic Power and World Order*
      (New York: Harcourt, 1946), 76; see also Bernard Brodie, "The Development of
      Nuclear Strategy," *International Security* 2 no. 4 (1978): 65–83.
[36]   Bernard Brodie, "The Atom Bomb as Policy Maker," *Bulletin of the Atomic
      Scientists* 4, no. 12 (1948): 277–383, at 383.
[37]   Hans J. Morgenthau, "Public Affairs: Death in the Nuclear Age," *Commentary*
      32, no. 3 (1961): 233.

sentiment. Since there is a broad agreement to the effect that war is destructive of human life and therefore morally undesirable, the only remaining task of an ethics of war is to specify under what conditions the use of force nevertheless might be permissible for the purpose of self-defense or to avert greater evils such as genocide or existential threats to humankind as a whole.[38]

But, as Michael Howard has argued, before the Enlightenment and its invention of peace and progress, war "was recognized as an intrinsic part of the social and political order."[39] The increased awareness of the destructiveness of war has sometimes been portrayed as an escape from an old world in which war was a natural part of the human condition into a new world in which war is at least in principle within human control thanks to the advancement of the social sciences in general and academic international relations in particular.[40] But this widespread belief in the destructiveness of war has been allowed to overshadow the existence of another way of viewing war that may help us understand why war came to be seen as a natural part of the human condition in the first place. This is the belief that war is a productive force in human affairs that ought to be harnessed for the right political purposes, such as the creation of order and peace. This belief and its performative consequences constitute the main focus of the coming chapters of this book. Yet the almost exclusive focus on this view of war should not be taken to imply that this view is exhaustive or even representative of the many ideas about war that we find in the history of international thought. The great variety and richness of the tradition of reflecting on war in international thought cannot be neatly subsumed under a

---

[38] See, for example, Michael Walzer, *Just and Unjust Wars: A Moral Argument with Historical Illustrations* (New York: Basic Books, 1977); Michael Howard (ed.), *Restraints on War: Studies in the Limitation of Armed Conflict* (Oxford: Oxford University Press, 1979); Larry May (ed.), *War: Essays in Political Philosophy* (Cambridge: Cambridge University Press, 2008); Jeff McMahan, *Killing in War* (Oxford: Oxford University Press, 2009). For a penetrating critique of such attempts, see Nicholas Rengger, *Just War and International Order: The Uncivil Condition in World Politics* (Cambridge: Cambridge University Press, 2013).

[39] Michael Howard, *The Invention of Peace: Reflections on War and International Order* (New Haven: Yale University Press, 2000), 10.

[40] Stanley Hoffmann, "An American Social Science: International Relations," *Daedalus* 106, no. 3 (1977): 41–60.

single conception of war, however abstractly defined.[41] Instead, my focus on the notion of war as a productive force in human affairs is motivated by its important but neglected role in the shaping of the modern political world and the role of war within this world: for want of a better term, I will henceforth refer to this view of war as ontogenetic war.

On this view, war does not require the identities of the belligerents to be known in advance but instead assumes that the belligerents are beaten into shape in the course of battle. Rather than standing in need of any explanation and justification, war is a mysterious and impersonal force that itself can be invoked to explain and justify political processes and their outcomes. The upshot of ontogenetic war is not that it takes two to tango but that it takes a tango to make two: war does not occur as a result of prior enmity between actors whose identities and interests are given and known but is that which produces identities and interests as well as the patterns of enmity and friendship within which actors become embedded by fighting. Thus understood, war is a primordial force that imposes structure on a world that otherwise would too chaotic to be accessible to understanding and hence also beyond the reach of human intervention. Making war is therefore also making sense: war is not only a means of imposing order onto chaos but also a way of imposing meaning onto an otherwise enigmatic political world. This implies that if war is a mysterious force beyond human control, the best we can hope for is to be able to tame its flames for more noble human ends and thus bestow some meaning on the suffering war invariably brings.

Should we subscribe to the view that the political world is war all they way down, we are likely to accept that politics is a continuation of war with other means rather than the other way around. Thus ontogenetic war implies that war is necessary precursor to the creation of political order but also that war is an important source of change in the political world. Indeed, before any recognizably modern notion of

[41] An ambitious attempt to classify conceptions of war in the Western tradition is Anatol Rapoport, "Introduction," in Carl von Clausewitz, *On War* (Harmondsworth: Penguin, 1984), 11–80. For the long legacy of internationalist thought critical of war, see Francis Harry Hinsley, *Power and the Pursuit of Peace: Theory and Practice in the History of Relations between States* (Cambridge: Cambridge University Press, 1967).

sociopolitical change had emerged – which it arguably did only with the French Revolution – war and other forms of organized violence were consistently invoked to explain major changes and upheavals within as well as between political communities, to the point of being regarded as *the* cause of transformation in the political world. And if we believe that war is the ultimate source of order and change in the political world, we will be inclined to maintain that war is justified in order to create the preconditions of political order whenever there is too much discord and suffering on the ground or whenever the authority necessary to uphold those preconditions is weak or absent.

Since this view of war makes little sense to a modern mind that recognizes no mysterious forces at the origin of things, those in search of philosophical support have often turned to Heraclitus. As he had it, "war [*polemos*] is father of all, king of all, and some he shows as gods while some as human beings, some he makes slaves, others free."[42] Yet many modern commentators have cautioned us not to interpret this fragment too literally.[43] As Heidegger remarked, "the *polemos* named here is a conflict that prevailed prior to everything divine and human, not a war in the human sense."[44] Hence the way in which Heraclitus uses the term *polemos* rather points to a cosmological principle of differentiation "that first caused the realm of being to separate into opposites, it first gave rise to position, order and rank."[45] When seen in the wider context of his cosmology, *polemos* signifies the mechanism through which the world is differentiated into recognizable beings placed in ontological opposition to each other.[46] As Heidegger goes on to explain, "the struggle meant here is the original struggle, for it gives rise to the contenders as such; it is not a mere assault on something already there."[47]

---

[42] Charles H. Kahn, *The Art and Thought of Heraclitus: A New Arrangement and Translation of the Fragments with Literary and Philosophical Commentary* (Cambridge: Cambridge University Press, 1981), fragment B, 53, 67.

[43] See, for example, *ibid.*, 204–10; Geoffrey Stephen Kirk, "Natural Change in Heraclitus," *Mind* 60, no. 237 (1951): 35–42.

[44] Martin Heidegger, "On the Grammar and Etymology of the Word 'Being,'" in *Introduction to Metaphysics*, trans. Ralph Mannheim (New Haven: Yale University Press, 1959), 62.

[45] *Ibid.*

[46] See Claudia Baracchi, "The Πόλεμος that Gathers All: Heraclitus on War," *Research in Phenomenology* 45, no. 2 (2015): 267–87.

[47] Heidegger, "On the Grammar and Etymology of the Word 'Being,'" 62.

Although we hear a distant echo of Heraclitus in Aristotle when he discusses the nature of friendship and enmity, the concept of *polemos* was given a more literal twist by the great historians of antiquity.[48] For instance, although hardly representative of the Greek understanding of war, Thucydides clearly alludes to the productive force of war when he describes the rise of the Hellenic world from what originally was but a disjointed set of communities. The scattered Greek cities "were before the Trojan War prevented by their want of strength and the absence of mutual intercourse from displaying any collective action."[49] And although the Romans recognized highly ritualized constraints on the legitimate use of force – as embodied in the *ius fetiale* – these were gradually overruled in the pursuit of imperial expansion and military glory so that without war, empire would not have been possible, and without empire, war would not have been necessary.[50] Hence, when Polybius recounted the causes of Roman expansion and the sources of imperial greatness, it was obvious to him that this was the result of military conquests and the successful projection of invincibility.[51] As Livy later described the birth of Rome in a similar spirit, "if any nation ought to be allowed to claim a sacred origin and point back to a divine paternity that nation is Rome. For such is her renown in war that when she chooses to represent Mars as her own and her founder's father, the nations of the world accept the statement with the same equanimity with which they accept her dominion."[52] Finally, although such conceptions were conspicuously absent from medieval doctrines of just war when applied to Christian princes, war appears to have been a potent source of

---

[48] Aristotle, *Nicomachean Ethics*, trans. Roger Crisp (Cambridge: Cambridge University Press, 2004), VIII:i.1155b, 144.

[49] Thucydides, *The Peloponnesian War* (London: J. M. Dent, 1910), I.i.

[50] See P. A. Brunt, "Laus Imperii," in P. D. A. Garnsey and C. R. Whittaker (eds.), *Imperialism in the Ancient World* (Cambridge: Cambridge University Press, 1978), 160–92; John Rich and Graham Shipley (eds.), *War and Society in the Roman World* (London: Routledge, 1993).

[51] Polybius, *Histories*, vol. I, trans. W. R. Paton (Cambridge, MA: LOEB Classical Library, 2010). For commentaries on the role of war in the *Histories*, see Donald Walter Baronowski, *Polybius and Roman Imperialism* (London: Bloomsbury, 2013); James Davidson, "The Gaze in Polybius' Histories," *Journal of Roman Studies* 81 (1991): 10–24.

[52] Titus Livy, *History of Rome*, vol. I, trans. Rev. Canon Roberts (New York: E.P. Dutton, 1912), preface, 7–8.

Christian cohesion whenever its fury was directed outward, against the infidel.[53] As Mastnak has argued, although the Crusades may have been born out of a genuine desire for peace, they also served the ultimate purpose of galvanizing Christendom. "[I]n its intentions and mythic self-perception, the crusade was an expression of the Christian unity that it was also creating."[54]

The purpose of this book in not to dig into the ancient foundations or medieval manifestations of this view of war but to tell the story of its revival in early modern Europe and how the outcomes of this revival continued to resonate throughout much of the modern period. This revival came as a consequence of sustained efforts to put political authority on secular foundations after the wars of religion and coincided neatly with the rediscovery of Roman sources from which notions useful to this end could be extracted. So when political authority no longer could be legitimized with reference to a divine will or a preordained cosmic order, Mars was invited back as the royal purveyor of political order, and his lingering presence was to remain crucial to secular statecraft well into the Enlightenment and beyond.[55]

Studying the return of this view makes it possible to freshly assess the transition from war as law enforcement to wars as an armed contest between legal equals. While this was never a clean break, the return of ontogenetic war helps us to understand what really was at stake in this transition. War as law enforcement made sense only as long as there was a law there to enforce, and some claim to jurisdiction and some political authority to back that latter claim up. Without any shared universalistic normative framework to lend prima facie legitimacy to such aspirations, the remaining way to create the preconditions of law enforcement in this sense was by means of prior expansion into what was essentially a legal void. By the same token, war as a contest

---

[53] James Muldoon, *Popes, Lawyers, and Infidels: The Church and the Non-Christian World 1250–1550* (Liverpool: Liverpool University Press, 1979); Julia Costa Lopez, "Beyond Eurocentrism and Orientalism: Revisiting the Othering of Jews and Muslims through Medieval Canon Law," *Review of International Studies* 42, no. 3 (2016): 450–70.

[54] Tomaz Mastnak, *Crusading Peace: Christendom, the Muslim World, and Western Political Order* (Berkeley: University of California Press, 2002), 95.

[55] See Friedrich Meinecke, *Machiavellism: The Doctrine of Raison d'état and Its Place in Modern History*, trans. Douglas Scott (New Haven: Yale University Press 1962); Hans Delbrück, *The Dawn of Modern Warfare*, trans. Walter Renfroe (Lincoln: University of Nebraska Press, 1990).

between legal equals makes sense only on condition that the belligerents in question are identifiable independently of the hostilities between
them, which means that they must be at peace with themselves. In the
absence of any traditional sources of legitimacy left undisturbed by the
Reformation and the wars of religion, the only remaining way to create
domestic order and peace out of the remnants of Christian unity was by
means of war.

The experiences of the two world wars paved the way for a forgetfulness concerning this troublesome part of the European past. Since
ontogenetic war is hard to reconcile with the pacifist self-images and
values of modern liberal and democratic societies, its historical importance in the formative phases of these societies has been conveniently
downplayed, if not forgotten. To cope with its consequences as they
were felt in trenches and concentration camps, its role in the shaping of
the modern world had to be denied. In this particular case, Nietzsche
was right when he insisted that a "poet could say that God has placed
forgetfulness as a doorkeeper on the threshold of the temple of human
dignity."[56] Something similar goes for the reception of this view within
the social sciences. While we all are familiar with the famous dictum
according to which "war made the state, and the state made war," the
fact that similar ideas about the constitutive powers of war indeed
inspired the very process of state making has largely escaped attention.[57] On those relatively rare occasions when this view has attracted
attention, it has been equated with different versions of militarism, but
without subjecting its assumptions or long historical pedigree to any
systematic inquiry.[58] But does this forgetfulness imply that its legacy
has been entirely lost to us? As some students of collective memory like
to maintain, "[n]ations can repress with psychological impunity, their

---

[56] Friedrich Nietzsche, *On the Genealogy of Morality*, trans. Carol Diethe
      (Cambridge: Cambridge University Press, 2006), 124. For accounts of the role
      of memory and forgetting in international politics, see Duncan Bell (ed.),
      *Memory, Trauma and World Politics: Reflections on the Relationship between
      Past and Present* (Basingstoke: Palgrave Macmillan, 2006); Jan-Werner Müller
      (ed.), *Memory and Power in Post-War Europe* (Cambridge: Cambridge
      University Press, 2002).
[57] Charles Tilly, "Reflections on the History of European State-Making," in
      Charles Tilly (ed.), *The Formation of National States in Western Europe*
      (Princeton, NJ: Princeton University Press, 1975), 42.
[58] See, for example, Karma Nabulsi, *Traditions of War: Occupation, Resistance,
      and the Law* (Oxford: Oxford University Press, 1999), 80–127.

collective memories can be changed without a returned of the repressed."[59] By contrast, I would like to argue that we are witnessing the return of the repressed insofar as a fair share of contemporary warfare is legitimized with reference precisely to its ontogenetic capacities. Rather than being contests between legal equals or a way of enforcing the law on the weak by the strong, many wars today are best understood as attempts to impose particularistic visions of political order in spaces and places where such order is deemed absent or weak due to prior conflicts.

Although the concept is largely absent from the study of international relations, Ruggie touches on the notion of ontogenetic war when he argues that during the early modern period, the wars of religion were constitutive wars in the sense that the nature and identity of the belligerents were not present beforehand but rather emerged gradually precisely as the consequence of these wars.[60] Perhaps symptomatically, this notion of war has recently been revived by critical theorists in search of a fresh approach to the study of war. As Jabri has argued, "[e]ven in its most instrumental articulation, therefore, violence has a constitutive manifestation and is hence seen as being formative of the subject."[61] Other critics have more specifically targeted the ontogenetic dimensions of modern liberal warfare. For example, as Dillon has remarked, "war … has been directly instrumental in making the political subjects of states and civil societies alike the very subjects that they are … War forms and transforms governmental institutions and practices as it does political rationalities and civic cultures."[62] In a similar vein, Evans takes the ontogenetic capacities of war as a starting point for a critique of contemporary liberal ways of war: "Liberal wars are intimately bound to the active production of political subjectivities.

---

[59] Claudio Fogu and Wulf Kansteiner, "The Politics of Memory and the Poetics of History," in Richard Ned Lebow, Wulf Kansteiner, and Claudio Fogu (eds.), *The Politics of Memory in Postwar Europe* (Durham, NC: Duke University Press, 2006), 284–310, at 289.

[60] John Gerard Ruggie, "Territoriality and Beyond: Problematizing Modernity in International Relations," *International Organization* 47, no. 1 (1993): 139–74, at 162.

[61] Vivienne Jabri, *War and the Transformation of Global Politics* (Basingstoke: Palgrave Macmillan, 2007), 12.

[62] Michael J. Dillon, "Introduction: From Liberal Conscience to Liberal Rule," in Michael J. Dillon and Julian Reid, *The Liberal Way of War: Killing to Make Life Live* (London: Routledge, 2009), 1–13, at 8–9

Security discourses have always had a particular affinity with political authenticity, which sets out who we are as people and defines what we are to become."[63] Finally, in what appears to be the most succinct statement to date, Barkawi and Brighton have argued that "war is a generative force like no other. It is of fundamental significance for politics, society and culture . . . War, the threat of war and the preparation for war mark the origins, transformation and end of polities."[64] As they go on to elaborate, the "transformative effect, the capacity to rework the reality of social and political existence, is . . . the objective of waging war."[65] To them, the most basic element of war is fighting broadly conceived, which produces consequences far beyond its immediate and contingent manifestations that should be made part of a renewed study of war. In terms of the present manifestations of this view, I think Massumi is right to point out that the current doctrines of preemptive war presupposes that war has the power to transform political reality in profound ways that extend far beyond its immediate effects.[66]

Yet, in contrast to the above-mentioned critics, I do not think that this view of war should be taken at face value and used as a starting point for a critical study of war but that it should be carefully contextualized and historicized with the aim of loosening its grip on our political imagination. Rather than passing moral judgment on ontogenetic war and its many manifestations, I would like to suggest that a historical inquiry into this notion of war should attend to its performative consequences in order to better understand how we got into the present predicament that critical theorists so lament. In my effort to explore the performative consequences of the notion of ontogenetic war, I shall attend to its *looping effects*, a concept that takes some

---

[63] Brad Evans, "The Liberal War Thesis: Introducing the Ten Key Principles of Twenty-First-Century Biopolitical Warfare," *South Atlantic Quarterly* 110, no. 3 (2011): 747–56, at 753.

[64] Tarak Barkawi and Shane Brighton, "Powers of War: Fighting, Knowledge, and Critique," *International Political Sociology* 5, no. 2 (2011): 126–43, at 126. For an interesting comment on the limitations of this view, see Astrid H. M. Nordin and Dan Öberg, "Targeting the Ontology of War: From Clausewitz to Baudrillard," *Millennium: Journal of International Studies* 43, no. 2 (2015): 392–410.

[65] Barkawi and Brighton, "Powers of War," 136.

[66] Brian Massumi, *Ontopower: War, Powers, and the State of Perception* (Durham, NC: Duke University Press, 2015), 1–19.

tweaking to become useful in this context. The idea of looping effects was originally introduced to capture how the grouping together of people on the basis of some of their characteristics affects their self-descriptions and the range of actions they can perform, as well as how they will reconstruct their past and envision their future. When people of a kind start thinking and acting differently as consequence of having been lumped together and labeled in a certain way, this transforms the grounds on which they initially were lumped together, which, in turn, produces new modes of knowing that feed into further change of the historical past and future possibilities available to them.[67]

But to what extent is the notion of looping effects applicable to concepts that subsume kinds of phenomena rather than kinds of people? Since war is neither a natural nor a human kind, the notion of looping effects seems not immediately suited to make sense of its performative consequences over time. But granted that the concept of war is used to refer to a class of phenomena, it is reasonable to assume that the ways in which this concept is used will affect which phenomena can thus be subsumed by telling us what war is and what war does and what war is not and what war does not. War is thus what we make of it through our creative tampering with the linguistic conventions that govern the use of its concept. As Hacking reminds us elsewhere, "human acts come into being hand in hand with our invention of the ways to name them."[68] And as Winch once pointed out, "to give an account of the meaning of a word is to describe how it is used; and to describe how it is used is to describe the social intercourse into which it enters."[69] Since the concept of war has been and still is used to denote instances of organized violence, its looping effects are confined to the ways in which war thereby is rendered distinct from other kinds of violence and the range of actions that can be legitimized by means of this concept by the actors involved, since, as Goodman once cleverly stated about the limits of what a standard constructivist account can hope to

[67] Ian Hacking, "The Looping Effects of Human Kinds," in Dan Sperber, David Premack, and Ann James Premack (eds.), *Causal Cognition: A Multi-Disciplinary Approach* (Oxford: Clarendon Press, 1995), 351–94, esp. 366–70.

[68] Hacking, *Historical Ontology*, 113.

[69] Peter Winch, *The Idea of a Social Science and Its Relation to Philosophy* (London: Routledge, 1958), 114–15.

achieve, "we are confined to ways of describing whatever is described."[70]

But what about the notion of ontogenetic war? Taking this view seriously means ascribing certain predetermined looping effects to war – such as the capacity to produce political order out of its negations or absences – while remaining oblivious to what such attributions do to the phenomenon of war itself. So, although I believe that we should refrain from attributing ontogenetic capacities to anything but ourselves, I also believe that we should recognize that the belief that some things have ontogenetic capacities might itself be ontogenetic, but not necessarily of what these beliefs are believed to be ontogenetic of. Hence what matters to the present inquiry is not whether war is really constitutive of political order or not, but the extent to which this belief has been constitutive of the meaning of war in international thought. Hence, taking ontogenetic attributions seriously means analyzing how they have given rise to and reinforced the belief that war is a necessary antidote to violence and disorder and how they have made war look as an inescapable part of the human condition and a natural fact of political life.

To substantiate this argument, I shall try to show how notions of ontogenetic war have been consistently invoked in order to explain and legitimize the existence of the modern state and the international system by demarcating them from what went before in time and what was outside in space, as well as by underpinning those legal frameworks intended to regulate the intercourse of states as well as their relations to the many others on the outside. Many of those things whose existence has been explained with reference to the productive force of war were later invoked to understand and legitimize the use of force, leading to a productive circularity in our understanding of what war possibly can mean. The limits and boundaries of the modern state and the international system have defined the conditions under which war is intelligible with reference only to those things that it is believed to have constituted in the past. If war is intelligible only with reference to these identities and boundaries, this means that if and when these identities and boundaries are challenged – as they arguably have been during the past decades – the modern concept of war will lose much of its coherence and analytical purchase, and the long-repressed view of

70   Nelson Goodman, *Ways of Worldmaking* (Indianapolis: Hackett, 1978), 3.

war as a productive force in human affairs is likely to resurface and to inform attempts to impose political order in times and places where it is believed to be absent, weak, or contested.

But how do we go about such an inquiry, given that the topic is vast and the evidence scattered across many different intellectual fields? Since my focus is on the historical ontology of war and its looping effects across historical contexts over a long period of time, I think some suggestions recently made by Armitage might be useful. Whereas contextualist historians have tended to focus on the use of political concepts within temporally quite limited contexts, Armitage has suggested that the scope of inquiry should be broadened to include comparisons *across* different historical contexts. What he has aptly termed "transtemporal history" consciously "links discrete contexts, moments and periods while maintaining the synchronic specificity of those contexts."[71] Furthermore, the writing of such a transtemporal history must proceed by means of what he calls serial contextualism. Doing this takes the "reconstruction of a sequence of distinct contexts in which identifiable agents strategically deployed existing languages to effect identifiable goals such as legitimation and de-legitimation."[72] Following these recommendations, I will focus on how war has been invoked by different actors for the purpose of legitimizing various aspects of the modern political order and how these strategies played themselves out within different intellectual fields both across time as well as across different national contexts. Yet, when doing this, I shall attend more to the presuppositions underlying different speech acts rather than to the rhetorical upshot of those speech acts. And given that the ambition of this book is to recover a specific conception of war rather than to provide a fair and full account of the entire range of conceptions of war that was available during the early modern and modern periods, I will pay less attention to those views of war that were developed in opposition to the productive view of war

[71] David Armitage, "What's the Big Idea? Intellectual History and the Longue Durée," *History of European Ideas* 38, no. 4 (2012): 493–507, at 498; David Armitage, Jo Guldi, and Jérôme Baudry, "Le Retour de la Longue Durée: une perspective Anglo-Américaine," *Annales. Histoire, Sciences Sociales* 70, no. 2 (2015): 289–318.
[72] Armitage, "What's the Big Idea?," 498.

but that have animated political and legal resistance to power politics ever since.[73]

The notion of ontogenetic war is in no way confined to distinct national contexts but traveled widely across them, as well as across different intellectual fields. Although the productive view of war is closely associated with the rise of nationalism, this view was intrinsically international, in the sense that its dissemination took place without the slightest regard for then-emerging territorial boundaries, as well as in the sense that it brought vague assumptions about the existence of an international system within which war was inevitable into being.[74] This has led me to believe that Wight simply was wrong when he lamented the absence of "a tradition of speculation about relations between states" or when he identified this tradition with "the kind of rumination about human destiny to which we give the unsatisfactory name of philosophy of history."[75] As I will demonstrate, there is indeed an extensive but neglected literature about war that extends far beyond the scattered remarks made by political philosophers or that was embodied in the classics of international law and the philosophy of history. When we venture beyond the established canon of legal and political thought, we will rediscover works that have long been forgotten by historians of international thought but that were widely disseminated among the political and military elites of the day and were read and appreciated as viable guides to political action by members of the same elites. Broadening the scope of inquiry to include narratives produced by courtiers and royal historians, memoires written by generals and diplomats, reports submitted by cartographers and military engineers, pieces of advice offered by ministers and strategists, and the commentaries provided by lawyers and philosophers, this will indicate that to the extent that there was something meriting the label of international theory during the early modern period, this was essentially a theory about war and its productive force. Reconstructing the assumptions of this theory makes it possible to reinterpret canonical

---

[73] I have attempted this elsewhere; see Jens Bartelson, *Visions of World Community* (Cambridge: Cambridge University Press, 2009).

[74] For an interesting overview of the study of international thought, see David Armitage, "The International Turn in Intellectual History," in Darrin M. McMahon and Samuel Moyn (eds.), *Rethinking Modern European Intellectual History* (Oxford: Oxford University Press, 2014), 232–52.

[75] Martin Wight, "Why Is There No International Theory?," *International Relations* 2, no. 1 (1960): 35–48, at 35 and 48.

texts in political and legal thought by showing how their scant accounts of war and warfare both informed and found ample support in writings from other intellectual fields and genres from the same periods but that have attracted less attention than have the great names of legal theory. So, although there is an element of comparison to my analysis, I will focus mainly on similarities across different fields and genres, sometimes downplaying their differences for the sake of maintaining a clear focus on shared conceptualizations of war and their presuppositions and implications.

Understanding War

But what can a historical ontology of war offer in terms of a better understanding of the phenomenon of war? Although this book does not directly address the causes of war, my account still has some important implications for our attempts to explain and understand the phenomenon of war itself. Since one upshot is to show how the meaning attributed to war is contingent on prior conceptualizations, it would be tempting to argue that war is but a looping effect of these conceptualizations. When war is invoked to explain and legitimize the existence of certain other things, this is bound to affect the conditions under which war itself can be understood and justified. For example, as long as we stay with conventional definitions of war as organized violence, justifications of war will remain essential to the very enterprise of war. If such justifications are understood as speech acts whose point is to command the approval of a given audience, justifications are indeed necessary to turn what otherwise might be but random outbursts of violence into an organized form and thus to war proper. And as long as we are willing to admit that justifications provided for a given action also can be a cause of that action under certain conditions, it would follow that an inquiry into the conditions under which war can be justified in different situations is a necessary precursor to an understanding of those among its possible causes that spring directly from human action.[76]

Before elaborating this further, we should note that we are very unlikely to find in the sociopolitical world anything that has not already

---

[76] See Donald Davidson, "Actions, Reasons, and Causes," *Journal of Philosophy* 60, no. 23 (1963): 685–700.

been put into it by ourselves or our predecessors. To treat war as a timeless concept or a transhistorical problem is therefore bound to lead attempts to understand war astray. This tendency is no more evident than in the efforts to reconstruct past thinking about war in order to better explain its causes in the present. A good example of this is the modern classic, *Man, the State and War* (1954), in which Waltz starts out by arguing that Collingwood was wrong when he "suggested that the best way of understanding the writings of philosophers is to seek out the questions they were attempting to answer" and instead proposes that "the best way to examine the problems of international political theory is to pose a central question and identify the answers that can be given to it."[77] By understanding war as a transhistorical problem, Waltz not only sacrifices the prohibition against anachronism on the altar of positivist explanation, but by ruling out that war might have meant very different things to different people in different times and places, he thereby precludes the possibility of a contextual explanation of the phenomenon of war. When Waltz proceeds further to make the variety of existing explanations of war manageable by classifying them, locating the causes of war within human nature, within the domestic makeup of states, or within the anarchic international system, he disregards the fact that this typology would have made little or no sense to most of the authors whose works he consulted in search for the most edifying examples. By doing so, Waltz also fails to note that some of these authors indeed were responsible for creating these categories and filling them with the kind of content that made their explanations stick and that they often did so with reference to the productive forces of war.

Another no less sophisticated example of this tendency to reconstruct past thinking about war from the vantage point of present concerns is found in *Ways of War and Peace* (1997) by Doyle. He opens this study by suggesting that theorists of war from Thucydides onward "are modern in a recognizable sense" because each begins with "the modern predicament – masterless men in modern society – and tries to speak across history to all who share it."[78] Faced with the uncertain outcomes of global change, Doyle then advises us to revisit

[77] Kenneth N. Waltz, *Man, the State, and War: A Theoretical Analysis* (New York: Columbia University Press, 1959), 12.

[78] Michael W. Doyle, *Ways of War and Peace: Realism, Liberalism, and Socialism* (New York: W.W. Norton, 1997), 10.

these classics in search for better explanations and prescriptions to guide us into the future. Grouping these together under the headings of realism, liberalism, and socialism, respectively, he proposes that these theories can offer competing but complementary guidance to the tricky moral issues underlying decisions about war and peace since "within this shared realization of anarchy, identities differ according to different assumptions about the content of interests and the meaning of institutions."[79] Yet this line of inquiry also presupposes that war is a transhistorical problem by virtue of possessing some timeless meaning and that theories grappling with war can be compartmentalized according to their assumptions about identities and interests. *Pace* Doyle, I argue that notions of ontogenetic war have been an integral part of all these worldviews and that this puts a limit on the amount of guidance they are able to offer us in the present.

Although a historical ontology of war cannot provide any good explanation of why there is war, it can supplement existing explanations by describing how the attributions of causes became possible in the first place. Take international anarchy. As Waltz famously argued with a little help from Rousseau, "wars occur because there is nothing to prevent them."[80] The task of historical ontology is not to contest the validity of this conclusion but to analyze how it acquired verisimilitude over time. Doing this is a matter of inquiring into its historical preconditions by describing the various functions attributed to war when explaining the genesis of the modern state and the transition from a stateless past to the modern international system. Exploring the looping effects of the notion of ontogenetic war helps us to understand how war became the evil twin of sovereignty and why political realism broadly conceived came to provide the best field guide to state conduct within the international system. Or take the notion that some states are more belligerent than others due to their domestic makeup. Although a historical ontology of war does not purport to explain why some states are more belligerent than others, it can help us to understand how the historical attribution of warlike qualities to some states have conditioned their internal makeup and shaped their interaction over time. Finally, take the view that war ultimately springs from the dark side of human nature. Again, historical ontology would have to remain agnostic on this score and instead point to the fact that human hostility has

[79] *Ibid.*, 24.   [80] Waltz, *Man, the State, and War*, 232.

been consistently invoked as the ultimate cause of war long enough to have become a self-fulfilling prophecy. But if the causes war in fact are nothing but cumulated looping effects of the belief that war is constitutive of something other than itself, my suggestion would be to abandon the quest for the causes of war in favor of a systematic inquiry into how different conceptions of war have shaped the range of actions and justifications available to actors in different contexts.

Given the failure to make good historical sense of past thinking about war documented earlier, a return to the practices of intellectual history would perhaps help us to avoid anachronistic reasoning of the worst kind, but it would not automatically help us to make any better sense of war itself.[81] Doing this would require us to pursue a contextualist line of inquiry one step further by studying not only how war was conceptualized in the past but also how the different meanings of war have affected the range of actions that possibly could be justified with reference to this concept. A transtemporal view would allow us to make inferences about how the range of available justifications has changed as a consequence of underlying changes in the meaning of war. The abandonment of the productive view of war after the end of the Second World War is a case in point, as is its sudden return after the end of the Cold War. Attending to the range of justifications will tell us who is entitled to wage war, for what reasons, and under what circumstances and under what conditions the relevant audiences are likely to accept some justifications while rejecting others: Although a historical ontology of war can never explain why there is war, it is a precursor to understanding why individual wars occur.

Plan of the Book

The rest of this book is organized as follows. In Chapter 2, I describe how war came to be understood as a transhistorical and ontogenetic state of affairs by early modern historians and how this notion transmuted into a recognizably modern notion of international anarchy. By focusing on the function of war in early modern and modern historical writing, I argue that this concept informs historical narratives of states and their emergence by dividing historical time into a stateless past and

---

[81] Robin G. Collingwood, *An Autobiography* (Oxford: Oxford University Press, 1939).

a statist present so that an international state of war is made to appear the natural correlate of state making. I end this chapter by describing what happens to the state of war when grafted onto theories of evolution and natural selection in early sociology, arguing that this goes some way to explain why the notion of ontogenetic war was so thoroughly discredited and repressed after the end of the two world wars. In Chapter 3, I explore some of the functions attributed to war in the creation of territories and the demarcation of boundaries between states in Europe, as well as between the European system of states and its non-European and stateless outside. Contesting the constructivist consensus on this issue, I argue that the process of territorial demarcation and unification was informed by and legitimized with reference to an ever-present possibility of war and domestic turmoil. I end by describing how these violent geographic imaginaries later blended with theories of natural selection and issued a generous license for imperial expansion and geopolitical competition during the late nineteenth century. In Chapter 4, I explore the functions attributed to human hostility and violence in some of the classics of international law, arguing that the attempt to restrict the use of force by means of law presupposes the prior existence of hostility among men and the concomitant possibility of discriminating between regular and irregular forms of violence. The propensity for irregular violence was initially projected backward in time onto a barbarous past in order to justify the use of force against threats to the legal order, such as pirates and brigands, thereby allowing for the legal regulation of violence between sovereigns. I end by arguing that when blended with doctrines of legal evolution, this notion of natural hostility was projected outward in space in order to legitimize the use of force against non-European peoples on the grounds that these peoples were predisposed to irregular forms of violence. In the concluding chapter, I discuss the recent return of the notion of ontogenetic war and its consequences for our understanding of allegedly new forms of war and warfare in world politics, arguing that its influence has been most strongly felt in the shifting legitimizations of military intervention after the end of the Cold War but that it then has been disseminated in the international system. Discussing the role of state weakness and failure in these legitimizations, I show how notions of ontogenetic war have informed recent justifications of humanitarian intervention and nation-building and how this has provoked similar responses from those who dispute the legitimacy of these policies and the ambitions they reflect. I end by pointing out that since some critics of war themselves subscribe to notions of ontogenetic war, they cannot hope to provide contemporary attempts to restrain the use of force with any solid moral or legal foundation. This raises important questions about limits of critical inquiry in international thought, questions that I briefly address toward the end.

2 | The State of War

Introduction

According to a contested commonplace of historical sociology, "War made the state, and the state made war."[1] On this view, the state is the outcome of violent competition between groups in society. As Weber famously argued, "having established the monopoly of physical violence as a means of rule within a territory," the state can then freely deploy its capacity for organized violence against other states.[2] By the same token, according to what has long been a common and no less contested view within academic international relations, relations between states are best characterized as a state of war. On this view, wars between states occur because there is no political authority in the international system there to prevent them from breaking out.[3]

---

[1] Charles Tilly, "Reflections on the History of European State-Making," in Charles Tilly (ed.), *The Formation of National States in Western Europe* (Princeton, NJ: Princeton University Press, 1975), 3–83, at 42; Charles Tilly, "War Making and State Making as Organized Crime," in Peter B. Evans, Dietrich Rueschemeyer, and Theda Skocpol (eds.), *Bringing the State Back In* (Cambridge: Cambridge University Press, 1985), 169–87; Charles Tilly, *Coercion, Capital, and European States AD 990–1990* (Oxford: Basil Blackwell, 1990); Thomas Ertman, *Birth of the Leviathan: Building States and Regimes in Medieval and Early Modern Europe* (Cambridge: Cambridge University Press, 1997); Anthony Giddens, *The Nation-State and Violence* (Berkeley: University of California Press, 1985). For a critical discussion, see Steven Gunn, "War and the Emergence of the State: Western Europe, 1350–1600," in Frank Tallett and D. J. B. Trim (eds.), *European Warfare 1350–1750* (Cambridge: Cambridge University Press, 2010), 50–73.

[2] Max Weber, "The Profession and Vocation of Politics," in Peter Lassman and Ronald Spiers (eds.), *Max Weber: Political Writings* (Cambridge: Cambridge University Press, 1994), 309–69, at 316.

[3] See, for example, Kenneth N. Waltz, *Man, the State and War: A Theoretical Analysis* (New York: Columbia University Press, 1959); Kenneth N. Waltz, *Theory of International Politics* (Reading, MA: Addison Wesley, 1979). For an ambitious restatement, see R. Harrison Wagner, *War and the State: The Theory of International Politics* (Ann Arbor: University of Michigan Press, 2007).

As Suganami has summarized the bottom line of those views, "if the practice of sovereignty is a sufficient condition of the possibility of arbitrary violence ... it follows ... that the possibility of arbitrary violence is a necessary condition of the practice of sovereignty."[4] And, as I argued earlier, there is indeed a double bind between sovereign authority and the use of force insofar as claims to political authority have been legitimized with reference to the violence that would ensue in its absence, while the use of force has consistently been justified with reference to sovereign authority.[5] But how did this double bind between the state and war come into being, and how did it become a crucial presupposition of historical sociology and academic international relations? These are the questions that will guide this chapter. As I shall argue, the double bind between war and the state is a result of a tendency within European historiography to explain the emergence of the state and the international system with reference to a *state of war*. From the beginning of the seventeenth to the end of the nineteenth century, the concept of war – however defined and understood – was used to define the temporal limits of states and the international realm by demarcating them from what allegedly existed before. Although the meanings ascribed to war varied considerably during this period, and although historical consciousness underwent substantial mutations during the same period, the attribution of ontogenetic functions to war represents a striking continuity that stretches from early modern historians of states to late nineteenth-century sociology. By focusing on the accounts of state formation that were widely disseminated and read by contemporary political elites in Europe, I will show how the double bind between war and the state was forged historically and how it informed and legitimized practices of state formation during this period. This means that when the mantra that war made the state and the state made war is repeated today, it might be the case that its apparent validity is nothing more than a result of its looping effects, since many of those who were involved in the making of states did so with cruder versions of this mantra firmly in mind.

---

[4] Hidemi Suganami, "Understanding Sovereignty through Kelsen/Schmitt," *Review of International Studies* 33, no. 3 (2007): 511–30, at 529.
[5] Jens Bartelson, "Double Binds: Sovereignty and the Just War Tradition," in Hent Kalmo and Quentin Skinner (eds.), *Sovereignty in Fragments: The Past, Present and Future of a Contested Concept* (Cambridge: Cambridge University Press, 2010), 81–95.

The intellectual obsession with war during this period is puzzling because it has frequently been portrayed as period of pacification and domestication. As Foucault pointed out, almost at the same time when the institutions of war were concentrated in the hands of the state and private warfare was abolished in favor of war between states, we witnessed the emergence of a historical and political discourse according to which society is constituted by conflicts; "we are therefore at war with one another; a battlefront runs through the whole of society, continuously and permanently, and it is this battlefront that puts us all on one side or the other."[6] While I am in broad agreement with Foucault that such imaginaries of war emerged simultaneously with the rise of the state in Europe, I would like to expand on his account in two ways. First, I think that we should pay more attention to the meaning and function of war in these imaginaries. Since Foucault implies that war has meant more or less the same across different contexts, he presupposes what has to be explained, namely, how this particular conception of war emerged and how it came to structure historical consciousness. Doing this, I would like to suggest that such violent imaginaries were much more pervasive than indicated by his account. To Foucault, the paradigmatic expression of such violent conflict is the clash of races, so "the conflictual relationship that that exists between the two groups that constitute the social body and shapes the state is in fact one of war, of permanent warfare. The State is nothing more than the way that the war between the two groups continues to be waged in apparently peaceful forms."[7] But rather than being restricted to the struggle between races within societies, however, I would like to suggest that such imaginaries involved a much wider range of collective subjects and were invoked to account for their identities. Finally, whereas Foucault's account is built on a rather sharp contrast between notions of struggle and war, on the one hand, and legalistic conceptions of sovereignty, on the other, I would like to argue that war finds its ultimate warrant in the quest for sovereignty and that this quest was frequently justified with reference to the violence that would ensue in the absence of supreme authority within the social body.

Second, I think that Foucault neglects a crucial aspect of the function of war in early modern political and historical writing. When he tries to show how the state emerges out of a continuous struggle between groups,

---

[6] Michel Foucault, *Society Must Be Defended* (New York: Picador, 2003), 51.
[7] *Ibid.*, 88.

Foucault takes the existence of temporally demarcated societies for
granted. Yet, as I will suggest below, the concept of war was crucial in
providing states and societies with their temporal limits. Early modern
accounts of war and the state are not primarily or exclusively concerned
with the legitimacy of particular forms of government but more often
invoke a state of war in order to constitute the temporal limits of individual
states in relation to their past. What is at stake in early modern histories of
the state is to explain a how a given state came into being as a result of
warfare, as a consequence of battles and conquests; how its population
gradually evolved into a people as a result of invasions, expulsions, and
subjugations; and how the state came into itself as a result of rebellions,
usurpations, and revolutions against a feudal or barbarous past. Thus, if
war indeed can be said to have *made* the state, this is because warfare
already was understood as being necessary to the constitution of states in
historical time, in relation to their own troubled past as well as to that of
their neighbors. Thus, expanding on the accounts by Fasolt and Davis, I
argue that notions of war and warfare have been integral to the very
practices of periodization that made it possible to distinguish between
states and premodern forms of political association and use that distinction
to arrange different forms of political association in sequences ranging
from the primitive to the more advanced and civilized. In other words,
this is partly a story of how the "Middle Ages" was assembled out of
myths of a violent past.[8]

The rest of this chapter is organized as follows. In the first section, I
describe how emergent conceptions of war and history during the late
sixteenth century paved the way for the rise of new forms of historical
writing that took particular states as their primary objects of inquiry.
I then provide a few examples of how the relationship between war
and the state was understood in some widely read treatises from the
seventeenth century. In the next section, I describe how themes from
these narratives found their way into Enlightenment histories of
progress and civilization and how war came to be understood as
the not-so-gentle civilizer of nations in the process. In the final section, I describe how these narratives blended with theories of evolution and natural selection and gave rise to theories of race struggle so

[8]   See Constantin Fasolt, *The Limits of History* (Chicago: University of Chicago
Press, 2004); Kathleen Davis, *Periodization and Sovereignty: How Ideas of
Feudalism and Secularization Govern the Politics of Time* (Philadelphia:
University of Pennsylvania Press, 2008).

dear to early social theory and sociology but so fatal to the modern world.

War and the Immemorial

Although we have grown accustomed to thinking of the state as the outcome of warfare, there is nothing new about this idea. Rather, as I argue in this section, such notions emerged in the early seventeenth century when new conceptions of war and new ways of understanding the past blended into new modes of historical writing that became preoccupied with the formation of particular political communities. From this point onward, reference to an ontogenetic and transhistorical state of war becomes the most common explanation for the emergence of particular states, as well as for the formation of an international arena characterized by intense rivalries between states.

Let us start with the concept of war. According to a widespread view, before war became a prerogative of sovereigns, no two parties could be equally justified in their resort to violence because the justness of one's cause implied the necessary injustice of that of the adversary. In the medieval "just war" tradition, war was widely conceptualized as an act of law enforcement between morally unequal parties through which legitimate authorities could impose law on their subjects and punish evildoers for their transgressions of these laws.[9] This implied that no sharp distinction between war and peace could be drawn, whether in theory or in practice. Since war was understood as an *action* undertaken by some legitimate authority with the aim of enforcing the law, it could well coexist with peaceful and orderly conduct among those not targeted for correction. Yet this unilateral conception of war gradually gave way to a bilateral one, according to which *both* belligerents could be equally justified in their resort to force. Drawing on Ulpian, civic humanists revived the Roman conception according to which war could be equally just on both sides. A first step in this direction had been taken by Fulgosius, who in his *In primam Pandectarum partem Commentaria* (*c.* 1400) argued that in the absence of any superior legal authority that could decide on the justness of their cause, belligerents

---

[9] See Stephen C. Neff, *War and the Law of Nations: A General History* (Cambridge: Cambridge University Press, 2005), 7–82; James Turner Johnson, *Just War Tradition and the Restraint of War: A Moral and Historical Inquiry* (Princeton, NJ: Princeton University Press, 1981).

had an equal right to fight precisely by virtue of being independent of any legal or moral authority.[10] On this view, war becomes less a matter of law enforcement and more akin to a duel between moral equals stuck in a condition devoid of objective right, a *state of war*.

The gradual acceptance of this view had profound implications for the grounds on which war could be fought and justified. In the absence of any shared and authoritative source of legal judgment, war becomes the final arbiter of conflict and hence also justifiable on grounds that it serves the causes of the political community, or at least parts thereof. So from the legal equality of belligerents follows the possibility of harnessing war for ends other than law enforcement and punishment, and although the nature of those ends could vary significantly, this shift implied that war could be used as a means to realize them. As Machiavelli states in the Preface to his *Arte Della Guerra* (1519–20), "For all the arts that are ordered in city for the sake of the common good of men, all the orders made there for living in fear of the laws of God, would be in vain if their defenses were not prepared."[11] The common good could be defined in terms of protection against external enemies and the preservation of domestic order but could also easily be stretched to include imperial aggrandizement and military glory.[12]

Since then, we have grown accustomed to regard war as a prerogative of sovereigns stuck in a condition devoid of common authority. In the absence of such authority, war becomes a natural condition of politics involving all parties in a constant test of strength believed to be the final arbiter of the moral and legal legitimacy of their claims. With no other method for resolving disputes at hand, "war was accepted as integral to the conduct of relationships between polities; *all* polities faced a struggle to maintain their relative position in what

[10] See Ryan Greenwood, "War and Sovereignty in Medieval Roman Law," *Law and History Review* 32, no. 1 (2014): 31–63; Gregory M. Reichberg, "Just War and Regular War: Competing Paradigms," in David Rodin and Henry Shue (eds.), *Just and Unjust Warriors: Moral Equality on the Battlefield* (Oxford: Oxford University Press, 2008), 193–213.

[11] Niccolò Machiavelli, *The Art of War*, trans. Christopher Lynch (Chicago: University of Chicago Press, 2003), 4.

[12] See Maurizio Viroli, *From Politics to Reason of State: The Acquisition and Transformation of the Language of Politics 1250–1600* (Cambridge: Cambridge University Press, 1992); Mikael Hörnqvist, "Machiavelli's Three Desires: Florentine Republicans on Liberty, Empire, and Justice," in Sankar Muthu (ed.), *Empire and Modern Political Thought* (Cambridge: Cambridge University Press, 2012), 7–29.

was a cut-throat environment."[13] As we shall see in this section, to conceptualize war as a default condition of political life implied that it was perceived to be beyond the full control of individual rulers and their policies but also that it could be harnessed for the purposes of making and preserving states. In the words of one eminent military historian, prior to the modern period, "war created policy rather than continued it."[14] Against this backdrop, it would hardly make sense to posit any distinction between civil and international wars, since warfare was widely believed to be the very means by which a distinction between the domestic and international realms could be drawn in practice.

So although it would be equally anachronistic to speak of a recognizably modern concept of the state at this point in time, I think it is possible to argue that such a conception emerges as a consequence of sustained efforts to harness the impersonal forces of war for the purposes of statecraft. If war has the power to pass verdicts on the actions of rulers, it has also the power to make or break states. As the Habsburg general Montecuccoli summarized his vast experiences of war in his *Mémoires* (1703), "Battles give Crowns and take them away, resolves disputes between Sovereigns without appeal, conclude the war and render the conqueror immortal."[15] And as he went on to elaborate the implications of a state of war among European states, "no State can be at peace, ward off attacks, defend its Laws, its Religion without Arms . . . its majesty will not be respected without them, neither among its subjects, nor among Foreigners."[16] If warfare indeed is a default condition of politics, the task of rulers is to harness its productive potentials for the singular purpose of creating and maintaining their states. Thus, in a widely read treatise titled *Tesoro Politico* (1589), Comino Ventura could persuasively argue that the foundation of the "machine of the state" lies in the systematic use of force both as an instrument of internal domination and to protect the state from foreign violence. Since wars are likely to occur anyway, or so Ventura believed,

---

[13] Frank Tallett and D. J. B. Trim, "'Then was then and now is now': an overview of change and continuity in late-medieval and early modern warfare," in Frank Tallett and D. J. B. Trim (eds.), *European Warfare 1350–1750* (Cambridge: Cambridge University Press, 2010), 1–26, at 22.

[14] George Clark, *War and Society in the 17th Century* (Cambridge: Cambridge University Press, 1958), 24–5.

[15] Raimundo Montecuccoli, *Mémoires* (Paris: Muzier, 1712), 183.

[16] *Ibid.*, 76.

it is a matter of prudence on behalf of the ruler to avoid the occurrence
of internal rebellions and foreign war at the same time. To maintain a
relative state of peace within their states, rulers have to face a peculiar
tradeoff: while mobilizing resources for the conduct of foreign war
easily leads to grievances at home that might issue in domestic rebel-
lion, failing to mobilize against external enemies might subject the state
to defeat and ruin at the hands of foreigners.[17] Consequently, it was
possible to argue that foreign wars sometimes were necessary to detract
attention from domestic problems. As Courtilz de Sandras argued, it is
a maxim of statecraft to always have some foreign war going on in
order to avoid internal strife and to keep up the martial spirit among
subjects.[18]

By the same token, while it would seem no less anachronistic to speak
of nationalism in a modern sense during the early modern period, the
constant possibility of war was frequently invoked in the construction of
rudimentary notions of national identity, which then were fed into contemporary justifications of war. As Hirschi has recently pointed out,
while the symbolic legacy of the Roman Empire was still very much
alive and widely shared among European elites, the obvious mismatch
between the imperial ideal of a single hegemonic power and the actual rise
of territorial states gave rise not only to a quest for supremacy among
them but also to attempts to reappropriate this symbolic legacy in order
to justify claims to supremacy with reference to superior national characters.[19] As Hirschi goes on to explain, "in a world of nations, one needs
to have an idea of how other nations see themselves in order to char-
acterize oneself."[20] Thus early modern varieties of nationalism emerged
in the context of rivaling claims to uniqueness and grandeur, each capitalizing on the same Roman legacy and each being formed in opposition
to the other. Accordingly, as Ventura observed, "not only are the customs
of Nations different, but often also opposed."[21]

Finally, while it would be historically inaccurate to speak of an international system during this period, efforts to achieve domestic order with

[17] Comino Ventura, *Trésor Politique* (Paris: Nicolas de Fossé, 1608), 1–23.
[18] Gatien Courtilz de Sandras, *Nouveaux Interets des Princes de L'Europe*
(Cologne: Pierre Marteau, 1686), 158–9.
[19] Caspar Hirschi, *The Origins of Nationalism: An Alternative History from
Ancient Rome to Early Modern Germany* (Cambridge: Cambridge University
Press, 2012), 34–49.
[20] *Ibid.*, 39.   [21] Ventura, *Trésor Politique*, 13.

violent means eventually resulted in the emergence of something akin to an international arena. Although lacking many of the characteristics we have come to associate with a modern international system or international society, this arena emerged as a consequence of territorial contests and relentless efforts at expansion. Whereas Renaissance warfare had been a local or regional affair at most, the geographic scope of early modern warfare expanded, as did the number of parties involved and the range of their strategic ambitions. As de Vries has shown, what was peculiar to early modern warfare was that the security of states increasingly depended on their ability to formulate strategies that spanned vast geographic areas and long periods of time and to implement those visions by projecting military power across equally vast stretches of time and space.[22]

Hence, when insights from the geographic and cartographic revolutions of the sixteenth century began to penetrate military and strategic thinking, it resulted in popular geopolitical guidebooks such as the *Relazioni Universali* (1591–8) by Giovanni Botero and *Les Estats, Empires, Royaumes et Principautes du Monde* (1625) by Pierre d'Avity. The geographic scope of these books extended far beyond the European continent into hitherto underexplored parts of the world. But whereas Botero is focused primarily on the Christian world and its relations with outside actors, d'Avity sets out to compare every known polity, from the great powers and the tiniest principalities in Europe to the most distant kingdoms of the Orient, providing thick, if often fanciful, descriptions of their geography, climate, customs, wealth, government, military capability, and religion, all in order to assess their relative power and to pass judgment on their foreign policies.[23]

In the next section, I attempt to provide some nuance to the transition from war as a method of law enforcement to idea of war as productive

[22] Kelly de Vries, "Warfare and the International System," in Frank Tallett and D. J. B. Trim (eds.), *European Warfare 1350–1750* (Cambridge: Cambridge University Press, 2010), 27–49.

[23] Giovanni Botero, *Relazioni Universali* (Venice: Appresso Giorgio Angelieri, 1599); Pierre D'Avity, *Les Estats, Empires, Royaumes et Principautes du Monde* (Paris: Pierre Chevalier, 1625). For analyses of Botero, see John M. Headley, "Geography and Empire in the Late Renaissance: Botero's Assignment, Western Universalism, and the Civilizing Process," *Renaissance Quarterly* 53, no. 4 (2000): 1119–55; Joan-Pau Rubiés, "Oriental Despotism and European Orientalism: Botero to Montesquieu," *Journal of Early Modern History* 9, nos. 1–2 (2005): 109–80.

force in human affairs. As I argue, war – both as a state of things and as a
mode of intercourse – was widely believed to be constitutive of states,
nations, and the international arena. Appeals to a state of war and war as
an activity were crucial to the framing of states as independent actors, to
the concomitant construction of nations as distinct and unique, and to the
creation of an international arena in which states could perform and
interact. Much of this depended on practices of historical rewriting,
through which a boundless state of war could be projected backward in
time to explain how individual states had first emerged and entered the
international arena by virtue of their ability to overcome internal and
external threats to their existence. What was buried in the past was
therefore also very much present in the present, as well as conversely.

Yet this backward projection of a state of war would hardly have been
possible without some prior changes in historical consciousness. Roughly
at the same time as the concept of war was being redefined along these
lines, European historiography underwent a corresponding transition
that greatly facilitated the backward projection of the state of war. As
Pocock has famously shown, the medieval concern with universal and
timeless preconditions of political community was then superseded by a
new focus on particular communities and their ability to withstand the
corrosive influence of time and change.[24] Whereas the great Renaissance
histories of Machiavelli and Guicciardini had assumed that historical
events would recur in cycles, much early modern historical scholarship
was informed by a quest for unbroken historical continuities that could
be used to support or debunk particular claims to political authority.
Because such claims were often justified with reference to purportedly
timeless and immutable principles of reason and nature, those who
wanted to defend their privileges and liberties against incursions by
royal authority had to argue that since these latter were founded in
ancient customs and fundamental laws of the realm, no ruler could ever
legitimately amend or revoke them. Those who wanted to resist absolutist
claims of authority often sought support in historical narratives in order
to demonstrate that some precious political and legal institutions indeed
antedated the rise of sovereign authority and were rooted in immemorial
customs that no king could ever alter. In France, this change took place in

[24] J. G. A. Pocock, *The Machiavellian Moment: Florentine Political Thought and
the Atlantic Republican Tradition* (Princeton, NJ: Princeton University Press,
1975), 3–80.

the context of religious warfare, with Huguenot writers asserting ancient rights and liberties with reference to the age-old institutions of popular sovereignty.[25] In England, authors such as Coke asserted the legal primacy of common law and the power of parliament against royal sovereignty and the arbitrary exercise of power through a recourse to historical tradition, a notion that later provided the ideological basis for a violent overthrow of the monarchy.[26]

The treatment law in these historical accounts was often paradoxical. On the one hand, the appeal to custom could be taken to entail that law is in constant change, as a consequence of the need to adapt customs to ever-changing circumstances. On the other hand, references to custom could be taken to imply that fundamental laws were unchanging and had remained the same since time immemorial. In either case, however, these laws were thought to be beyond the scope of sovereign intervention and thereby also thought to constitute effective bridles on its exercise.[27] Much of this scholarship emerged in opposition to other tendencies in early modern political and legal thought. In contrast to theories of sovereignty that sought to justify sovereign authority in abstract and contractual terms, legal histories were written with the more or less explicit intention to support or debunk particular claims to authority but had little, if anything, to say about the sources of sovereignty and its legitimacy in general terms.[28] Furthermore, in contrast to attempts to deduce universal principles of political order from Stoic notions of human reason and sociability, these histories explain the formation of states in terms of violent conflicts about the content of their fundamental laws, often in opposition to the timeless categories of natural law.[29]

---

[25] Michael Walzer, *The Revolution of the Saints: A Study in the Origins of Radical Politics* (Cambridge, MA: Harvard University Press, 1965); Donald R. Kelley, *Foundations of Modern Historical Scholarship: Language, Law, and History in the French Renaissance* (New York: Columbia University Press, 1970).

[26] See J. G. A. Pocock, *The Ancient Constitution and the Feudal Law: A Study of English Historical Thought in the Seventeenth Century* (Cambridge: Cambridge University Press, 1987), 30–55; Harold J. Berman, "The Origins of Historical Jurisprudence: Coke, Selden, Hale," *Yale Law Journal* 103, no. 7 (1994): 1651–738, esp. 1686–94.

[27] Pocock, *Ancient Constitution*, 36.

[28] Harro Höpfl and Martyn P. Thompson, "The History of Contract as a Motif in Political Thought," *American Historical Review* 84, no. 4 (1979): 919–44.

[29] Martyn P. Thompson, "The History of Fundamental Law in Political Thought from the French Wars of Religion to the American Revolution," *American Historical Review* 91, no. 5 (1986): 1103–28.

If appeals to unbroken historical continuities were a source of political legitimacy, claims to absolute sovereignty were nothing but attempts to usurp the rights and liberties that had existed since time immemorial. As Pocock has summarized the efforts to trace the origin of fundamental laws and constitutions back into a distant past in order to endow them with immunity from royal interference, "the concept of the immemorial encouraged the fabrication of myths about immensely remote times, and the fact that the appeal to early national history took the form of partisan controversy between sovereign and constitution enhanced this tendency."[30] Following this appeal to the immemorial, "laws must be either absolutely immemorial or subject to an absolute sovereign."[31]

Since this kind of historiography projected the concerns of the present back onto a distant and mythic past in search for legitimacy, it thereby presupposed that national traditions of constitutional and political development were distinct and continuous. This entailed that any disruptions those traditions had undergone could be twisted into evidence of prior usurpations and thus be used to contest the legitimacy of royal authority in the present. Wars of conquest were paradigmatic instances of such disruptions, and their consequences for constitutional continuity and the legitimacy of royal authority were hotly contested during the seventeenth and eighteenth centuries. In England, the Norman Conquest was a recurring source of political and legal discord in which the rights of the people and parliament were pitted against those of the king. While Coke held that common law antedated the arrival of the Normans, he also maintained that the institutions introduced by them formed part of law by virtue of having been confirmed by William the Conqueror. This was later vehemently disputed by the Levellers, to whom the very idea of common law was but an offspring of the Conquest and hence nothing but a usurpation of the ancient liberties of the Anglo-Saxon peoples.[32] In France, the conquest of Gaul by the Franks performed a similar function in political historiography. To Huguenot historians, the invasion by the Franks was in effect a war of liberation from the legacy of Roman absolutism, which helped restore continuity to France and produced a sense of national

---

[30] Pocock, *Ancient Constitution*, 19.   [31] *Ibid.*, 52.

[32] R. B. Seaberg, "The Norman Conquest and the Common Law: The Levellers and the Argument from Continuity," *The Historical Journal* 24, no. 4 (1981): 791–806.

identity.[33] For example, to Boulainvilliers, although the Frankish conquest of Gaul signified liberation from the Roman yoke, it also marked a happy resurrection of the aristocratic values of a German warrior culture.[34]

Yet, in all these examples, violent conflict is systematically invoked to contest the monopolization of political authority in the hands of a single sovereign, as well as to account for the constitution of cohesive societies that could raise more legitimate claims to authority by virtue of the historical continuity of their customs and traditions. But, as such, these accounts remain firmly focused on what had taken place *within* societies rather than with how those societies had come into being in the first place and how they had been demarcated in relation to their own tumultuous past as well as to their neighbors. In short, while the preceding accounts indicate the rise of a new historical consciousness that takes armed struggle as the organizing principle of historical writing in order to debunk royal claims to sovereignty, they had little to say about the temporal origins and limits of states and their relations to other states.

From the State of War to the State

During the later part of the seventeenth century, the quest for the immemorial issues in a new form of historiography that is supportive of royal sovereignty and statehood. Reflecting the concerns of secular statecraft, some historians now begin to narrate histories of individual states in terms of an imagined or desired congruence between sovereigns, nations, and territories into what we retrospectively have come to consider *modern* states. What is at stake in this kind of historiography is not the question of whether particular authority claims raised by kings, nobles, and popular assemblies are legitimate or not, but to what extent states – despite their sometimes profound internal divisions and questionable historical continuity – can be said to exist independently of their rulers and ruled and, by implication, whether they are able to act autonomously in an emergent international arena and attain legal personality in the eyes of international lawyers.[35] The task at hand was thus

---

[33] Zachary Sayre Schiffman, "An Anatomy of the Historical Revolution in Renaissance France," *Renaissance Quarterly* 42, no. 3 (1989): 507–33.

[34] See Foucault, *Society Must Be Defended*, 144–65.

[35] See, for example, Ben Holland, *The Moral Person of the State: Pufendorf, Sovereignty and Composite Polities* (Cambridge: Cambridge University Press,

to reconstruct the past of individual states in such a way that temporal discontinuities and moments of internal discord could be rearranged into a progressive sequences taking us from its primitive and violent origins in the past into its full unity and splendor in the present. As such, these historians were in the process of creating new practices of periodization, insofar as they had to reconstruct the past of states in ways that made that past clearly distinguishable from the present.

But in order to write histories of such dubious entities as states, nations, and their territories, these entities must be taken to exist in the first place, albeit in some rudimentary or embryonic form. During the early modern period, such entities were very much works in progress, calling for rigorous definitions and careful distinction from other forms of political association.[36] Hence, in the kind of historiography we will consider shortly, states are demarcated from a distant past when the conditions of their existence were more uncertain – when they lacked a locus of sovereign authority, fixed populations, and territorial boundaries – in order to make credible that even despite all these apparent historical discontinuities and the recurrent threats to their temporal continuity represented by conquests and usurpations, each individual state remains essentially the same across time precisely *by virtue of* the constant contestation of its sovereignty and its territorial integrity and the shifting composition of its population. To this end, it seemed necessary to assume that states had been constituted through a constant rivalry between primordial groups stuck in a state of war since time immemorial.

In contrast to the histories of law and government discussed in the preceding section, these histories of states could capitalize on themes and concepts salient in contemporary natural law and universal history without much contradiction being felt between them. Assumptions about social antagonism, human sociability, and stages of human development that had been used to justify the existence of sovereign authority in theories of natural law could now be used to reconstruct

2017); Jens Bartelson, "Sovereignty and the Personality of the State," in Robert Schuett and Peter M. R. Stirk (eds.), *The Concept of the State in International Relations: Philosophy, Sovereignty, and Cosmopolitanism* (Edinburgh: Edinburgh University Press, 2015), 81–107; Quentin Skinner, "A Genealogy of the Modern State," in *Proceedings of the British Academy* 162 (2009): 325–70.
36 For this point, see Annabel S. Brett, *Changes of State: Nature and the Limits of the City in Early Modern Natural Law* (Princeton, NJ: Princeton University Press, 2011).

the historical trajectory of actually existing states, provided that they were reinterpreted as *empirical* assumptions and then allowed to structure the available historical evidence accordingly. What counted as admissible historical evidence was, in turn, somewhat circularly determined by pointing to the extent to which it could be used to corroborate these conjectural accounts or not. Rather than being written in opposition to the abstract justifications of sovereignty provided by Grotius or Hobbes, much of this historiography can be understood as a means to substantiate these justifications with "empirical" evidence. The appeal to reason and nature that was used during this period to back claims to sovereignty was thereby supplemented with historical narratives that purported to show that the violent origin of states was not merely a fiction invented to demonstrate the necessity of sovereign authority but also had a very real basis in the prehistory of each state. By implication, to question the legitimacy of sovereign authority was tantamount to inviting that prehistory right back into the present, with all the violence and disorder this would bring.

Yet what had antedated the formation of states, and what would most likely return in their absence, was not a simple *bellum omni contra omnes* with individuals fighting each other out of fear or pride. Since there was no historical evidence to support the idea that individuals had ever coexisted in such a sordid condition, the starting point was that men had banded together into primordial groups glued together by kinship and paternal authority and that these groups then had entered into bellicose relations for reasons of passion and expediency. Because kinship was thought to be the basis of these groups, the preoccupation with race in the archaic sense of this term came naturally to many early modern historians. So roughly at the same point in time when Boulainvilliers turned to history to defend aristocratic privilege against royal claims to sovereignty, the latter claims had already found ample support in a new kind of historiography that portrayed royal sovereignty and state formation as the natural outcomes of wars fought successfully against the enemies of the state, a category to which those parts of the nobility that Boulainvilliers so valiantly defended certainly counted. Hence there was no longer any need to invoke mythological-lawgivers such as a Solon or a Lycurgus to account for the origin of individual states. When the immemorial had been equated with a general state of war, there were no ancient customs or fundamental laws left uncontaminated by brute force to which those who wanted to dispute royal claims could appeal. History was war all the way down.

The theoretical principles governing this kind of historical writing were derived from what I earlier termed the *analysis of interests*.[37] Integral to this analysis was the idea that the politics is, or at least ought to be, governed by strict considerations of self-interest rather than being motivated by religious zeal or blind passion.[38] As Rohan argued in his *De l'interest des Princes et Estats de la Chrestienté* (1643), "princes command the people and interest commands princes," and since "knowledge of this interest is as much elevated above that of the actions of princes, as they are above the peoples," then identifying and sticking to rational interest become imperative to the survival and flourishing of princes and their states.[39] The aim of this analysis was to infer maxims from the past that could be used to benchmark state conduct in the present. Since the interests of a given state were thought to include its security, reputation, and wealth, and since these were believed to vary according to the geopolitical situation and form of government of each state, knowledge of these factors was believed to be an important requirement for rational action in domestic and foreign politics during the early modern period.[40]

Thus the rather loose precepts of "Reason of State" found in Botero and Ventura now morphed into what was to become the foundational principle of state historiography during the modern period, namely, that political actors were and always had been primarily motivated by their self-interest. Given that the principle of self-interest itself was supposed to be valid across time and space, it furnished not only a viable guide to the

---

[37] Jens Bartelson, *A Genealogy of Sovereignty* (Cambridge: Cambridge University Press, 1995), 154–85.

[38] See, for example, J. A. W. Gunn, "'Interest Will Not Lie': A Seventeenth-Century Political Maxim," *Journal of the History of Ideas* 29, no. 4 (1968): 551–64; J. A. W. Gunn, *Politics and the Public Interest in the Seventeenth Century* (London: Routledge, 1969); William Farr Church, *Richelieu and Reason of State* (Princeton, NJ: Princeton University Press, 1972); Albert O. Hirschman, *The Passions and the Interests: Political Arguments for Capitalism before Its Triumph* (Princeton, NJ: Princeton University Press, 1977).

[39] Henri Duc de Rohan, *De l'Interest des Princes et Estats de la Chrestienté* (Paris: Augustin Courbé, 1643), 1. Rohan's text was widely imitated during the seventeenth and early eighteenth centuries, yet sometimes with value added. See, for example, Anon., *Interests et Maximes des Princes et des États Souverains* (Cologne, 1666); Jean Rousset, *Les Interets Presens des Puissances de l'Europe* (La Haye, 1734).

[40] Ryan Walter, "The Analysis of Interest and the History of Economic Thought," *Parergon* 28, no. 2 (2011): 129–47.

conduct of states in the present but also provided a recipe for historical writing insofar as the past of states could be reconstructed as the outcome of prior clashes between self-interested actors. The analysis of interest thereby made it possible to narrate the history of each state as a process of individuation propelled by perpetual conflicts of interest and shifting patterns of friendship and enmity. But since the notion of self-interest only can claim to have explanatory power in a world populated by other equally self-interested parties, it also brought a change in the criteria for what counted as valid historical knowledge. Since self-interested actors presumably speak and act according to their interest, their words and actions must be interpreted accordingly. What actors say about themselves cannot be taken at face value but must be seen as clever attempts to promote and conceal their claims to power, and what actors say about others are no less clever attempts to delegitimize *their* claims to power. Thus the analysis of interests furnishes the seed values of what later was to be known as source criticism, since it allows the historian to evaluate statements as inherently partisan and thus base his or her own claims to historical truth on a juxtaposition or triangulation of such statements. Yet claims to an unbiased historical truth were by no means innocent, not only because they served to legitimize claims to power but also because they helped naturalize the state of war as a productive and inescapable condition of political life.

If the earliest examples of this mode of historical writing still owed much to the exemplary historiography of the Renaissance, it grew more sophisticated as the analysis of interest was brought to bear on available historical records and sources and allowed them to be organized in accordance with its principles. In this process, the initial preoccupation with the history of particular states gradually gives way to more of a comparative perspective, with a growing focus on the relations between states rather than on their inner characteristics. While most of these comparative histories were devoted to the major players on the European scene and their relations, some of them purported to cover polities outside the European context as well.[41]

---

[41] For a similar perspective on the role of historiography in the formation of states and the international system, see Richard Devetak, "Historiographical Foundations of Modern International Thought: Histories of the European States-System from Florence to Göttingen," *History of European Ideas* 41, no. 1 (2015): 62–77.

Perhaps the foremost and most systematic exponent of this mode of historical writing is Samuel von Pufendorf. While he is widely known for his contributions to natural law and the law of nations, his historical works have received less scholarly attention. Written during his appointment as a court historian in Stockholm, they were translated into numerous languages and widely read as viable guides to European great power politics well into the eighteenth century.[42] True to the methodological principles described earlier, von Pufendorf felt no contradiction between his ambition to write in a style at once impersonal and impartial in order to uncover the truth from authentic sources while simultaneously purporting to interpret and express the motives of the states whose history he wrote.

As von Pufendorf writes in the Preface of his *Einleitung zu der Historie der vornehmsten Reiche und Staaten, so itziger Zeit in Europa sich befinden* (1682), "he who has no Relish for History, is very unlikely to make any great Progress in the Way of Knowledge."[43] He then criticizes the contemporary focus on ancient history in favor of the "considerable Advantage it is to understand the Modern History as well as of our Native Country, as of its neighbouring Nations."[44] In order to provide the reader with valid historical knowledge of the past of each individual state and its relations with other states, von Pufendorf sets out to describe the "good and bad qualifications of each Nation . . . [and] what concerns the Nature, Strength and Weakness of each Country, and its form of Government."[45] To this end, he introduces a distinction between the imaginary and the real interests of states. Whereas the former "consists in such things as cannot be performed without disquieting and being injurious to a great many other states," real interests are further subdivided into perpetual and temporary ones. While the former "depends chiefly on the Situation and Constitution of the Country, and the natural

---

[42] For a general background, see Leonard Krieger, "History and Law in the Seventeenth Century: Pufendorf," *Journal of the History of Ideas* 21, no. 2 (1960): 198–210; Pärtel Piirimäe, "Politics and History: An Unholy Alliance? Samuel Pufendorf as Official Historiographer," in M. Engelbrecht, U. Hanssen-Decker, and D. Höffker (eds.), *Rund um die Meere des Nordens. Festschrift für Hain Rebas* (Heyde: Boyens Buchverlag, 2008), 237–52. On von Pufendorf's influence on the Swedish court, see R. M. Hatton, *Charles XII of Sweden* (London: Weidenfeld & Nicolson, 1968), 50, 111.

[43] Samuel von Pufendorf, *Introduction to the History of the Principal Kingdoms and States in Europe* (London: Peele, 1719), preface, ii.

[44] *Ibid.*, ii–iii.   [45] *Ibid.*, iv.

Inclinations of the People," the latter is determined by the "Condition, Strengths and Weakness of the neighbouring Nations."[46] Drawing on existing histories of European states, von Pufendorf sees no reason to correct them but rather wants to take them as indicative of the perceptions these states entertain of their own past and present. That these histories are biased and are based on all sorts of myths is of less concern to him, as long as these biases and myths can be taken as expressions of their distinct identities and interests. Since he regards these narratives to be indicative of claims to dynastic and territorial sovereignty, it does not really matter to him whether they are based or ascertainable historical facts or not, as long as they can be made intelligible with reference to a general state of war between seemingly cohesive and self-interested actors.

But if states are, or at least should be, governed by the maxims of real interests in their relations with each other, how did individual states come into being, and how did they manage to consolidate themselves into independent actors and legal persons? To the same extent that the precepts of secular statecraft are reflected in the relations of states, states have invariably been constituted through violent conflict between primordial groups. Thus, as if to empirically substantiate the speculative account of the origin of civil societies we find in the first pages of *De jure naturae et gentium* (1672), the real reason why mankind left behind paternal forms of government after the Deluge is that "among the Neighbouring Families, sometimes Quarrels used to arise, which being often decided by Force, drew along with them very great Inconveniences . . . And to guard off such Injuries, the Neighbours that lived so near as to be able to assist one another in case of Necessity, did enter into a society to defend themselves against their common Enemies."[47] But this state of war did not end with the constitution of societies but was now instead manifested in the relations between these, eventually culminating in the consolidation of distinct and bounded states. To von Pufendorf, as to many of his contemporaries, one of the main propellants of state formation is foreign invasion, which compels otherwise rivaling groups to unite against the intruders. Thus we learn that Spain "was in ancient times divided into a great many States, independent of one another ... But this multiplicity or partition exposed this otherwise Warlike Nation to the Inroads of Foreign Enemies."[48] Likewise, England was originally divided into "a great

---

[46] *Ibid.*, v.   [47] *Ibid.*, 2.   [48] *Ibid.*, 25.

many petty States," which "exposed them to the danger of being overcome by their Foreign Enemies."[49] And although the Gauls initially
had conquered both Italy and Greece, "this potent People, ignorant of
their own Strength and Power, were in no capacity to exert it sufficiently against other Nations, because they were not then under
the Government of one Prince, but divided into a great many petty
States, which were always at variance with one another. This contributed much to facilitate the Conquest of the Romans over them."[50]
After the Frankish invasion, it was evident that "the Race of the ancient
Gauls was not quite extinguished, but that both Nations were by
degrees united into one, though with this difference, that the Frankish
families made up the Body of the Nation."[51]

But a state could also originate as a result of expulsion or colonization in the distant past. As we learn from the posthumous compilation
entitled, *The Compleat History of Sweden from Its Origin to This Time*
(1702), although little is known of the ancient origins of this kingdom,
"it is probable that the first Inhabitants for a long time retained the free
State of Paternal Authority."[52] After having noted that "we are equally
in the dark of the exploits of their ancient Kings, since what we know of
them is only taken from old Ballads and fabulous Legends,"[53] von
Pufendorf embarks on a critical discussion of two earlier and well-
known accounts of Scandinavian history written by Johannes Magnus
and Johannes Messenius, respectively.[54] According to Magnus,
Denmark had been created when King Erik had "sent all the useless
and dissolute sort of People into the Isles of Denmark, and gave them
Judges who were subject to the Empire of the Goths."[55] This view had
later been disputed by Messenius, who had been responsible for organizing the royal archives that von Pufendorf used as the basis for his
own account. According to Messenius, Magnus had merely been interested in deprecating the Danes, when in fact "these colonies were only
planted in order to ease the Country which was over-stocked with

---

[49] *Ibid.*, 84.   [50] *Ibid.*, 148.   [51] *Ibid.*, 149.
[52] Samuel von Pufendorf, *The Compleat History of Sweden from Its Origin to This Time* (London: Wild, 1702), 3.
[53] *Ibid.*
[54] The source subject to contestation by both these authors is *Gesta Danorum* by Saxo Grammaticus. See Kurt Johannesson, *Saxo Grammaticus. Komposition och världsbild i Gesta Danorum* (Stockholm: Almqvist & Wiksell International, 1978).
[55] von Pufendorf, *History*, 5.

Inhabitants ... and ... there were a great many Worthy and Brave Persons concerned in such Expeditions."[56] But regardless of whether the Danish nation is made up of wicked men once expelled from Gothic soil or founded by praiseworthy men colonizing what then had been but a *terra nullius*, Denmark and the Danes nevertheless owed their existence to the most ancient and noble kingdom of Scandinavia and were therefore stuck in a position of perpetual inferiority vis-à-vis that kingdom. The reader should not be surprised to find that the relations between Denmark and Sweden had since been marked by nothing but mutual suspicion, deceit, and treachery.[57]

This provides the starting point for a long narrative leading toward the liberation of Sweden from the Danish yoke, culminating in its role as the vanguard of Protestant liberty against the imperial ambitions pursued by Ferdinand II. Indeed, the main reason why Sweden entered the Thirty Years War was that the "Emperor had formed a design to ruine the Protestants and make himself absolute Soveraign of Germany: This done, he meant to make himself Master of the Northern Kingdoms, which were necessary for establishing the Universal Monarchy over Europe, that he aspires after."[58] But in order to achieve the goals of this war of liberation, it was absolutely necessary that "the Protestants should act in Concert, and joyn their Forces together; for that otherwise, the peace would no sooner be concluded, but the Imperialists would resume their old Game, and ruine the Confederates one after another."[59] Hence, in this account, it is the Thirty Years War that compels Protestant states to consolidate and unite against a common enemy.

This account represents a first version of the idea that the Peace of Westphalia constitutes a point of transition from the world of empire to a world of states. But, in contrast to the modern version of this idea, Westphalia does not mark the emergence of a system of territorially bounded and mutually recognizing sovereign states but represents the end result of a war of independence and liberation from imperial authority pursued by a rather loose coalition of disparate actors.[60] To von Pufendorf, what made the world of states was not so much the Peace of Westphalia but the war that preceded that peace. So

---

[56] *Ibid.*   [57] *Ibid.*, 88ff, 168ff.   [58] *Ibid.*, 437–8.   [59] *Ibid.*, 462.
[60] For a discussion, see Derek Croxton, "The Peace of Westphalia of 1648 and the Origins of Sovereignty," *International History Review* 21, no. 3 (1999): 569–91; Andreas Osiander, "Sovereignty, International Relations, and the Westphalian Myth," *International Organization* 55, no. 2 (2001): 251–87.

however glorious, this peace cannot but result in new wars, since states are now stuck in a state of war among themselves, much as a consequence of their violent prehistory and the outward projection of that violent past that followed naturally on their quest for independence. As von Pufendorf tells us, soon after his coronation, Charles Gustavus "was indispensably obliged to prepare himself and take up Arms, not only least the Courages of so many Brave officers would droop by too much ease, and that way obscure the Lustre and Glory of the Swedish Nation; but because the Fire of War, which was kindled between the Poles and Muscovites, was come even to the Frontiers of Sweden."[61] Thus the unity of nations gave way to a proliferation of internal divisions, invasions, and conquests, yet rivalries between groups as well as with foreign foes pushed forward a consolidation of state power in the hands of successive sovereigns, ending with an outward projection of violent impulses onto the emergent international arena.

So to the nadir of empire corresponds the genesis of that arena where the interests of states are bound to clash. But the Protestant myth of Westphalia also gave rise to the first attempts to write what later came to be known as diplomatic history. Rather than tracing the history of particular states backward in time in order to assert their uniqueness and glory in the present, works in this genre take Westphalia to be a formative moment in history and then recount the history of the states that owed their independence to the preceding war. One of the first efforts in this direction was made by the Dutch diplomat Abraham de Wicquefort, whose *L'Ambassadeur et ses Fonctions* (1682) had quickly become the standard manual of contemporary diplomatic practice. Wicquefort later turned out to be a skilled and prolific writer of diplomatic history. As we learn from his *Histoire de Provinces-Unies des Pais-Bas* (1704), it was the treaty of Münster that led to the "perfect establishment" of the Dutch republic. Whereas von Pufendorf had struggled to make sense of a distant past in terms consonant with the precepts of secular statecraft, Wicquefort faces the easier task of making sense of contemporary great power politics in the same terms. Yet, admittedly, "it is a very delicate matter to write of the affairs of those who are living through and handling them, and following their execution with Justice and Truth, through so much as their interests differ

---

[61] von Pufendorf, *History*, 560.

and their passions are directly opposed."[62] To this end, he purports to advance nothing that cannot be verified from archives, registers, and memoirs and whose truth can be ascertained by readers who themselves were witnesses of the events to be recounted. In his account, the Thirty Years War was indeed constitutive of some states, since prior to the Peace of Westphalia, one cannot speak of the United Provinces as a state proper because "there was no other Sovereignty in this state than that which resided in the provinces of which it was composed."[63] Thus it becomes possible to speak of the United Provinces as a single state as a consequence of the conquests of territories from the Spaniards. France, and England, being "jealous of the formidable power of the King of Spain and the House of Austria," thereby facilitated the birth of the United Provinces, which was first to discover the weakness of Spain.[64] Noting that the king of Spain "can be properly called the veritable enemy of this State," Wicquefort proceeds to describe the liberation of the Dutch from the Spanish yoke, from the onset of the Dutch revolt to what he optimistically believes to be its conclusion at Münster.[65] What transpires from his account is the contention that these wars had shaped the United Provinces as an independent actor on the international stage and made it able to entertain diplomatic relations with other European states on formally equal terms.

Yet the mode of historical writing exemplified in this account raises a series of important questions. How could the state of war be projected back onto time immemorial and structure historical narratives, and how was it possible to assume that European countries – at least in some embryonic form – had been present since the dawn of history? This is puzzling given that early modern historical consciousness was still largely under the spell of universal history, according to which humanity traversed a series of preordained historical stages contained in a providential plan.[66] Since the precepts of secular statecraft were regarded as immoral and destructive, those Protestant historians who used them to structure their historical narratives were facing an away game. In order to understand why such statist historiography won the day, we must pay attention to the rhetorical functions performed by these

---

[62] Abraham de Wicquefort, *Histoire de Provinces-Unies des Pais-Bas* (La Haye: Johnson 1719), 2.
[63] Wicquefort, *Histoire*, 6, 16   [64] *Ibid.*, 26.   [65] *Ibid.*, 44; 45–59.
[66] See for example, Jacques-Bénigne Bossuet, *Discours sur l"Histoire Universelle* (Paris: S. Mabre-Cramoisy, 1681).

historical accounts. First, and most obviously, projecting a state of war onto the immemorial served to establish continuities between past and present that were used to legitimize power politics in the present, precisely against those who disputed such conduct on moral grounds. By establishing continuities between past and present, it was possible to argue that since the state of war was a transhistorical condition beyond the scope of human volition, it necessitated recourse to political practices that otherwise would have been considered profoundly destructive of the political order.

Second, I think it is equally obvious that the assumption that states had been present in some embryonic form since time immemorial served not only to reinforce claims to sovereignty by their rulers but also to sustain the early forms of nationalism that had accompanied the rise of ontogenetic war. This is no more evident than in the attribution of national characters during this period. As I argued in the preceding section, ideas of nationhood could be traced back to the reappropriation of Roman ideals of empire and patriotism. Drawing on this rich symbolic legacy, many writers were busy constructing accounts of national identities in support of sovereignty claims raised by individual rulers. Frequently fanned by the flames of war, these accounts were used to galvanize compatriots into action and to stigmatize foreigners into enemies so that each story of nationhood developed in opposition to other similar stories until a system of self-reinforcing stereotypes and prejudices had taken hold of European elites and thoroughly tainted their perceptions of their neighbors.

The creation of such national identities is very present in the early modern histories discussed earlier. Here d'Avity and Pufendorf stand out as the most creative and dynamic exponents, and the fact that their accounts are separated by more than half a century allows for some interesting comparisons. As an important step in assessing the strengths and weaknesses of European states, d'Avity provides elaborate descriptions of the customs and manners of their inhabitants. While he draws heavily on Roman authorities such as Strabo, Pliny, and Tacitus when describing the past, his way of characterizing present customs provides us with nice glimpses into seventeenth-century proto-nationalism at work. Thus we learn that although the English were originally barbarous, they have gradually become more polite and civilized, now being capable of arts and science and displaying courtesy and hospitality to strangers.[67] Yet their original barbarism remains alive and well among the lower classes, since "with the exception of those well born and nourished, the nature of all others is extremely fierce, and their way of living intolerable to anyone with sentiment and courage."[68] Hence the occasional visitor to England should be forewarned that "the leftovers of this nation are indeed born into thievery."[69]

Likewise, the Spaniards are "of a warm and dry nature, and of a brown color" and "surpass almost all the rest of mankind in their superstition."[70] They receive foreigners with little courtesy and "keep their solemnity with a feigned sincerity, which makes them detested by all other nations."[71] Their haughtiness aside, the Spaniards are also constantly conniving and "love tricks and lies in all matters," including those of faith: "they pretend great reverence of the Church and things sacred, and some of them hold that their professed piety ... have [sic] rendered the Heavens favorable, and has made God give them a new world through conquest."[72] By contrast, and unsurprisingly, the French excel at bonhomie. The French, being "good and straightforward," and while threatened by the malicious designs of their neighbors in the South, these plots are to no avail because the French were literally born in war and their nobility the most valiant and gentle.[73]

Similarly, each chapter of Pufendorf's *History* ends with a brief sketch of the peculiarities of each nation, making it valuable as a catalogue of early modern stereotypes. But underneath the surface of prejudice is an analysis of the virtues and vices that help explain why some states have been successful and others have failed to survive and prosper. Among the former, the French and the Swedes stand out for their valor and military prowess. The French nation "has been always warlike ... they were very brave at the first Onset; but after their first Fury was a little cooled, their Courage used to slacken, if they met with stout and brave Resistance."[74] We also learn that the French are "also brisk, forward, of a merry Constitution: as to their outward appearance in their Apparel and Behaviour, they are generally very comely."[75] The Swedes, despite having descended from barbarians, also embody Roman valor; "they were ever reputed very Warlike; they always had the character of a People that are not Afraid of their Skin, or annoyed by the smell

[67] D'Avity, *Les Estats, Empires, Royaumes et Principautes du Monde*, 6.
[68] *Ibid.*, 7.   [69] *Ibid.*   [70] *Ibid.* 146.   [71] *Ibid.*   [72] *Ibid.*, 147.
[73] *Ibid.*, 90–1.   [74] von Pufendorf, *Introduction*, 210.   [75] *Ibid.*, 211.

of Gunpowder." But Pufendorf is quick to add some qualifications, noting that since even if they are "very well versed in the Art of Dissimulation, they remain 'extremely jealous and distrustful' ... as well as 'very invidous,' insomuch that one Swede does not commonly love to see another thrive."[76] The Spaniards receive an unfavorable treatment by Pufendorf. Thus we learn of the Spaniards that although they "are very fit for War ... their sober way of living, and spare Bodies, qualify them to bear Hunger and Thirst ... they maintain their Gravity by highflown Words and proud Behaviour." Furthermore, "they are seldom fit for any Trade or Business where hard Labour is required." And "Their Pride, Covetousness, and rigorous Proceedings make them hateful to all that are under their Command."[77]

These accounts are indicative of how political competition among early modern states was reinforced by an appeal to national characteristics, how the notion of a primordial state of war found additional nourishment in the attribution of warlike characteristics, and how the distribution of virtues and vices among these peoples reflected an emergent stratification between the Protestant North and the Catholic South. While the nations of the North are governed by rational interest, those in the South remain prey to passions and superstition. And while the former are described as diligent and trustworthy, the latter are inclined to be proud and dishonest in their dealings.

But these nations are also internally stratified. While the nobility is distinguished by its valor, gentleness, and hospitality, the lower strata still bear the stigma of barbarism that originally had characterized each nation before the struggle between races had propelled the process of state formation forward and given rise to virtuous elites. Thus these authors are characteristically ambivalent about the nature of barbarism and its relation to the state. On the one hand, barbarism is present at the foundation of each state since time immemorial and thus remains an indispensable force behind its formation. On the other hand, as soon as the state has been formed and warfare has become the privilege of a warrior class, what remains of barbarism becomes a threat that must be either expelled from the social body or harnessed for the purposes of foreign war. To d'Avity, since the violent energies of the lower classes represent a threat to the cohesion of society, their members must be subjugated, disciplined, and punished. Only in that way can other

[76] von Pufendorf, *History*, 610, 612.   [77] von Pufendorf, *Introduction*, 59, 60.

nations aspire to the perfection already attained by the French. To Pufendorf, "the boors" constitute a whimsical and dangerous force that a ruler may neglect only at his own peril. But when properly tamed, however, the boors can become useful; as evidenced by the military reforms of Gustavus Adolphus, their enlistment and training can be a source of great military success.

From Barbarism to Civilization

When we enter the eighteenth century, it is widely accepted as axiomatic that war had made the state. What had begun as a series of historical conjectures intended to legitimize sovereign authority now found support in a rich historiography that portrayed the formation of states and their intercourse as the inevitable result of a state of war that had been present since time immemorial. For example, to Hume, government found its origin in war: "[I]t is probable, that the first ascendant of one man over multitudes begun during a state of war; where the superiority of courage and of genius discovers itself most visibly, where unanimity and concert are most requisite, and where the pernicious effects of disorder are most sensibly felt."[78] And as Smith contended, "the first duty of the sovereign, that of protecting the society from the violence and invasion of other independent societies, can be performed only by means of a military force."[79]

But whereas philosophers and historians of the seventeenth century had been focused on war as an instrument of secular statecraft, their Enlightenment successors were more concerned with its undesirable fallout. Many authors during this period lamented that war perpetuated despotic governments at home and imperial rule abroad but simultaneously regarded an international state of war as an inevitable outcome of domestic pacification. To Rousseau, it was obvious that the formation of states merely had pushed the state of war outward so that "bodies politic, remaining thus in a state of nature among themselves, presently experienced the inconveniences which had obliged individuals to forsake it; for this state became still more fatal to these great bodies than it had been to the individuals of whom they were composed. Hence arose

[78] David Hume, "On the Origin of Government," in *Essays* (Indianapolis, IN: Liberty Fund, 1987), I.V, 6.
[79] Adam Smith, *An Inquiry into the Nature and Causes of the Wealth of Nations* [1776], ed. Edwin Cannan (London: Methuen & Co., 1904), II.V.1.0.

national wars, battles, murders, and reprisals, which shock nature and outrage reason."[80]

To accept that war had made states made it hard to deny that states also made war and hence also that the abolition of warfare within states had turned the state of war into a permanent condition of humankind, which was irreversibly divided into distinct and bounded communities, each claiming sovereignty over its territory and population. As Rousseau went on to argue, "the state of war is the natural relation of one Power to another ... Who then are those between whom war takes place and who alone can truly be called enemies? I answer that they are public persons. And what is a 'public person'? I answer that it is that moral creation called a Sovereign, which owes its existence to a social compact and all the decisions of which go by the name of 'laws.'"[81]

According to Howard, many Enlightenment authors regarded war "not as part of the natural order or a necessary instrument of state power, but as a foolish anachronism, perpetuated only by those who enjoyed or profited from it."[82] But although many Enlightenment authors certainly were critical of contemporary practices of war and empire, they were also struggling to come to terms with the role of war and the prospects of popular sovereignty.[83] Catering to the latter concerns, they sometimes invoked war as an important cause of human progress and civilization and, by implication, as the not-so-gentle civilizer of nations. Thus Enlightenment historians and philosophers were inclined to argue two things. First, given the widely shared assumption that human history could be subdivided into distinct stages ranging from the primitive to the more advanced, they argued that since the art of war had been crucial to the progress of the human species, civilized states enjoyed a military advantage over less civilized ones.

---

[80] Rousseau, "Discourse on the Origin of Inequality," in Jean-Jacques Rousseau, *The Social Contract and Discourses*, trans. G. D. H. Cole (London: Dent, 1990), 100. For an analysis of Rousseau's view of war that remains valuable, see Stanley Hoffmann, "Rousseau on War and Peace," in Stanley Hoffmann, *The State of War: Essays on the Theory and Practice of International Politics* (New York: Praeger, 1965), 54–87.

[81] Jean-Jacques Rousseau, "L'État de Guerre," in Jean Jacques Rousseau, *The Political Writings of Jean Jacques Rousseau*, vol. I, ed. C. E. Vaughan (Cambridge: Cambridge University Press, 1915), 293–307, at 301.

[82] Michael Howard, *The Invention of Peace: Reflections on War and International Order* (New Haven: Yale University Press, 2000), 26.

[83] See Richard Whatmore, *Against War and Empire: Geneva, Britain and France in the Eighteenth Century* (New Haven: Yale University Press, 2012).

Second, since many Enlightenment historians were critical of imperial practices of war on the grounds that they hampered political progress and corrupted commercial advances, it was not uncommon to argue that popular sovereignty was desirable for strategic rather than moral or ideological reasons, insofar as it could be expected to give republics a distinctive edge in an international system characterized by fierce political and economic competition between great powers.

Yet these arguments assumed that nations were sufficiently cohesive to maintain the conditions of popular sovereignty in order to augment their external power. While the early modern authors discussed earlier had construed nations in support of claims to sovereign authority, these nations were hardly conceived as acting subjects in their own right but multitudes held together by common characteristics. To speak of nations as actors took some rather profound changes in the meaning of this concept and its range of applicability. From having been used to refer to groups divided along kinship lines, the concept of nation was now being used to refer to entire populations under the presumption that prior conflicts between these groups had been resolved or at least mitigated to such an extent that nations now could be conceived as collective subjects.[84]

The second source of change concerns the appeals to popular sovereignty that made their way into treatises in legal and political theory from the mid-eighteenth century onward. If nations constitute collective subjects, and if they enjoy legal independence within an international system devoid of supreme authority, it was a short step to argue that they also were entitled to govern themselves internally. Hence arose the connection between claims to external sovereignty, on the one hand, and pleas to self-determination, on the other.[85] In the present context, however, a new understanding of how this connection was forged allows us to question a common understanding of the relationship between nationalism and popular sovereignty. According to this understanding, nationalism and nations arose in close conjunction with the quest for popular sovereignty and democratic legitimacy that

---

[84] Foucault, *Society Must Be Defended*, 215–38.

[85] See David Armitage, *The Declaration of Independence: A Global History* (Cambridge, MA: Harvard University Press, 2007); David Armitage, *Foundations of Modern International Thought* (Cambridge: Cambridge University Press, 2013), 191–232.

ensued from the American and French revolutions. As Greenfeld argued some time ago, "[n]ationalism was the form in which democracy appeared in the world, contained in the idea of the nation as a butterfly in a cocoon."[86] And as Hunt has pointed out, "the displacement of the ruler by the nation required the building of a citizenry in which individuals ... identified with each other as part of a nation."[87] But although this was undoubtedly true in many cases, this should not detract attention from the fact early versions of popular sovereignty were justified with reference to the increase in social cohesion and state power that popular participation in politics was expected to bring. The first recognizably modern pleas for popular sovereignty are therefore perhaps better understood as responses to problems of security and war rather than as harbingers of revolutions to come.

To grasp this peculiar connection between war and popular sovereignty, let us briefly revisit the notions of an international system that started to emerge in the literature during this period. Many contemporary authors struggled to make sense of what they perceived to be a radical break with the foreign policies of the seventeenth century. Whereas war had been seen as a tool for consolidating state sovereignty and boosting the power and prestige of monarchs, it was now increasingly taken to be a consequence of economic and geopolitical competition between states that resulted from mercantile ideology and practices.[88] As Hume commented on the trade rivalries between the great powers, "nothing is more usual, among states which have made some advances in commerce, than to look on the progress of their neighbours with a suspicious eye, to consider all trading states as their rivals, and to suppose that it is impossible for any of them to flourish, but at their expence."[89] Mercantile practices made earlier maxims of statecraft

---

[86] Liah Greenfeld, *Nationalism: Five Roads to Modernity* (Cambridge, MA: Harvard University Press, 1992), 10. For other accounts that emphasize this connection, see Christopher A. Bayly, *The Birth of the Modern World 1780–1914* (Oxford: Blackwell, 2004), 199–243; Bernhard Yack, "Popular Sovereignty and Nationalism," *Political Theory* 29 no. 4 (2001): 517–36.

[87] Lynn Hunt, "The French Revolution in Global Context," in David Armitage and Sanjay Subrahmanyam (eds.), *The Age of Revolutions in a Global Context, c. 1760–1840* (Basingstoke: Palgrave Macmillan, 2010), 20–36, at 35.

[88] See Istvan Hont, *Jealousy of Trade: International Competition and the Nation-State in Historical Perspective* (Cambridge, MA: Harvard University Press, 2005), 1–159.

[89] David Hume, "Jealousy of Trade" [1742], in *Essays* (Indianapolis, IN: Liberty Fund, 1987), II.VI, 1.

appear outdated because they had been derived from the attributes of individual states rather than from their relative power position in the *system* of states that now was believed to be emerging and whose modus operandi was thought to be outside the control of individual statesmen. As Mably argued, what determine the interests and conduct of states are no longer their inner attributes but their relative power in the international political system. To him, and now irrespective of their different customs and laws, the great powers of Europe can be subdivided into two broad categories – dominant and rival ones – while all lesser powers will have to conduct their foreign policies with an eye to the balance of power between the great powers.[90]

In this new system, it was imperative to maintain the balance of power in order to prevent any state from achieving dominance, thereby preserving the independence of individual states while upholding a modicum of international order and peace. While the international system was a potent source of discord in its own right due to its anarchic character, it was also widely perceived to be a means to preserve the independence of states and the liberties of peoples. As Gibbon remarked in his *Decline and Fall of the Roman Empire* (1776–8), in sharp contrast to the Roman Empire, "the division of Europe into a number of independent states, connected, however, with each other, by the general resemblance of religion, language, and manners, is productive of the most beneficial consequences to the liberty of mankind."[91] As historical narratives of states now were restructured, the Protestant myth of Westphalia was superseded by narratives that located the origin of the international system even further back in time but that again gave preeminence to the constitutive force of war when explaining the genesis of states and nations in Europe.[92]

For example, as we learn from Voltaire in his *Siècle de Louis XIV* (1751), the progress from barbarism to civilization had been propelled by the gradual perfection of arts and manners that started with the Greeks and culminated during the reign of Louis XIV. But even well before his

---

[90] Gabriel Bonnot de Mably, *Des Principes des Négociations, pour servir d'introduction au Droit Publique de l'europé, fondé sur les traités* (La Haye, 1757), 31–2.

[91] Edward Gibbon, *The Decline and Fall of the Roman Empire*, vol. 1 (New York: Modern Library, n.d.), 72–3.

[92] For an overview of such themes in Enlightenment historiography, see Bruce Buchan, "Enlightened Histories: Civilization, War and the Scottish Enlightenment," *European Legacy* 10, no. 2 (2005): 177–92.

reign, Europe "might be considered as a great republic divided into several states" whose intercourse was characterized by "the prudent policy of preserving, as far as they are able, an equal balance of power among themselves."[93] Voltaire then describes the preconditions for the cultural and scientific refinement attained during the reign of Louis. As it turns out, his greatest feat was to consolidate the French state and to abolish factionalism, discord, and superstition that had long stifled progress. Since "politics and arms seem unhappily to be the two professions most natural to man, who must always be either negotiating or fighting," the measurement of true greatness was the ability to master both.[94] Thus, at the height of his reign, "Louis increased his dominions even in peace, and always kept himself in readiness for war, fortifying the frontier towns, augmenting the number of his troops, keeping them well disciplined, and frequently reviewing them in person."[95] And as a result of his endeavors, the French "state became one regular whole, every line of which terminated in the centre."[96] This made it possible to turn a nation hitherto divided and turbulent into "a peaceable people, who were dangerous only to the enemy."[97]

Another example of this new periodization is found in Robertson's *History of the Reign of the Emperor Charles V* (1769). Whereas both Voltaire and Hume had emphasized the importance of balance of power in maintaining the European system of states, Robertson was more concerned with how and why the latter had emerged.[98] As he states in the Preface, since modern history begins with the advent of secular statecraft, this makes it imperative to confine "study of history in detail chiefly to that period in which the several states of Europe having become intimately connected, the operations of one power are so felt by all as to influence their councils, and to regulate their measures."[99] Tracing the origin of the modern international system to the

---

93 Voltaire, *The Age of Louis XIV* [1751], vol. 12, in *The Works of Voltaire: A Contemporary Version* (New York: E.R. Dumont, 1901), 13. For a valuable account of the historiographic context, see J. G. A. Pocock, *Barbarism and Religion*, vol. II: *Narratives of Civil Government* (Cambridge: Cambridge University Press, 1999), 289–99.
94 Voltaire, *The Age of Louis XIV*, 30.   95 *Ibid.*, 115.   96 *Ibid.*, 256.
97 *Ibid.*, 257.
98 For a comparison, see Frederick G. Whelan, "Robertson, Hume, and the Balance of Power," *Hume Studies* 21, no. 2 (1995): 315–32.
99 William Robertson, *The History of the Reign of the Emperor Charles V, with a View of the Progress of Society in Europe, from the Subversion of the Roman*

reign of Charles V, this system emerges largely as an unintended consequence of his policies of conquest and counter-reformation, and especially through the resistance these policies provoked among the French. As Robertson continues, "it was during his administration that the powers of Europe were formed into one great political system, in which each took a station, wherein it has since remained with less variation than could have been expected after the shocks occasioned by so many internal revolutions, and so many foreign wars."[100] The cornerstone of this system was the balance of power, and the moment of its inception was the Peace of Cateau-Cambrésis in 1559. At this point, the belligerents had been compelled by recent historical developments to acknowledge that "no prince was so much superior to the rest in power, as to render his efforts irresistible, and his conquests easy ... the advantages possessed by one state were counterbalanced by circumstances favourable to others and this prevented any from attaining such superiority as might have been fatal to all."[101] But the reign of Charles had further consequences insofar as it had forced European states to consolidate in order to counteract his ambitions so that "the different kingdoms of Europe acquired internal vigour; that they discerned the resources of which they were possessed; that they came both to feel their own strength, and to know how to render it formidable to others."[102] True to the practices Enlightenment historiography, Robertson projects contemporary concerns onto the past and allows them to organize a narrative in which war, together with scientific and moral progress, become the driving force behind the consolidation of states in Europe and the formation of "one great political system, in which each took a station, wherein it hath remained since that time with less variation than could have been expected after the events of two active centuries."[103] While allowing for differences of culture and religion, there was not among European states "that wide diversity of character and of genius which, in almost every period of history, hath exalted the Europeans above the inhabitants of the other quarters of the globe, and seems to have destined the one to rule, and the other to obey."[104]

Empire to the Beginning of the Sixteenth Century, vol. I [1769] (London: Routledge, 1857), vii. For the historiographic context, see Pocock, *Barbarism and Religion*, vol. II, 83–96.
[100] Robertson, *The History of the Reign of the Emperor Charles V*, vol. I, viii.
[101] Robertson, *The History of the Reign of the Emperor Charles V*, vol. II, 470.
[102] *Ibid.*, 471.   [103] *Ibid.*   [104] *Ibid.*, 470.

But before this great system could be projected backward in time, it had first to become a social fact in its own right, and this is where the prerevolutionary pleas for popular sovereignty start to make sense. Important clues to this development can be found in the republican tradition and its understanding of the relationship between popular sovereignty and warfare. As Nabulsi has summarized the core assumptions of this tradition, "if freedom is to be understood as independence ... then one needs to find the means to avoid becoming dependent not only on tyrants who arise (by means of faction) from within but also from without (by way of conquest)."[105] This is why the strategic defenses of popular sovereignty articulated by Mably and d'Argenson become so important. Both authors seek to revive tenets of classical republicanism in French foreign policy in the decades before the Revolution not because they wanted to overthrow the monarchy but rather because they wanted to augment the relative power of France in relation to its competitors during a period of relative decline. To Mably, diplomatic ties between states is the outcome of a natural tendency among humans to form alliances: "like humans when united into a society ... have formed a defensive league against violence, it is natural that less powerful peoples unite themselves once more to oppose who would abuse their superiority of power."[106] Invoking familiar republican themes and virtues, Mably argues that to preserve the independence of the state from foreign powers, it is necessary to preserve the liberty of the citizens from arbitrary exercises of power. Republican governments are best equipped in this regard because they stand internally united and can thus better withstand foreign pressure. They are therefore in a good position to maintain peaceful relations with other states but also to deal most forcibly with states that wish to expand their influence at the expense of others.[107] So whereas Mably sometimes has been credited with having reconceptualized the French nation in terms more democratic and inclusive than some of his contemporaries, I think it is important to recall that his vindication of

---

[105] Karma Nabulsi, *Traditions of War: Occupation, Resistance, and the Law* (Oxford: Oxford University Press, 1999), 177–240, at 238–9; cf. Nicholas Greenwood Onuf, *The Republican Legacy in International Thought* (Cambridge: Cambridge University Press, 1998).
[106] Mably, *Principes*, 2.   [107] *Ibid.*, 151–70.

republican virtues and institutions was to some extent motivated by concerns with external security and internal legitimacy.[108]

Another example of how the connection between popular sovereignty and national interest could be conceptualized is found in *Considérations sur le Gouvernement Ancient et Présent de la France* (1764–5), by Marquis d'Argenson, who had briefly served as foreign minister under Louis XV.[109] In a world characterized by swift and unforeseen reversals of fortune among states, good government must maximize both the strength of the state and the happiness of the people at the same time. Yet these objectives often turn out to be difficult to reconcile in practice because a strong state calls for a rule that is likely to deprive the people of their happiness and infringe on their liberty, whereas promoting the latter risks undermining the strength of the state and thereby rendering it more vulnerable to external enemies. D'Argenson seeks to handle this tradeoff by an appeal to a very peculiar form of popular sovereignty: "I hope to show through this examination, that popular administration can be exercised under sovereign authority, without diminishing but rather increasing public power, and that this is a source of people's happiness."[110] Since direct rule by the people will necessarily degenerate into mob rule and eventually result in anarchy, true democracy is only possible when deputies are elected by the people and thereby constitute a public power in its own right.[111] Since the state is composed of many particular and often conflicting interests, the sovereign must know when to hamper their expression and when to give them free reign for the sake of the general good. To that end, different parts of the people must be allowed to gather together to discuss and act with a certain degree of independence.[112] And "if the public interest is listened to and allowed to act without confusion, it will produce a movement towards continuity and renewal that will further increase and perfect it."[113] Again, popular sovereignty is justified not with reference to the civic virtues it is

---

[108] Compare François Furet and Mona Ozouf, "Deux Légitimations Historiques de la Société Française au XVIIIe Siècle: Mably et Boulainvilliers," in *Annales. Économies, Sociétés, Civilisations* (1979): 438–50.

[109] René Louis de Voyer de Paulmy D'Argenson, *Considérations sur le Gouvernement Ancient et Présent de la France* (Amsterdam: Reys, 1765). For an interesting analysis, see Péter Balázs, "Philosophie et Histoire dans l'œuvre du marquis d'Argenson," *Dix-Huitième Siècle* 1 (2010): 561–79.

[110] D'Argenson, *Considérations*, 2. [111] *Ibid.*, 7–8. [112] *Ibid.*, 28.
[113] *Ibid.*, 34.

supposed to foster but as a means to increase the legitimacy of royal authority and the power of the state as a whole. Thus the importance of this early version of illiberal democracy lies in its ability to preserve rather than to subvert monarchical institutions. This being so, popular sovereignty makes it possible to reconcile conflicting interests for the common good and align those interests with those of the sovereign, thereby creating the kind of national unity that is best equipped to withstand foreign threats and revolutionary upheaval at home. This reconceptualization of republican ideas not only antedated the famous reconceptualization of the nation undertaken by Sieyès but was informed by political imperatives very distinct from those that animated the works of Rousseau and Diderot.

The idea that war is productive of national cohesion found ample support in more erudite works of the same period. While some Enlightenment authors saw war as detrimental to human happiness and conducive only of despotism and imperialism, others regarded war as the main driver of progress in human affairs and tried to explain the genesis of sociopolitical order in terms of perpetual conflict. Thus Ferguson, in his *Essay on the History of Civil Society* (1767), starts out from the assumption that "mankind not only find in their condition the sources of variance and dissension; they appear to have in their minds the seeds of animosity, and to embrace the occasions of mutual opposition, with alacrity and pleasure."[114] At earlier stages of human development, this violent predisposition manifested itself in perpetual struggles among rude nations, yet without "the rivalship of nations, and the practice of war, civil society itself could scarcely have found an object or a form."[115] Thus a comparison of the prehistory of the

---

[114] Adam Ferguson, *An Essay on the History of Civil Society* (London: Millar & Cadell, 1767), 30. For some recent interpretations, see Lisa Hill, "Eighteenth-Century Anticipations of the Sociology of Conflict: The Case of Adam Ferguson," *Journal of the History of Ideas* 62, no. 2 (2001): 281–99; Craig Smith, "'We Have Mingled Politeness with the Use of the Sword': Nature and Civilisation in Adam Ferguson's Philosophy of War," *The European Legacy* 19, no. 1 (2014): 1–15; Bruce Buchan, "Civilisation, Sovereignty and War: The Scottish Enlightenment and International Relations," *International Relations* 20, no. 2 (2006): 175–92; Hans Joas and Wolfgang Knöbl, *War in Social Thought: Hobbes to the Present* (Princeton, NJ: Princeton University Press, 2013), 31–7; Iain McDaniel, *Adam Ferguson in the Scottish Enlightenment: The Roman Past and Europe's Future* (Cambridge, MA: Harvard University Press, 2013).

[115] Ferguson, *Essay*, 35.

Greeks, the Romans, and the contemporary condition of the native tribes of America reveal that "in every rude state, the great business is war; and that in barbarous times, mankind, being generally divided into small parties, are engaged in almost perpetual hostilities. This circumstance gives the military leader a continued ascendant in his country, and inclines every people, during warlike ages, to monarchical government."[116] From this, Ferguson was able to infer that "such therefore appears to have been the commencement of history with all nations, and in such circumstances are we to look for the original character of mankind."[117] Yet, however belligerent and ferocious, rude and barbarian nations must "always yield to the superior arts, and the more discipline of more civilized nations."[118] So when nations evolve into a more civilized stage, they not only become less belligerent but also more skilled in the art of war and thus better equipped to subjugate their more rude enemies. And while rude nations are "for the most part separated by jealousy and animosity; yet when pressed by wars and formidable enemies, they sometimes unite in greater bodies"[119] and have thereby been forced to embark on the road toward a more civilized and polite stage. Hence "the enjoyment of peace, and the prospect of being able to exchange one commodity for another, turns, by degrees the hunter and warrior into a tradesman and a merchant."[120] At this point, Ferguson reiterates a familiar point, since having escaped their original rudeness and barbarism, "they require the exercise of foreign wars to maintain domestic peace: when the enemy no longer appears from abroad, they have leisure for private feuds, and employ that courage in their dissensions at home."[121]

But even if some civic virtues and military valor unfortunately had been lost in the transition from barbarous to commercial and civilized societies, an international state of war between such societies is nevertheless preferable to the boundless state of war between uncivilized nations that had preceded it, since the civilizing process also extends into the European system of states "we have improved on the laws of war ... we have mingled politeness with the use of the sword; we have learned to make war under the stipulations of treaties and cartels ... This is, perhaps, the principal characteristic, on which, among modern nations, we bestow the epithets of *civilized* or of *polished*."[122] Yet,

---

[116] *Ibid.*, 226.   [117] *Ibid.*, 114.   [118] *Ibid.*, 144.   [119] *Ibid.*, 155.
[120] *Ibid.*, 277.   [121] *Ibid.*, 157.   [122] *Ibid.*, 306.

however much subject to legal regulation and territorial compartmentalization, war will remain a productive force in human affairs because
it "furnishes mankind with a principal occupation of their restless
spirit" and "serves, by the variety of its events, to diversify their
fortunes. While it opens to one tribe or society, the way to eminence,
and leads to dominion, it brings another to subjection, and closes the
scene of their national efforts."[123] As Kalyvas and Katznelson have
concluded in their analysis of Ferguson's work, "modernity generates
diversity that is always conflictual."[124] Hence the international state of
war can be understood as a consequence of the modernizing process,
since that process pushes the remnants of barbarism and hostility outward, into the *nowhere* of the international system. Against the backdrop of this understanding of war as the first mover of the civilizing
process, it made perfect sense not only to argue that republican forms of
government were better adapted to the more refined circumstances of
civilized nations but that they also gave such nations a distinctive
advantage compared with their less civilized opponents in times of war.

Similar themes recurred and were further elaborated by Smith in his
Inquiry into the Nature and Causes of the Wealth of Nations (1776).
To him, it was evident that the capacity to wage war increased with the
level of civilization and that this gave civilized states an advantage over
uncivilized ones because "in modern times the poor and barbarous find
it difficult to defend themselves against the opulent and civilized."[125]
Developing the capacity for warfare is thus absolutely crucial for the
modern state because "the art of war, however, as it is certainly the
noblest of all arts, so in the progress of improvement it necessarily
becomes one of the most complicated among them."[126] Since standing
armies enjoy a distinctive advantage over citizen militias, the former
must be "maintained by an opulent and civilized nation, so it can alone
defend such a nation against the invasion of a poor and barbarous
neighbour. It is only by means of a standing army, therefore, that the
civilization of any country can be perpetuated, or even preserved for
any considerable time."[127] And, by the same token, standing armies
represent the best means to impose civilization on other parts of the

---

[123] *Ibid.*, 316.
[124] Andreas Kalyvas and Ira Katznelson, "Adam Ferguson Returns: Liberalism
through a Glass, Darkly," *Political Theory* 26, no. 2 (1998): 173–97, at 191.
[125] Smith, *Wealth of Nations*, II.V.1.43.   [126] *Ibid.*, II.V.1.13.
[127] *Ibid.*, II.V.1.38.

world because such armies "establish with an irresistible force, the law of the sovereign through the remotest provinces of the empire, and maintain some degree of regular government in countries which could not otherwise admit of any."[128]

It could of course also be argued that republics are more disposed to peaceful conduct than are monarchical governments and that the international state of war eventually will give way to a state of international peace, at least among the former. But although the belief that republics are predisposed to peace long had been a salient theme in republican thought, this belief was further reinforced by the expectation that progress and civilization would eventually make war redundant, and such expectations were commonly voiced in the more optimistic strands of Enlightenment political thought.[129] Yet, as Kant famously argued in his *Idee zu einer allgemeinen Geschichte in weltbürgerlicher Absicht* (1784), "the unsocial sociability of men, that is, their tendency to come together in society, coupled, however, with continual resistance which constantly threatens to break this society up" will ultimately propel mankind toward a state of peace.[130] Having established commonwealths based on the rule of law and the reciprocal freedom of their members, mankind is then faced with the final challenge of overcoming discord in its external relations. The same unsociability that once compelled mankind to form states now manifests itself *between* states; "each must accordingly expect from any other precisely the same evils which formerly oppressed individual men and forced them into a law-governed civil state."[131] In response to this predicament, though, "nature has thus again employed the unsociableness of men, and even of the large societies and states which human beings construct, as a means of arriving at a condition of calm and security through their inevitable antagonism."[132] And "wars, tense and unremitting military preparations, and the resultant distress which every state must feel within itself, even in the midst of peace" are the mechanisms that could be expected to compel states to enter into a federation for the purpose of securing a lasting peace among themselves.[133]

---

[128] *Ibid.*, II.V.1.39.
[129] Sankar Muthu, *Enlightenment against Empire* (Princeton, NJ: Princeton University Press, 2003); Jens Bartelson, *Visions of World Community* (Cambridge: Cambridge University Press, 2009), 115–70.
[130] Kant, "Idea for a Universal History with a Cosmopolitan Purpose," in Hans Reiss (ed.), *Kant: Political Writings* (Cambridge: Cambridge University Press, 1991), 41–53, at 44.
[131] Kant, *Idea*, 47. [132] *Ibid.* [133] *Ibid.*

Although both Ferguson and Kant saw war as an underlying source of human progress and civilization, they also saw progress and civilization as the main antidotes to the unrestricted use of force in international politics. To Ferguson, the civilizing process would temper the bellicose spirit of rude nations by compelling them to become civilized in the face of international competition and the threat of ultimate annihilation. To Kant, the innate unsocial sociability of men would compel them to enter into a pacific federation and ultimately into a world community governed by cosmopolitan law. Both these arguments give rise to pragmatic paradoxes, however, because they are vulnerable to the objection that if war indeed is the driving force behind progress and civilization, then to abolish war would be tantamount to removing the springs of progress and civilization, thereby plunging mankind back into the primordial state that allegedly had conditioned the emergence of states and civil societies in the first place. Hence some antagonism needs to be cultivated for constructive purposes rather than being abolished, lest the springs of human development should be altogether lost.[134] In a similar vein, it was also possible to object that even if a lasting peace would be possible to attain among republican states by forming a federation between them, such a federation would just make other states band together in opposition, thereby reproducing the international state of war between more powerful entities. As Hegel famously argued in his *Grundlinien der Philosophie des Rechts* (1821), "even if a number of states join together as a family, this league, in its individuality, must generate opposition and create an enemy."[135] Once the idea of an international state of war had taken hold, conservatives could always pour cold water on hopes for transcendence or reform. Reform and resistance would be either futile or

---

[134] See Michaele Ferguson, "Unsocial Sociability: Perpetual Antagonism in Kant's Political Thought," in Elisabeth Ellis (ed.), *Kant's Political Theory: Interpretations and Applications* (University Park, PA: Pennsylvania State University Press, 2012), 150–69.

[135] Georg Wilhelm Friedrich Hegel, *Elements of the Philosophy of Right*, trans. H. B. Nisbet (Cambridge: Cambridge University Press, 1991), § 324, 362. For discussions of the wider ramifications of this passage, see Shlomo Avineri, "The Problem of War in Hegel's Thought," *Journal of the History of Ideas* 22, no. 4 (1961): 463–74; Steven B. Smith, "Hegel's Views on War, the State, and International Relations," *American Political Science Review* 77, no. 3 (1983): 624–32; Colin Tyler, "Hegel, War and the Tragedy of Imperialism," *History of European Ideas* 30, no. 4 (2004): 403–31.

counterproductive and would merely serve to reproduce the logic of hostility and enmity that had brought the international state of war into being. In the gloomiest of days, as much as such a state of war spurred a quest for eternal peace, that quest must inevitably issue in perpetual war.[136] States and nations – now being thought of as congruent – are stuck in an international system where every attempt to transcend its underlying logic will only serve to transpose antagonism to ever higher levels of aggregation while pushing war further beyond the purview of human freedom and responsibility and further into the realm of historical necessity.

By the beginning of the nineteenth century, a recognizably modern notion of international anarchy had begun to inform the now-proliferating historical writing about the intercourse of states. Looking back on the formative phases of that system in what later was to become a foundational text for the modern study of international relations, Heeren started out by carefully delimiting his topic. A study of the international system "must not be confounded with the history of the separate states of which it is composed." Rather, it is a history of their *relations* as constituted by their internal freedom, "that is, the stability and mutual independence of its members."[137] This reciprocal freedom is what distinguishes the European system from its opposite, "where an acknowledged preponderance of one of the members exists."[138] But this focus on relations between states did not mean that the internal makeup of states was unaffected by their interaction or vice versa. Even if his primary task was to furnish a sketch of the changes that the European system had undergone since its formation, Heeren also wanted to show how the characters and modes of action of the leading states had been shaped by their intercourse.[139] Although the European system had reached a stage of maturity in which "princes and nations do not exist to make war on each other,

---

[136] See Andreas Behnke, "Eternal Peace, Perpetual War? A Critical Investigation into Kant's Conceptualisations of War," *Journal of International Relations and Development* 15, no. 2 (2012): 250–71.

[137] Arnold Hermann Ludwig Heeren, *Geschichte des Europäischen Staatensystems und seiner Kolonien* (1809/1819). I have used the following translation: *A Manual of the History of the Political System of Europe and Its Colonies from Its Formation at the Close of the Fifteenth Century to Its Reestablishment upon the Fall of Napoleon* (London: Henry G. Bohn, 1834), 5.

[138] *Ibid.*, viii.   [139] *Ibid.*, ix.

unless forced by necessity," this had not always been the case.[140] In fact, much of what had happen in the European system before it had reached that mature stage had happened as a result of wars motivated by religion, succession, or territorial aggrandizement and the ability of that system to resist quests for preponderance and to restore the balance of power. For example, of the consequences of the War of the Austrian Succession, we learn that these "were important, not merely to the separate states, who had been engaged in it; they were still more so as regards the mutual relations between them."[141] As for the American Revolutionary War, we are informed that "no other war has led to such vast consequences as this in the history of mankind."[142] But the Seven Years' War stands out in terms of its creative powers because it "had called forth a spirit of activity which peace could not allay." Apart from its tangible effects on the balance of power, a principal character of the activity now displayed "was the facility with which the growing intelligence of the age enabled it to employ itself upon a variety and multiplicity of objects unknown to it before; especially upon the mutual relations of men and states, which now began to be known and understood."[143] Accordingly, war was the source of that reflexivity because the productive forces of war had not only brought the international system into being but also had given rise to a certain awareness of its existence that was to become the sine qua non of its maturity.

As Ranke was to remark on Heraclitus in *Die Grossen Mächte* (1833), "out of the clash of opposing forces, in the crucial moments of danger – collapse, resurgence, liberation – the most decisive new developments are born ... In their interaction and succession, in their life, in their decline and rejuvenation ... lies the secret of world history."[144] But this kind of statist and bellicist historiography was soon challenged by the rise of cultural history and its new practices of periodization. To historians such as Burckhardt, it was the Renaissance revival of the ideals of antiquity and the refinement of the arts that had provided a happy escape out of barbarism and feudalism, not the incessant warfare between primordial groups of people. With the invention of the Renaissance, a temporal buffer zone was thus inserted between the dark past of barbarism and the coming of modernity that made it possible to posit the state as a work of

---

[140] *Ibid.*, 477.   [141] *Ibid.*, 235.   [142] *Ibid.*, 284.   [143] *Ibid.*, 250.
[144] Leopold von Ranke, "The Great Powers," trans. Theodore von Laue, in Theodore von Laue (ed.), *Leopold Ranke: The Formative Years* (Princeton, NJ: Princeton University Press, 1950), 181–218, at 214 and 217.

art rather than as an outcome of war.[145] But given the undeniably statist foundations of modern international relations, many of those who later advocated a historical approach to its study would rather turn to Heeren and Ranke for support.[146]

Universal War

Almost at the same time as statist history came under challenge from cultural historians such as Burkhardt and Lamprecht, war became an object of abstract philosophical inquiry, and its study gradually pushed in a more nomothetic direction. To many early modern and Enlightenment historians, war had been a productive force that could and should be harnessed for the purposes of secular statecraft and perhaps even be celebrated as a cause of human progress and civilization. But even if war was widely understood as an impersonal and productive force by these historians, it was rarely, if ever, considered separately from its particular historical instantiations. Even if there was a tendency to use the concept of war as if war had a life of its own, it was rarely conceived of in abstract terms. War was an essential part of social and political life, but only by virtue of its lack of an essence; war was capable of producing substances only because it lacked a substance of its own.

This changed during the nineteenth century when war became the subject of philosophical rather than merely politicohistorical analysis. While Clausewitz' definition of war as a "duel on a larger scale" echoes a view of war well established already during the sixteenth century, he is among first to insist that this is the universal and timeless meaning of war, a meaning that transcends all its particular manifestations, and that this meaning first needs to be grasped before we can hope to come to terms with particular wars. As we learn from the opening pages of *Vom Kriege* (1832), "war is an act of force, and there is no logical limit to the application of that force. Each side, therefore, compels its opponent to follow suit; a reciprocal action is started which must lead, in

---

[145] See Jacob Burckhardt, *The Civilization of the Renaissance in Italy* [1860] (London: Phaidon Press, 1951), esp. 1–80; Donald R. Kelley, "The Old Cultural History," *History of the Human Sciences* 9, no. 3 (1996): 101–26.

[146] Hedley Bull, "International Theory: The Case for a Classical Approach," *World Politics* 18, no. 3 (1966): 361–77; Gordon A. Craig, "The Historian and the Study of International Relations," *American Historical Review* 88, no. 1 (1983): 1–11.

theory, to extremes."[147] Yet, if the essence of war always remains the same, the practices of war are open to endless modification because "if wars between civilized nations are far less cruel and destructive than wars between savages, the reason lies in the social conditions of the states themselves and in their relationships to one another. These are the forces that give rise to war; the same forces circumscribe and moderate it."[148]

To Clausewitz, wars are the result of hostile feelings or hostile intentions or both. Whereas the former motive is likely to predominate among savage peoples and subside with civilization, the latter constitutes a universal and transhistorical precondition of war. Yet "even the most savage, almost instinctive, passion of hatred cannot be conceived as existing without hostile intent; but hostile intentions are often unaccompanied by any sort of hostile feelings."[149] But the fact that civilized states fight wars for different reasons and with different methods must not lead us to conclude that the essence of war has changed or to hope for its imminent abolishment because "it would be an obvious fallacy to imagine war between civilized peoples as resulting merely from a rational act on the part of their governments and to conceive of war as gradually ridding itself of passion, so that in the end one would never really need to use the physical impact of the fighting forces."[150] Thus, although the actual conduct of war is contingent on shifting historical and political circumstances, absolute war has a timeless and universal essence that always will remain the same across time and space.[151]

Given their background understanding of war as a philosophical category, it is revealing that both Marx and Engels, both of whom struggled to make sense of contemporary wars in terms of the contradictions of capitalism, nevertheless felt compelled to posit war as a productive force in human affairs when explaining the ancient foundations of class differences and the division of labor. To Marx, the difficulties confronted by early forms of communal life stem from the presence of other communities, so "war is therefore the great comprehensive task, the peat communal labour which is required either to occupy the objective conditions of being there alive, or to protect and perpetuate the occupation. Hence the commune consists of families

---

[147] Carl von Clausewitz, *On War*, trans. Michael Howard and Peter Paret (Oxford: Oxford University Press, 2007), 15.
[148] *Ibid.*, 14.   [149] *Ibid.*   [150] *Ibid.*
[151] For a good treatment of the conceptual underpinnings, see Raymond Aron, *Penser La Guerre, Clausewitz*, vol. I (Paris: Gallimard, 1976), 108–48.

organized in a warlike way."[152] And even when Engels tried to explain the rise of social classes in purely economic terms, he conceded that during antiquity, additional slave labor was "provided by war, and war was as old as the simultaneous existence alongside each other of several groups of communities."[153] This notion of war as a productive force in human affairs was also reflected in Marx's comments on the Indian Revolt of 1857. Rather than being a mere mutiny, as many of his contemporaries had it, this was indeed a *national* revolt that galvanized the Indians into a community through their brave resistance to the British. As such, the so-called revolt was more a war of independence because now "Mussulmans and Hindoos, renouncing their mutual antipathies, have combined against their common masters," something that "has coincided with a general disaffection exhibited against English supremacy on the part of the great Asiatic nations."[154]

This nascent universalistic conception of war continued to resonate with military strategists until it found its way into early sociology toward the end of the nineteenth century. This development was conditioned by – and to some extent also conditioned – other and largely simultaneous conceptual changes. The first of these concerned the concept of the nation, which long had evolved in tandem with that of war. Whereas early modern authors had used this concept to denote primordial groups whose existence allegedly antedated the rise of states, and although Sieyès had later bequeathed an understanding of the nation as an emergent political unity under a common authority, late nineteenth-century writers now redefined the nation in biological or cultural terms and then used this concept to describe the violent race struggles they thought to be characteristic of the modern international system.[155]

Second, and much as a consequence of the preceding, the meaning of the concept of barbarism changes, and its range of applicability is

[152] Karl Marx, *Grundrisse: Foundations of the Critique of Political Economy* [1859], trans. S. W. Ryazanskaya (Moscow: Progress Publishers, 1964), 246. One of the best treatments remains W. B. Gallie, *Philosophers of Peace and War: Kant, Clausewitz, Marx, Engles and Tolstoy* (Cambridge: Cambridge University Press, 1979), 66–99.

[153] Friedrich Engels, *Anti-Dühring* [1894], trans. Emile Burns (New York: International Publishers, 1966), 205.

[154] Karl Marx, "The Revolt in the Indian Army," *New York Daily Tribune*, July 15, 1857.

[155] See Mike Hawkins, *Social Darwinism in European and American Thought 1860–1945* (Cambridge: Cambridge University Press, 1997), 184–5.

widened to encompass new peoples and societies. We have already
noted how early modern writers often invoked this notion to explain
the origins of the state. While they differed somewhat about the
temporal limits and defining characteristics of barbarism and the
barbarian, they were in broad agreement that barbarism represented
a historical stage without which the rise of the state would not have
been possible and which states and societies also had effectively
transcended in the process of becoming civilized. The barbarian
had embodied all the violent energies that found their paramount
expression in the primordial state of war until those energies were
tamed and converted into military valor once the state was in place.
Yet remnants of barbarism continued to pose an imagined threat to
political order from within as well as from without. The lower strata
of society were often described as barbarous and therefore dangerous, as were peoples on the fringes of the European system, such as
Swedes and Turks. During the later part of the nineteenth century,
however, peoples outside Europe were being identified as barbarous
on the basis of a blend of cultural and biological features, whereas
those Europeans previously saddled with such epithets were rede-
scribed in eugenicist terms as weak, degenerate, or simply morally
defective.

These conceptual changes have largely been attributed to the
impact of Darwinism on social and political thought during this
period.[156] But perhaps this influence was more reciprocal in kind.
As Crook has argued, "Darwin transferred metaphors taken from
European military and imperial experience directly to nature."[157]
But although Darwin accepted that a struggle for existence was
necessary to human development and that this struggle might well
have taken violent forms during the early stages of civilization, he
thought that it might ultimately engender sympathy and more peaceful forms of competition between civilized peoples.[158] While some of his

---

[156] See, for example, Richard Hofstadter, *Social Darwinism in American Thought*
(Boston: Beacon Press, 1992); Paul Crook, *Darwinism, War and History: The
Debate over the Biology of War from the "Origin of Species" to the First World
War* (Cambridge: Cambridge University Press, 1994), 63–97; Casper Sylvest,
British Liberal Internationalism, 1880–1930: Making Progress? (Manchester:
Manchester University Press, 2009).

[157] Crook, *Darwinism, War and History*, 15.

[158] *Ibid.*, 24–28; Hawkins, *Social Darwinism*, 33.

followers – such as Spencer – interpreted the theory of evolution in largely pacifist terms, others extended the assumption that conflict was a necessary feature of natural selection to cover the sociopolitical realm as well, until social Darwinism became "an omnipresent reality for the practitioners of the social sciences during this period."[159] Early social scientists were thus left with the choice of arguing either that social and cultural evolution was dependent on, and therefore reducible to, the biological characteristics of human beings or that social and political evolution occurred through analogous processes of selection and adaption, mirroring the mechanisms operative in nature, yet without being fully identical with them.[160] That nation and race were used interchangeably greatly facilitated the spread of such analogies across domains. This, in turn, made it easier to transfer naturalistic notions of struggle to the sociopolitical realm and paved the way for the conclusion that nature and culture were governed by the same underlying and immutable laws of human existence.

While ideas of race and race struggle certainly antedated the work of Darwin – notably those of Knox and Gobineau – such theorizing received additional scientific legitimacy with the rather swift but also very selective uptake of the Darwinian worldview described earlier.[161] And although some Social Darwinists believed that competition between nations gradually would assume more peaceful forms as they became more civilized, others subscribed to the view that human progress is driven by ceaseless and violent competition between distinct races.[162] Since notions of race and nation blended biological and cultural elements together, it became obvious to social scientists not only that conflict between races was natural but also that such conflict was indispensable to our understanding of society. As Le Bon claimed, "without the conflict of individuals, races, and classes – in a word,

---

[159] Hawkins, *Social Darwinism*, 13.   [160] *Ibid.*, 34–5.

[161] See Robert Knox, *Races of Men: A Fragment* (Philadelphia: Lea & Blanchard, 1850); Arthur de Gobineau, *Essai sur l'Inegalité des Races Humaines* (Paris: Firmin Didot, 1853–5).

[162] As Duncan Bell has shown, racial theories of international relations constitute an important part of the prehistory of the democratic peace thesis; see Duncan Bell, "Before the Democratic Peace: Racial Utopianism, Empire, and the Abolition of War," *European Journal of International Relations* 20, no. 3 (2014): 647–70.

without universal conflict, man would never have emerged from savagery, would never have attained to civilization."[163] This being so, "the
only process that Nature has been able to discover for the amelioration of
species is to bring into the world far more creatures that she is able to
nourish, and to establish between them a perpetual struggle in which only
the strongest and the best adapted can survive."[164] Yet to Le Bon, the
attainment of civilization offered no escape from the universal struggle of
races and nations that has animated history from the beginning. Thus Le
Bon maintained that "equally among the savage and the civilized man,
the state of war against his fellows is the natural state, and the struggle is
all the more cruel . . . when the people among whom it rages have attained
a higher degree of civilization."[165] The history of peoples, he continued,
"is in reality only a narrative of facts resulting from their efforts to surpass
their neighbours in military strength."[166] History therefore "tells us that
the nations have always been struggling, and that since the beginning of
the world the right of the strongest has always been the arbiter of their
destinies."[167] Those immutable laws governing history were equally valid
in the present because "international relations are to-day what they have
been since the beginning of the world, when different interests are in
question, or when it is merely a matter of a nation wishing to enlarge
itself. Right and justice have never played any part in relations of unequal
strength."[168]

Similar views of universal war loomed large in the racial psychology of
Gumplowicz. To him, the state originates in the successful subjection of
weaker ethnic groups by stronger ones. Once accomplished, such subjection gives rise to a hierarchy between rulers and ruled, where the former
governs the latter by virtue of their mental and military superiority: "The
one party commands; the other labors and accommodates itself to superior force. As every war must cease raging and the weaker party must give
up fruitless opposition, so nature helps to make the situation peaceful and
lasting. But peace and permanence are the elements of order, out of which
come habit, custom, rights."[169] Once consolidated, the state enters a

[163] Gustave Le Bon, *The Psychology of Socialism* (New York: Macmillan, 1899),
323.
[164] *Ibid.*, 331.
[165] Gustave Le Bon, *L'Homme et les Sociétés: leurs orgines at leur histoire*, vol. II
(Paris: Rotschild, 1881), 88.
[166] *Ibid.*, 95.   [167] Le Bon, *Psychology of Socialism*, 326–7.   [168] *Ibid.*, 329.
[169] Ludwig Gumplowicz, *Outlines of Sociology* [1885], trans. Frederick W. Moore
(Philadelphia: American Academy of Political and Social Science, 1899), 121.

perpetual struggle for survival with other nations because its "object is always defence against attacks, increase of power and territory, that is, conquest in one form or another."[170] The existence of universal struggle implies that "even the least aggressive state will be drawn in spite of itself into the stream of 'history'; evolution cannot stop. As wants increase, the state, which was called into being to satisfy them, is driven to further conquests of territory and power."[171] As a result, international relations become a constant struggle for power between races; "it is generally recognized that states oppose each other like savage hordes; that they follow the blind laws of nature; that no ethical law or moral obligation, only the fear of the stronger holds them in check."[172] Yet war cannot continue continuously, lest the ends for which it is undertaken should be defeated. "Peace is as necessary as occasional war, for both are the result of a natural law of strife; and so it was possible to establish states, since otherwise the more powerful must have had to exterminate the weaker."[173]

Since history offers no escape out of endless struggle, even civilized and powerful states must always face threats to their existence from without as well as from within. With barbarism embodied in both the lower races and the lower classes, Gumplowicz fears that these might join forces in the destruction of civilization. As he goes on to explain:

[T]he fall of many a powerful civilized state under the assault of rather small barbarian hordes could not be comprehended if it were not known that domestic social enemies of the existing order let the secretly glimmering hatred of the property and ruling classes burst into bright flame in the moment of danger; and this alone is often sufficient to turn the toilsome labor of centuries into dust and ashes.[174]

Given this logic of might and right, rise and decay, the only valid moral precept on offer is that "to make war upon strangers and over-power them is a virtue; to betray one's fellow citizens is a crime."[175] Theories of race and race struggle were also central to early American sociology.[176] Two of its founding fathers subscribed to conceptions of race similar to that of Gumplowicz and held that race struggle was

---

[170] *Ibid.*, 117.   [171] *Ibid.*, 125.   [172] *Ibid.*, 147.   [173] *Ibid.*, 126.
[174] *Ibid.*, 206.   [175] *Ibid.*, 210.
[176] See Hofstadter, *Social Darwinism in American Thought*, 51–84; Dorothy Ross, *The Origins of American Social Science* (Cambridge: Cambridge University Press, 1992), 85–97.

inevitable and desirable as a source of human progress and civilization. Sumner – who was a card-carrying Social Darwinist – started his analysis of war by contesting the then widespread assumption that warfare was endemic among primitive peoples. From available anthropological evidence he was able to infer that "we cannot postulate a warlike character or a habit of fighting as a universal or even characteristic trait of primitive man."[177] Instead, war only arises between more developed societies as a result of a differentiation between insiders and outsiders. As Sumner states, "the sentiment which prevails inside the 'we-group,' between its members, is that of peace and cooperation; the sentiment which prevails inside of a group towards all outsiders is that of hostility and war."[178] This differentiation between insiders and outsider is itself explained with reference to competition for scarce resources. As Sumner goes on to explain, "war arises from the competition of life, not from the struggle for existence. In the struggle for existence a man is wrestling with nature to extort from her the means of subsistence. It is when two men are striving side by side in the struggle for existence, to extort from nature the supplies they need, that they come into rivalry and a collision of interest with each other takes place."[179] This struggle leads further to the formation of more or less cohesive groups stuck in competition for scarce natural resources. "It is the competition of life, therefore, which makes war, and that is why war always has existed and always will."[180]

This violent competition for life also explains how and why states emerged in history. The same conditions that made men hostile toward outsiders also made them yield to domestic authority and to "submit to discipline, obey law, cultivate peace, and create institutions inside."[181] As men fought wars, "they were acquiring discipline and cohesion; they were learning cooperation, perseverance, fortitude, and patience." Thus, by necessitating concord on the inside in order to cope with external competition, "war forms larger social units and produces states."[182] And in order to survive the no less fierce competition in the international system, the state must be a "true peace-group in which there is sufficient concord and sympathy to overcome the antagonisms of nationality, race, class etc., and in which are maintained institutions adequate to adjust interests and control passions."[183] And since "no

[177] William Graham Sumner, "War" [1903], in *War and Other Essays* (New Haven: Yale University Press, 1919), 3–40, at 7.
[178] *Ibid.*, 9.   [179] *Ibid.*   [180] *Ibid.*, 10.   [181] *Ibid.*, 11.   [182] *Ibid.*, 15.
[183] *Ibid.*, 28.

one has yet found any way in which two races, far apart in blood and culture, can be amalgamated into one society with satisfaction to both," this entails that to maintain the cohesion necessary to ward off external aggression, states must be racially and culturally homogeneous.[184] In his concluding remarks, Sumner addresses the question of whether universal peace is possible. But given his ontology of race struggle, the notion of universal peace is but an intellectual fallacy and ultimately a very dangerous doctrine. Peace can never embrace all of mankind, since whenever a peace group grows bigger, "differences, discords, antagonisms, and war begin inside of it on account of the divergence of interests."[185] By assuming that the struggle for life is the ultimate driving force in nature, Sumner could argue not only that war is a universal feature of human history but also that war is constitutive of the modern state. By further assuming that war is a perennial feature of the struggle for existence among states, Sumner could conclude that war indeed is universal and inescapable and also the main source of progress in human affairs. Sumner thereby provided the historical conception of war found in Ferguson and Kant with a scientific foundation consonant with the Darwinist consensus of his day. By so doing, he also took important steps toward elevating the state to the penultimate vehicle of universal and racial war. And, by understanding race and nation as congruent, he was able to assume that the struggle for existence that had animated the premodern period and the international wars of his own present were instantiations of the same underlying and immutable laws.

A similar line of argument was presented by the statistician and eugenicist Pearson in his attempt to put nationalism on a scientific footing. Guided by the question of what part the nation plays in the universal struggle for existence, he contended that the scientific view of the nation requires that we regard it as "an organized whole, kept up to a high pitch of internal efficiency by insuring that its numbers are substantially recruited from the better stocks, and kept up to a high pitch of external efficiency by contest, chiefly by way of war with inferior races, and with equal races by the struggle for trade-routes and for the sources of raw material and of food supply."[186] Thus the nation itself is constituted through race struggle, and once nations become racially homogeneous,

---

[184] *Ibid.*, 35. [185] *Ibid.*, 36.
[186] Karl Pearson, *National Life from the Standpoint of Science* [1900] (London: Adam & Charles Black, 1901), 43.

this struggle will perpetuate itself as a conscious quest for dominance in
the international system, a struggle in which the white man ultimately
must prevail.

   Although the other founding father of American sociology spent much
time debunking Social Darwinism for what he took to be its misguided
cosmological starting points, Ward was no less inclined to see universal
struggle as the constitutive force in the historical and social evolution of
mankind. To him, all social structures owe their existence to "some form
of struggle among the social forces whereby the centrifugal and destructive character of each force acting alone is neutralized and each is made to
contribute to the constructive work of society."[187] Whereas Sumner held
war to be a perennial feature of human history from its primitive past to
the present day, Ward regarded universal struggle as the condition of
possibility of the social realm and the key to its differentiation from mere
nature, this being so because human beings have first to subjugate or
domesticate other species in their quest for survival before they can enter
a state of war among themselves. Yet, having done so, a struggle between
human races will inevitably follow, since "each race looks upon all others
as utterly unlike itself, and usually there exists among different races the
most profound mutual contempt. Whenever two races are brought into
contact it usually means war."[188] Drawing heavily on the earlier works
by Gumplowicz and Ratzenhofer, both of whom "have abundantly and
admirably proved that the genesis of society as we see it and know it has
been through the struggle of races," Ward goes on to describe the
historical development that has led to the formation of states and the
subsequent transposition of universal struggle to the international
realm.[189] The first step is the conquest and subjugation of one race by
another. After a conclusive victory, the conquering race needs the assistance of the conquered race. "After a long trial of the stern policy of
repression the physically superior race tires of the strain and relaxes in the
direction of general law, of calling in the aid of the best elements of the
weaker race, and at length reaches the stage marked by the formation of a
state."[190] But the formation and consolidation of states does not end of
race struggle but rather marks its transposition to another level. As Ward
goes on to argue, "races, states, peoples, nations are always forming,

[187] Lester F. Ward, *Pure Sociology: A Treatise on the Origin and Spontaneous
      Development of Society* [1903] (New York: Macmillan, 1916), 193.
[188] *Ibid.*, 193.   [189] *Ibid.*, 203.   [190] *Ibid.*, 208.

always aggressing, always clashing and clinching, and struggling for the mastery, and the long, painful, wasteful, but always fruitful gestation must be renewed and repeated again and again."[191] Like Sumner before him, Ward could not see how this struggle between races ever could end other than by the conclusive dominance of the superior race over all others, unless all impetus behind human progress should be irretrievably lost and barbarism should return with a vengeance. Propelled by the natural hatred between races, "the movement must go on, and there seems no place for it to stop until, just as man has gained dominion over the animal world, so the highest type of man shall gain dominion over all the lower types of man."[192]

But what are we to make of these accounts of race struggle and its role as a driver of historical progress? Many scholars have seen these ideas and their subsequent dissemination as an important ideational cause of the First World War. Especially when combined other noxious ingredients, such as *Realpolitik* and ethnic nationalism, these theories offered not only new ways of legitimizing imperialism and colonialism abroad, but by portraying war among European states as inevitable and sometimes even desirable, they also furnished a recipe for disaster. Their preoccupation with race and race struggle also made these theories complicit in policies of racial extermination.[193] Yet, by focusing more or less exclusively on the meaning and function of the concept of race in those theories, existing scholarship has missed what I take to be a more important point. This has to do with the primacy accorded to struggle in their accounts of the genesis of political order. Even though the authors discussed earlier took racial differences to be constitutive of states and the international system, they accorded explanatory priority to the concept of struggle over that of race. Races – whether conceived in biological or cultural terms or in any conceivable blend thereof – are not understood as preconstituted entities whose identities and boundaries are immutable but are themselves seen as outcomes of multiple struggles in the past.

[191] *Ibid.*   [192] *Ibid.*, 239.
[193] See, for example, Richard Weikart, "Progress through Racial Extermination: Social Darwinism, Eugenics, and Pacifism in Germany, 1860–1918," *German Studies Review* 26, no. 2 (2003): 273–94; Richard Weikart, *From Darwin to Hitler: Evolutionary Ethics, Eugenics, and Racism in Germany* (New York: Palgrave Macmillan, 2004); Beatrice Heuser, *The Evolution of Strategy: Thinking War from Antiquity to the Present* (Cambridge: Cambridge University Press, 2010), 123–37.

The mechanisms of racial differentiation invoked by Social Darwinists presuppose that the struggle for existence is a cosmological principle whose applicability extends to all living beings from the beginning of the world. When tailored to fit certain political purposes, this obsession with struggle resulted in a celebration of the productive forces of war, whose looping effects were manifest in the many atrocities that were to follow during the twentieth century. In its more extreme versions, this celebration of war also brought a profound suspicion of peace. As the German general Bernhardi argued just before the onset of the First World War, the aspiration to peace is "directly antagonistic to the great universal laws that rule all life. War is a biological necessity of the first importance, a regulative element in the life of mankind that cannot be dispensed with, since without it an unhealthy development will follow, which excludes every advancement of the race, and therefore all civilization."[194]

In this chapter, we have seen how different conceptions of war have been invoked in order to explain the genesis of the modern state and the international system by contrasting them with a stateless past of barbarism. Despite significant discontinuities in terms of historical consciousness across different historical contexts, war – however defined – bestows order to history to the extent that the temporal limits of statehood would appear enigmatic in its absence. As I pointed out in Chapter 1, this is why the concept of war seems to lack a history of its own, since war is a condition of possible history, at least in the shape in which the past has become known to us within Western historiography.

We have also noted that while the meaning of war changes almost imperceptibly in response to ontological and epistemological mutations underlying the practice of historical writing, the range of subjects allegedly constituted through warfare varies considerably across time, taking us from primordial kinship groups via states and nations to races. Hence those who want to explain the occurrence of war with reference to the characteristics of states or the international system should be reminded that since these entities long have been believed to be nothing but avatars of war, their explanations cannot be but fancy restatements of already well-entrenched but long-forgotten looping effects of the ontogenetic view of war. We have also seen how the quest for temporal limits led many historians to posit a stateless past

---

[194] Friedrich von Bernhardi, *Germany and the Next War*, trans. Allen H. Powles (New York: Longmans, Green, 1914), 18.

from which states could emerge only by escaping the barbarism that made them possible in the first place. Yet such escape was possible only by projecting the most undesirable characteristics of that barbarous past onto non-European peoples, now believed to be stuck with political institutions and practices of a kind that the Europeans thought they had left behind. To fully understand how this act of wholesale political exorcism was accomplished, however, we have to inquire into how the spatial limits of the modern state and the international system were defined and defended with reference to the productive force of war. That is the task of Chapter 3.

3 | Fortifying the State

Introduction

Territoriality has long been a defining characteristic of the modern state and the international system. As John Herz once pointed out, what accounts for the coherence of the modern state is the fact of its physical extension, "an expanse of territory encircled for its identification and its defense by a 'hard shell' of fortifications."[1] And since the international system is composed of such territorial states, it has also been widely accepted that "every international order, down to our own day, has been essentially territorial."[2] Hence, at least since Leibniz insisted that sovereignty entails jurisdiction over a bounded portion of space, territoriality has been what distinguishes the modern state and the modern international order from what allegedly existed before, a feudal order characterized by multiple authorities with overlapping jurisdictions ruling unbounded and heterogeneous political spaces.[3] Being an essential attribute of states, territory has also been regarded as a potent source of discord in international politics. "War, whether interstate or guerilla, is a political process that has as its purpose the control of territory to enable subsequent projections of power."[4] Since many

---

[1] John H. Herz, "Rise and Demise of the Territorial State," *World Politics* 9, no. 4 (1957): 473–93, at 474.

[2] Raymond Aron, *Peace and War: A Theory of International Relations* (Cambridge: Cambridge University Press, 1966), 161. For an analysis of this assumption, see Alexander B. Murphy, "The Sovereign State System as Political-Territorial Idea: Historical and Contemporary Considerations," in Thomas J. Biersteker and Cynthia Weber (eds.), *State Sovereignty as Social Construct* (Cambridge: Cambridge University Press), 81–120.

[3] See, for example, Hendrik Spruyt, *The Sovereign State and Its Competitors* (Princeton, NJ: Princeton University Press, 1994); Saskia Sassen, *Territory, Authority, Rights: From Medieval to Global Assemblages* (Princeton, NJ: Princeton University Press, 2006), 25–73.

[4] Colin Flint, "Introduction: Geography of War and Peace," in Colin Flint (ed.), *The Geography of War and Peace: From Death Camps to Diplomats* (Oxford: Oxford University Press, 2005), 1–15, at 6.

wars have been caused by disputes over territory or aimed at territorial conquest, the preservation of territorial integrity has long been a paramount concern of state security until it eventually became a sacrosanct principle of modern international order.⁵ So even if we should agree with those who today argue that political authority has become increasingly deterritorialized and that territory therefore has lost much of its former importance to international politics, the fact remains that by most definitions state sovereignty denotes supreme authority within a given territory.⁶

But how did territoriality become a defining characteristic of the modern state and a perennial apple of discord in international politics? This is puzzling, especially given that early modern theories of the state rarely made any explicit references to the concept of territory nor implied that political authority had to be spatially bounded to be legitimate. As Brett has eloquently pointed out, "the drive to define the city as a unity possessed of sovereign power, and to show how that entity and that power can have been created by individual human agents, militates against the definition of the state in terms of place or even of territory."⁷ Although Bodin maintained that sovereignty was confined to a commonwealth composed of a multitude of households, he did not assume that this multitude had to be spatially bounded.⁸ Furthermore, while Grotius held that *imperium* could be exercised over places as well as peoples, the primary subjects of sovereign power were the latter.⁹ And since Hobbes recognized no limits to the scope of sovereignty, its territorial extension is at best implicit in his account.¹⁰ In sum, as Benton has pointed out, the conceptions of space implied by early modern theories of the state were heterogeneous and elastic ones

⁵ See, for example, John Vasquez, *The War Puzzle* (Cambridge: Cambridge University Press, 1993); Mark W. Zacher, "The Territorial Integrity Norm: International Boundaries and the Use of Force," *International Organization* 55, no. 2 (2001): 215–50; Monica Duffy Toft, "Territory and War," *Journal of Peace Research* 51, no. 2 (2014): 185–98.

⁶ See, for example, Ayelet Banai, Margaret Moore, David Miller, Cara Nine, and Frank Dietrich, "Symposium 'Theories of Territory beyond Westphalia'," *International Theory* 6, no. 1 (2014): 98–104.

⁷ Annabel S. Brett, *Changes of State: Nature and the Limits of the City in Early Modern Natural Law* (Princeton, NJ: Princeton University Press, 2011), 212.

⁸ See Stuart Elden, *The Birth of Territory* (Chicago: University of Chicago Press, 2013), 240.

⁹ *Ibid.*, 259–68; Brett, *Changes of State*, 199, 210.

¹⁰ Elden, *The Birth of Territory*, 301; Brett, *Changes of State*, 212.

at best, and it was not until later that the concept of sovereignty came to connote exclusive control over a bounded territory.[11]

In response to this puzzle, many scholars have tried to explain when and how the connection between political authority and territory first emerged. According to a pioneering effort by John Ruggie, the quintessentially modern congruence between authority and territory was made possible by the Renaissance invention of linear perspective and its subsequent incorporation in political and legal thought. As Ruggie argued, "what was true in the visual arts was equally true in politics: political space came to be defined *as it appeared from a single fixed viewpoint.* The concept of sovereignty, then, was merely the doctrinal counterpart of the application of single-point perspectival forms to the spatial organization of politics."[12] In what since has crystallized into a constructivist consensus on this issue, many authors have affirmed the historical contingency of modern conceptions of space and emphasized the importance of geographic and cartographic practices in the shaping of the modern state and the modern international system.[13] As Branch has claimed in what arguably is the most sophisticated statement of this position to date, the invention of modern techniques of mapping was necessary, if not sufficient, for the emergence and consolidation of the modern state and the international system. The dissemination of cartographic representations of linear and homogeneous space restructured conceptions of political authority among actors, thereby legitimizing territorial forms of rule at the expense of nonterritorial ones. Although modern mapping techniques evolved independently of political

---

[11] Lauren Benton, *A Search for Sovereignty: Law and Geography in European Empires, 1400–1900* (Cambridge: Cambridge University Press, 2010), 1–39, 279–99.

[12] John Gerard Ruggie, "Territoriality and Beyond: Problematizing Modernity in International Relations," *International Organization* 47, no. 1 (1993): 139–74, at 159; Richard Ned Lebow, "Constitutive Causality: Imagined Spaces and Political Practices," *Millennium* 38, no. 2 (2009): 211–39. See also Samuel Y. Edgerton, *The Renaissance Rediscovery of Linear Perspective* (New York: Basic Books, 1975); John Agnew, "The Territorial Trap: The Geographical Assumptions of International Relations Theory," *Review of International Political Economy* 1, no. 1 (1994): 53–80.

[13] See, for example, Elden, *The Birth of Territory*; Jordan Branch, *The Cartographic State: Maps, Territory, and the Origins of Sovereignty* (Cambridge: Cambridge University Press, 2014); Jeppe Strandsbjerg, *Territory, Globalization and International Relations: The Cartographic Reality of Space* (Houndsmills: Palgrave Macmillan, 2010).

considerations, their implicit notions of homogeneous and demarcated spaces were gradually translated into political practice, as indicated by the increasing salience of references to territorial boundaries in peace treaties from the early modern to the modern period.[14]

In another no less comprehensive account of the congruence between political authority and territory, Elden argued that while the treaties that concluded the Thirty Years War did not contain any modern notion of territorially bounded sovereignty, they nevertheless granted territorial rights to individual princes, and subsequent attempts to spell out the implications of these rights led Leibniz to argue that "sovereign is he who is master of a territory." Although this definition of sovereignty echoed medieval conceptions of territorial jurisdiction and was articulated against the backdrop of lingering claims to imperial authority, it was the first time supreme authority was explicitly *equated* with territorial control.[15]

Yet the question of how such conceptions of territorial authority were translated into facts on the ground has rarely been raised, and the few answers available portray this as a process of rationalization through which cartographic representations were translated more or less directly into actual territorial demarcations. As Biggs has described this process, "as lands were surveyed and mapped, they were reshaped into a territory: a homogenous [*sic*] and uniform space, demarcated by linear boundaries."[16] But, although both Biggs and Branch describe in detail how mapping techniques were gradually harnessed for political purposes and how they shaped perceptions of what constituted legitimate political authority, they do not have much to say about how this conversion was carried out in practice. Thus, as Shah pointed out, there seems to be a missing link in much recent constructivist scholarship on territoriality. While constructivists help us to make sense of territorial sovereignty in the abstract form, it appears in legal and political theories that they have failed to account for how the physical substratum of the

---

[14] Branch, *Cartographic State*, 1–67.   [15] Elden, *Birth of Territory*, 318–21.
[16] Michael Biggs, "Putting the State on the Map: Cartography, Territory, and European State Formation," *Comparative Studies in Society and History* 41, no. 2 (1999): 374–405, at 385.

state – the *res* of the *respublica* – came into being and became a natural point of reference for these theories.[17]

To the same extent that cartography constituted the object of state formation, though, state authorities constituted the object of cartography by creating its referents through concrete practices of demarcation and unification.[18] Taking this suggestion seriously would imply that we should not confine our inquiry to the changing representations of territory on maps but that we ought to pay attention to how the corresponding referents were created as well. Hence, in this chapter, I focus on the process of conversion through which claims to sovereign authority represented on maps were translated into facts on the ground and how the outcome of this process became naturalized and taken for granted by historical geographers. As I suggest, the conversion of symbolic claims to territorial authority we find on early modern maps into the kind of demarcated territory we have come to associate with the modern state was to a large extent carried out and justified with reference to the productive forces of war and warfare, forces that were held capable of generating geographic facts on their own. This is evident from the consistent appeals made by cartographers and geographers to the need to keep foreign enemies at bay and to the desire to prevent unclear jurisdictions from causing domestic unrest.

Yet my argument must be distinguished from the view according to which territoriality and boundaries originate in political violence. This view has a long pedigree within social theory and is implicit in some theories of state formation.[19] As Lefebvre argued some time ago, state sovereignty "implies a space against which violence, whether latent or overt, is directed, a space established and constituted by violence."[20] By the same token, Virilio has emphasized how the territoriality of the modern state was shaped by the strategic imperatives of war from the Middle Ages to the French Revolution.[21] According to a recent version

[17]   Nisha Shah, "The Territorial Trap of the Territorial Trap: Global
       Transformation and the Problem of the State's Two Territories," *International
       Political Sociology* 6, no. 1 (2012): 57–76.
[18]   Biggs, "Putting the State on the Map," 391.
[19]   See Anthony Giddens, *The Nation-State and Violence* (Berkeley: University of
       California Press, 1985), 35–60.
[20]   Henri Lefebvre, *The Production of Space* [1974] (Oxford: Blackwell, 1991),
       280.
[21]   For the idea that human geography is conditioned by war, see Paul Virilio,
       L'Insecurité du Territoire (Paris: Galilée, 1993); Paul Virilio, *Speed and Politics*

of this view, while maps were certainly instrumental in the process of state making insofar as they helped demarcate legitimate claims to political authority from illegitimate ones, they also helped to "mask the violence that brings the state into being and the interests that sustain the ideological preponderance of the state system."[22] From this point of view, the territoriality of the modern states owes its existence to violent disputes over territory that only later resulted in stable demarcations. As Brenner and Elden have stated this point, "[t]erritory is always being produced and reproduced by the actions of the former and through political struggles over the latter."[23]

But to say that territory was an object of struggle before it settled into an organizing principle raises the question of how this connection between territory and political violence emerged in the first place. My intention in this chapter is not to contest or corroborate the above-mentioned views but to describe how they became possible to entertain and why they were able to acquire verisimilitude over time. To answer these questions, I believe that we must attend to the productive forces attributed to war in cartographic and geographic theory and practice. Doing this should not mean, of course, that we commit ourselves to any aspect of this view or that cartographic representations of political space were themselves constitutive of territoriality. As I will argue, much in the same way as the temporal limits of the state and the international system were drawn with reference to a primordial state of war, so the spatial boundaries of states as well as the less tangible lines of demarcation separating the civilized world from its barbarous outside were informed by violent imaginaries that emphasized the ever-present possibility of warfare and domestic unrest as the main drivers behind processes of territorial demarcation and unification. Such imaginaries were further reinforced by cartographic representations of space that rendered the outcome contingent on the successful use of force. Hence the fact that we have come to understand the territoriality of the state and the international system as an outcome of war and

(New York: Semiotext(e), 1986), 29–41; for an analysis, see Tim Luke and Gearóid Ó Tuathail, "The Spatiality of War, Speed and Vision in the Work of Paul Virilio," in Mike Crang and Nigel Thrift (eds.), *Thinking Space* (London: Routledge, 2000), 360–79.

22 Mark Neocleous, "Off the Map: On Violence and Cartography," *European Journal of Social Theory* 6, no. 4 (2003): 409–25, at 422.

23 Neil Brenner and Stuart Elden, "Henri Lefebvre on State, Space, Territory," *International Political Sociology* 3, no. 4 (2009): 353–77, at 367.

warfare testifies to the potent looping effects of such imaginaries in and out of cartography, with profound consequences for the ways in which we have come to understand the causes of war within the modern international order.

The rest of this chapter is organized as follows. In the next section, I will sketch some of the main features of the geographic and cartographic revolutions and the reconceptualization of space that they brought into being. I will then proceed to describe how the largely symbolic claims to sovereignty embodied in early modern maps were translated into actual claims to territorial authority. Doing this, I will analyze how different conceptions of territoriality were disseminated among political elites and gradually translated into facts on the ground, arguing that violent geographic imaginaries acted as the main conveyors in this process. In the third section, I focus on the art of fortification and the quest for natural boundaries. Although I believe that Virilio overstated this point when he argued that the modern state is but the outcome of a long process of fortification, I think that it is helpful to regard fortification as a shorthand for the process by which abstract conceptions of territory were turned into facts on the ground, for the simple reason that fortification was seen as a model by many of those who were busy bringing this process of conversion about. In the final section, I dwell on how the imagined congruence of political authority and territory was naturalized and taken for granted as a consequence of attempts to reconceptualize geography as a struggle between nations and races.

Mapping the State

As I have described in some detail elsewhere, the geographic and cartographic revolutions of the early modern period were conditioned by changes in cosmological? outlook that took place during the late sixteenth century.[24] These changes made it possible to conceptualize the world as a spherical object, a globe. This was a precondition for the compartmentalization of that spherical object into distinct portions by

[24] See Jens Bartelson, *Visions of World Community* (Cambridge: Cambridge University Press, 2009); Jens Bartelson, "The Social Construction of Globality," *International Political Sociology* 4, no. 3 (2010): 219–35.

means of geometric methods, as well as for the subsequent subjection of such portions to exclusive claims to sovereign authority by their rulers.[25] To this end, "the machine of discovery ... not only produced an immense perceptual challenge and epistemological problem but also the realization of an almost totally accessible and inhabitable global arena in which to contend with this problem."[26] On this emergent global arena, the discipline of cosmography "could reign as an absolute sovereign over the terraqueous globe ... It manipulated at will the natural frontiers of rivers and mountains; determined the future of peoples by fixing their migrations and boundaries."[27] As Sloterdijk summarized the ideological temptations brought by this development, "as soon as the form of the sphere could be constructed in geometrical abstraction and gazed upon in cosmological contemplation, there arose forcefully the question of who should rule over the represented and produced sphere."[28] Hence dreams of unbounded sovereignty "found the beginnings of its realization in the map or sphere that was dedicated to the monarch, framed by his arms and traversed by his ships, and that opened up to his dreams of empire a space of intervention stretching to the limits of the terraqueous globe."[29] Hence the appropriation of space on a global scale was as much a source of knowledge as a source of sovereignty by rising imperial powers.[30] But while such

[25] See Denis Cosgrove, *Apollo's Eye: A Cartographic Genealogy of the Earth in the Western Imagination* (Baltimore: Johns Hopkins University Press, 2001); Denis Cosgrove, "Globalism and Tolerance in Early Modern Geography," *Annals of the Association of American Geographers* 93, no. 4 (2003): 852–70.

[26] John Headley, "The Sixteenth-Century Venetian Celebration of the Earth's Total Habitability: The Issue of the Fully Habitable World for Renaissance Europe," *Journal of World History* 8, no. 1: 1–27, at 24.

[27] Frank Lestringant, *Mapping the Renaissance World: The Geographical Imagination in the Age of Discovery* (Cambridge: Polity Press, 1994), 3.

[28] Peter Sloterdijk, "Geometry in the Colossal: The Project of Metaphysical Globalization," *Environment and Planning D: Society and Space* 27 (2009): 29–40, at 33. For the full story, see Peter Sloterdijk, *Globes, Spheres,* vol. II: *Macrospherology* (Los Angeles: Semiotext(e), 2014).

[29] Lestringant, *Mapping the Renaissance World*, 23. See also David Turnbull, "Cartography and Science in Early Modern Europe: Mapping the Construction of Knowledge Spaces," *Imago Mundi* 48, no. 1 (1996): 5–24.

[30] Jerry Brotton, *Trading Territories: Mapping the Early Modern World* (Ithaca, NY: Cornell University Press, 1997), 83; Brian J. Harley, "Silences and Secrecy: The Hidden Agenda of Cartography in Early Modern Europe," *Imago Mundi* 40, no. 1 (1988): 57–76; John Harley and Paul Laxton, *The New Nature of Maps: Essays in the History of Cartography* (Baltimore: Johns Hopkins University Press, 2002).

representations of space inspired visions of empire and world community, they were also harnessed for the purpose of buttressing particularistic claims to territorial sovereignty.[31] As Branch has aptly described this, "a mutually constitutive relationship exists between representations of political space, the ideas held by actors about the organization of political authority, and actors' authoritative political practices manifesting those ideas."[32]

To some extent, this was a result of claims to political authority already being symbolically embodied in maps. As Jacob has pointed out, "[m]aps reflect a desire for completeness, a dream of universality, a yearning for power in which seeing from a point of view forbidden to all others ... is equivalent to possession."[33] Thus, before invading Provence in 1536, Charles V had convinced himself that possessing a map of this province was tantamount to possessing a title to the province proper.[34] But since we should be careful to attribute causal powers to inanimate objects such as maps, contentions such as the preceding raise questions about how abstract conceptions of space represented on maps were translated into actual territoriality and how they spurred quests for territorial control. Granted that maps are nothing more and nothing less than instruments of power – albeit arguably very potent ones – how can we understand the process through which the authority claims they embody were realized?

Although I am sympathetic to those who argue that advances in cartography and techniques of mapping played an important role in the creation of modern states and the international system, I would like to add that the role of cartography in this process ought to be understood against the backdrop of contemporary beliefs about the productive nature of war and warfare. The territorialization of political authority was not the result of a rationalization of space through the agreed imposition of neat geometric demarcations but a process to a

---

[31] See Marcelo Escolar, "Exploration, Cartography and the Modernization of State Power," *International Social Science Journal* 49, no. 151 (1997): 55–75.

[32] Branch, *Cartographic State*, 69.

[33] Christian Jacob, *The Sovereign Map: Theoretical Approaches in Cartography throughout History* (Chicago: University of Chicago Press, 2006), 1.

[34] Martin Du Bellay, *Mémoires de messire Martin Du Bellay, in Choix de chroniques et mémoires sur l'histoire de France*, vol. 11, ed. J. A. C. Buchon (Paris: A. Desrez, 1836), 582. Quoted in John Hale, "Warfare and Cartography, ca. 1450 to ca. 1640," in David Woodward (ed.), *The History of Cartography*, vol. 3 (Chicago: University of Chicago Press, 2007), 719–37, at 719.

large extent driven by perceptions of military necessity on behalf of ruling elites in Europe, and many of these perceptions were, in turn, informed by ontogenetic conceptions of war and warfare. Although mapmaking at first evolved independently of such concerns and catered to many different needs, historians of military thought have emphasized how later advances in cartography were prompted by military necessity and how these advances, in turn, contributed to the evolution of military strategy.[35]

As Foucault pointed out, territory was a strategic concept before it became a geographic one. According to him, the traditional problem of sovereignty was a matter of holding onto or conquering territory, which gave rise to the questions that came to preoccupy geographers and cartographers during the early modern period: how can territories be demarcated, fixed, protected, or enlarged?[36] Raising successful claims to territorial authority and jurisdiction presupposed that questions such as these could be answered with sufficient precision and the answers then effectively implemented. Thus, when Jomini famously defined strategy as "the art of making war upon the map," he was thereby taking for granted what in fact was the result of a long process through which the concerns of cartography and warfare had been allowed to cross-fertilize so that the lines drawn on the map by means of the pen also could be drawn on the ground by means of the sword. Without the mapping of territory, no modern military strategy could succeed, as well as conversely.[37] In this section, I try to show how this confluence of concerns took place during the seventeenth and eighteenth centuries and how this ushered in the territorial demarcations that we have come to associate with the modern state and the international system. Doing this, I focus mainly on developments in Britain and France. Both these states were early adopters of new technologies of surveying and mapmaking that had emerged during the cartographic

---

[35] See, for example, Azar Gat, *A History of Military Thought: From the Enlightenment to the Cold War* (Oxford: Oxford University Press, 2001), 76–8.

[36] Michel Foucault, *Security, Territory, Population. Lectures at the Collège de France 1977–1978* (New York: Picador, 2007), 64–5. For a useful commentary, see Stuart Elden, "How Should We Do the History of Territory?," *Territory, Politics, Governance* 1, no. 1 (2013): 5–20.

[37] Baron Antoine Henri de Jomini, *The Art of War*, ed. and trans. G. H. Mendell and W. P. Craighill (Philadelphia: Lippincott, 1862), 69.

revolution and were quick to harness them for political and military purposes in ways that were widely emulated by other European states.[38] Although significant cartographic resources were developed by Portugal and Spain, these were mainly devoted to the mapping of their overseas possessions, even if detailed maps of the Iberian Peninsula such as the Escorial Atlas were produced during the late sixteenth century. Given that the land frontiers of Spain were comparatively short, its government faced no strong incentives to produce domestic maps.[39]

While many early modern maps were produced for commercial and artistic reasons, many European governments started to commission maps and undertake major mapping projects during the sixteenth and seventeenth centuries. One of the most important functions of early maps was to embody representations of royal power and to disseminate these representations in order to legitimize royal claims to power. In 1579, Saxton produced his *Atlas of the Counties of England and Wales*, its frontispiece embellished with a portrait of an enthroned Elizabeth I. Similar developments soon followed in France, with Bouguereau's *Le Théâtre Francoys* celebrating the rise of Henri de Navarre to the throne in 1594 by depicting the lands under his control.[40] During the reign of Louis XIV, the making and dissemination of maps became important in order to legitimize royal authority and territorial conquests to those on the receiving end, as indicated by the appearance of *Les Glorieuses Conquestes de Louis Le Grand* by Sébastien de Beaulieu in 1662.

But although the rise of cartography was closely connected to royal claims to power, it was also driven by more practical considerations,

---

[38] See Peter Barber, "England I: Pageantry, Defense, and Government – Maps at Court to 1550," in David Buisseret (ed.), *Monarchs, Ministers, and Maps: The Emergence of Cartography as a Tool of Government in Early Modern Europe* (Chicago: University of Chicago Press, 1992), 26–56; Peter Barber, "England II: Monarchs, Ministers, and Maps, 1550–1625," in Buisseret, *Monarchs, Ministers, and Maps*, 57–98; David Buisseret, "Monarchs, Ministers, and Maps in France before the Ascension of Louis XIV," in Buisseret, *Monarchs, Ministers, and Maps*, 99–123.

[39] Geoffrey Parker, "Maps and Ministers: The Spanish Habsburgs," in Buisseret, *Monarchs, Ministers, and Maps*, 124–52.

[40] Christine Petto, *Mapping and Charting in Early Modern England and France: Power, Patronage, and Production* (Lanham, MD: Lexington Books, 2015), 4–13.

and new methods of surveying and mapping were often invented in direct response to pressing needs for taxation and administrative reform.[41] Reflecting such needs, surveys by means of triangulation were made by Jacob van Deventer in the Duchy of Brabant and were followed by similar efforts in other northern provinces of the Low Countries during the mid-sixteenth century. Some of these maps were later incorporated into the undisputed masterpiece of Renaissance cartography, the *Theatrum Orbis Terrarum* (1570) by Abraham Ortelius.[42] One of the first land surveys that covered an entire realm was undertaken in Sweden well before it had achieved great power status.[43] The Swedish Land Survey (*Lantmäteriet*) was established by a royal decree in 1628 and given the task of surveying the entire kingdom "not only to protect his land and realm against the enemy, but also to use every opportunity and means to improve their condition."[44] While the precise motives for undertaking this massive task have been disputed by historians, it now seems clear that mapping the realm was prompted by the Swedish aspirations to great power status at the time.[45]

Similar projects followed elsewhere. When Colbert launched the first geodetic survey of France in 1660, it was motivated by the need for administrative reform and the desire to advance commerce. The latter remained an important rationale for surveying and mapping well into the next century, when Cassini de Thury justified his undertaking in the following way: "as much as it is necessary for the sovereign to know the

[41] Monique Pelletier, "Cartography and Power in France during the Seventeenth and Eighteenth Centuries," *Cartographica: The International Journal for Geographic Information and Geovisualization* 35, nos. 3–4 (1998): 41–53.

[42] Cornelis Koeman and Marco van Egmond, "Surveying and Official Mapping in the Low Countries, 1500–ca. 1670," in Woodward, *The History of Cartography*, vol. 3, part II, 1246–94, esp. 1257ff.

[43] See Elizabeth Baigent, "Swedish Cadastral Mapping 1628–1700: A Neglected Legacy," *Geographical Journal* 156, no. 1 (1990): 62–9; Roger J. P. Kain and Elizabeth Baigent, *The Cadastral Map in the Service of the State: A History of Property Mapping* (Chicago: University of Chicago Press, 1992).

[44] Kunglig Instruktion, April 4, 1628, quoted in Viktor Ekstrand (ed.), *Samlingar i Landtmäteri, första samlingen, instruktioner och bref, 1628–1699* (Stockholm: Isaac Marcus, 1901), 1.

[45] See Staffan Helmfrid, "De geometriska jordeböckerna – 'skattläggningskartor,'" *YMER* 79 no. 3 (1959), 224–31; Baigent, "Swedish Cadastral Mapping 1628–1700," 64, 67.

country under his dominion well, it is useful to the subjects to know the location of places where their interests can be furthered and commerce conducted."[46]

Although boundaries and administrative divisions were often delineated on these maps, such boundaries rarely corresponded to the actual jurisdictions of early modern states but rather reflected the working methods of cartographers and their desire to impose a sense of order on a world whose intelligibility had been all but lost during the age of discoveries.[47] Sometimes cartographers produced maps that conveyed the impression of more territorial homogeneity and political centralization than was actually the case, but which were deemed suitable to further such ambitions.[48] Whether produced for propagandistic or practical purposes, maps and atlases conditioned subsequent claims to territorial authority by secular rulers in Europe and elsewhere. So "while atlas structure was defining political territory ever more precisely ... it was also giving form to the political territoriality and geopolitical appetites of particular nations."[49] In the case of France – which might be taken as paradigmatic in this regard – there was a striking lack of correspondence between the "natural" boundaries delineated by cartographers and the actual extent of its governmental jurisdiction. As Sahlins has remarked, "the stylized depiction of rivers and mountains within a growing commercial cartography provided a language that lent itself to the more general political project of building an idealized representation of the state."[50] But, however inaccurate they were, such representations of territory were not only essential to the conduct of foreign policy but also were important in fostering a sense of identity by defining populations with reference to their location. As we have seen, the idea that the political authority ought to be exercised over a sufficiently

---

[46] César-François Cassini de Thury, *Description Géométrique de la France* (Paris: Desaint, 1783), 5.

[47] For this theme, see Charles W. J. Withers, *Placing the Enlightenment: Thinking Geographically about the Age of Reason* (Chicago: University of Chicago Press, 2007), 87–110.

[48] Josef W. Konvitz, "The Nation-State, Paris and Cartography in Eighteenth- and Nineteenth-Century France," *Journal of Historical Geography* 16, no. 1 (1990): 3–16.

[49] James R. Akerman, "The Structuring of Political Territory in Early Printed Atlases," *Imago Mundi* 47, no. 1 (1995): 138–54, at 152.

[50] Peter Sahlins, "Natural Frontiers Revisited: France's Boundaries since the Seventeenth Century," *American Historical Review* 95, no. 5 (1990): 1423–51, at 1428.

homogeneous population antedated the notion that its exercise should be territorially bounded, yet cartography provided one important means for aligning populations and territories under the same sovereign gaze. Given imperatives such as these, early modern cartographic projects aimed at establishing more precise boundaries in order to settle issues of jurisdiction and loyalty in contested areas, such as in the frontier zones between France and the Netherlands.[51] As cartographic methods became more precise and the resulting maps more accurate, not only did they become more useful in settling territorial disputes but also in order to bring territories and populations to coincide by turning territorial boundaries into national boundaries.[52] But this was not always without complications; since maps could be used to promote different interests depending on the cartographic techniques used, they sometimes fueled territorial and national disputes rather than contributed to their resolution.[53]

Simultaneously, the early modern period was marked by great changes in the art of war in Europe. As armies grew in size and the importance of artillery increased, the need for effective field command increased in proportion. Since the art of command now consisted of combining the strengths of the various branches of the army, this was a matter of making optimal use of the terrain for defense as well as attack.[54] As Machiavelli advised a captain marching through foreign territory, "the first thing [you] must do is to have the whole territory described and pictured so that [you] know the places, the number, the distances, the roads, the mountains, the rivers and marshes, and the nature of them."[55] Thus, although some maps were widely disseminated to bolster royal claims to authority and foster a sense of national identity, military maps were often surrounded by secrecy. In Portugal,

---

[51] David Buisseret, "The Cartographic Definition of France's Eastern Boundary in the Early Seventeenth Century," *Imago Mundi* 36, no. 1 (1984): 72–80.

[52] See, for example, Daniel Nordman, "Des Limites d'État aux Frontières Nationales," in Pierre Nora (ed.), *Les Lieux de Memoire, vol. II: La Nation* (Paris: Gallimard, 1997), 1125–46.

[53] See, for example, Mary Pedley, "Map Wars: The Role of Maps in the Nova Scotia/Acadia Boundary Disputes of 1750," *Imago Mundi* 50, no. 1 (1998): 96–104.

[54] For the impact of the military revolution on cartography and mapping, see David Buisseret, *The Mapmakers' Quest: Depicting New Worlds in Renaissance Europe* (Oxford: Oxford University Press, 2003), 113–38.

[55] Niccolò Machiavelli, *The Art of War*, trans. Christopher Lynch (Chicago: University of Chicago Press, 2003), 111.

the government kept all cartographic information under strict surveillance and on several occasions ordered the destruction of all maps and globes for reasons of national security.[56] And when Charles IX of France was presented with a map of his country by a cartographer, he had it locked up "because maps are useful in war, enabling a foreign enemy to lead an army without the aid of a guide who knows the country across the terrain shown on the said maps, utilizing only a quadrant."[57]

With some hindsight, such suspiciousness seems unfounded and even paranoid. Although geographic knowledge had long been deemed useful to military planning, military concerns were initially of limited importance to the evolution of cartography and the production of maps. As Hale has shown, the knowledge required for successful campaigns was not primarily transmitted through maps but rather orally or in writing. Though commercial maps were widely available from the late sixteenth century onward, they did not cater that well to the needs of the field commander. Because such maps rarely contained any strategically important information about the precise locations of roads, river crossings, and mountain passes or the nature of the terrain, military leaders rather relied on written or oral topographic accounts when planning and conducting campaigns in foreign lands. Although administrative maps contained potentially valuable information, they were used in the settlement of legal disputes rather than being appropriated for military purposes. Well into the seventeenth century, "the demand for multipurpose topographical information prevented the evolution of a cartography primarily geared to the needs of war."[58]

But this was soon to change in response to new methods of war. As the preferred way of warfare changed from siege to battle, knowing the terrain became more important to both attack and defense. This made topographic surveying of paramount importance to success on the battlefield. Already during the seventeenth century, French topographic mapping was had been entrusted to a corps of geographical

---

[56] A. Teixeira da Mota, "Some Notes on the Organization of Hydrographical Services in Portugal before the Beginning of the Nineteenth Century," *Imago Mundi* 28 (1976): 51–60.

[57] Quoted in Geoffrey Parker, "Maps and Ministers: The Spanish Habsburgs," in Buisseret (ed.), *Monarchs, Ministers, and Maps*, 124–52, at 125.

[58] John Hale, "Warfare and Cartography, ca. 1450 to ca. 1640," in Woodward, *The History of Cartography*, vol. 3, 719–37, at 735.

engineers whose work was seen as an important preparation for future wars.[59] In 1624, geographical engineers had begun to accompany French forces into battle, and by the beginning of next century, geographical engineers were tasked with the undertaking of land surveys and the design of fortifications. Since topographic mapping provided information essential to the location of fortifications, topographic mapping was understood as an integral part of defensive warfare.[60] As such, the cartographic activities of military engineers during the seventeenth century resulted in the mapping of large parts of France, especially of the frontier regions.[61]

Similar developments took place in England. As the instructions to the principal military engineer from the *Board of Ordnance* read in 1663, he was supposed to "take surveys of land ... to have always by him ... Engineers useful in Fortifications and Sieges, to draw and design the Situation of any Place in their due Prospects."[62] A decade later, considerations of war and peace had become integral to the mapmaking enterprise in England. As John Ogilby claimed in the dedicatory epistle in his road atlas *Britannia* (1675), "[h]ere then I present your sacred majesty with an important novelty, the scale of peace and war, whereby ... a true prospect of this your flourishing kingdom may be taken, pregnant hints of security and interest gathered."[63] In order to dissipate any remaining doubts about the usefulness of his masterpiece, Ogilby advices the reader "not to press the infallible notions deducible in order to the security against civil dissension and foreign invasion."[64] Such mundane motives would become even more salient as mapmaking went from being a way of propagating claims to territorial authority to

---

[59] Josef W. Konvitz, *Cartography in France, 1660–1848: Science, Engineering, and Statecraft* (Chicago: University of Chicago Press, 1987), 1–31.

[60] Henri Marie Auguste Berthaut, *Les Ingenieurs Geographes Militaires, 1624–1831*, vol. 1 (Paris: Imprimerie du Service Géographique, 1901), 1–10.

[61] Buisseret, *Mapmaker's Quest*, 131; Anne Godlewska, *Geography Unbound: French Geographic Science from Cassini to Humboldt* (Chicago: University of Chicago Press, 1999).

[62] Quoted in Carolyn Jane Anderson, "State Imperatives: Military Mapping in Scotland, 1689–1770," *Scottish Geographical Journal* 125, no. 1 (2009): 4–24, at 7.

[63] John Ogilby, *Britannia or, an Illustration of the Kingdom of England and Dominion of Wales* (London: Ogilby, 1675), dedication to Charles II. For the background of this work, see Petto, *Mapping and Charting in Early Modern England and France*, 27–30.

[64] Ogilby, *Britannia*, preface, folio 1.

an instrument for actively asserting and implementing such claims on the ground.

During the following century, cartography underwent a phase of intense militarization. This brought an emphasis on the natural frontiers of each country as the proper locus of defense and attack, an emphasis that was difficult to reconcile with the long-standing obsession among cartographers with purely geometric methods of demarcation. Since cartography had long been an offspring of cosmography, the foundations of mapmaking were sought in the axioms of geometry. And since surveying was based on measurement of distance through triangulation, mapmaking presupposed that the physical environment was static enough to be rendered intelligible via empirical observation. Simultaneously, the map was a potent metaphor for all knowledge, and the art of mapmaking was closely aligned with the interests and ideologies of ruling elites.[65] Whereas commercial mapmaking had imposed intelligibility on the world with little regard for the actual extent of jurisdictions, the military preoccupation with geography was conditioned by the need to determine the natural frontiers of each country in order to protect it from attack or to use frontier regions as launching pads for assaults on neighboring countries. Thus, in the 1740s, the English army began to employ draftsmen to chart areas where campaigns were planned, and in Prussia, Frederick the Great insisted that the most detailed and accurate maps should be used because "knowledge of a country is to a general is what a rifle is to an infantryman and what the rules of arithmetic are to a geometrician."[66]

Similar developments ensued in France. A *Dépôt Général de la Guerre et de la Géographie* was established in 1743 and was charged with the task of directing the strategic needs of military geography in times of war. As Withers has remarked about this enterprise, "military geography was a handmaiden to state politics."[67] Such efforts yielded the first comprehensive manuals in military geography, such as *Les Principes de la Guerre de Montagnes* (1775) by Pierre Bourcet. Having started his career by conducting clandestine reconnaissance operations in the Alps and having then planned the French invasion of Piedmont during the War of the Austrian Succession, Bourcet devoted the first

---

[65]   Matthew H. Edney, "Mathematical Cosmography and the Social Ideology of British Cartography, 1780–1820," *Imago Mundi* 46, no. 1 (1994): 101–16.

[66]   Quoted in Buisseret, *Mapmakers' Quest*, 118.

[67]   Withers, *Placing the Enlightenment*, 198.

chapters of his manual to the methods of topographic reconnaissance and its importance to strategic planning. When undertaking reconnaissance missions in frontier areas, the first step is to acquire knowledge about the limits separating the territories of different sovereigns from each other.[68] This was a matter of identifying the natural frontiers of each country. Following a curious geographic doctrine, Bourcet proposed that in order to localize the natural frontier in mountainous areas, one needed to obtain information about the location of the waterways separated by a given mountain range.[69] Having thus determined the proper line of demarcation between two countries with reference to what was termed *les eaux pendants*, the commander is advised not to remain content consulting existing maps but to supplement the information contained therein by scouting and taking careful notes on the terrain, its relative accessibility, and the nature and severity of the various obstacles to be overcome by an advancing force.[70] This method for determining natural frontiers in mountainous areas was the result of peculiar looping effects because it had first been introduced as a method for settling territorial disputes during peace negotiations before it was turned into a tool of military planning by Bourcet.[71] As the century progressed, awareness of the importance of surveying and mapmaking to military planning increased further. As General Roy stated 1785, "accurate surveys of a country are universally admitted to be ... the best means of forming judicious plans of defence ... Hence it happens, that if a country has not actually been surveyed, or is but little known, a state of warfare generally produces the first improvements in its geography."[72] In response to this predicament, many European states charged military officers with conducting

---

[68]   Pierre de Bourcet, *Principes de la Guerre de Montagnes* (Paris: Imprimerie Nationale, 1888), 7.

[69]   For a background, see Bernard Debarbieux, "La (M)montagne comme figure de la frontière: réflexions à partir de quelques cas," *Le Globe. Revue Genevoise de Géographie* 137 (1997): 145–66.

[70]   Bourcet, *Principes de la Guerre de Montagnes*, 9–10.

[71]   See Georg Friedrich von Martens, *Nouveaux Supplémens au Receuil de Traités* (Göttingen: Dietrich, 1839), 11; *Traité de Paix entre La France et La Savoye conclu à Utrecht le 11 April 1713* (Paris: Fournier, 1713); *Traité entre le Roi et le Roi de Sardaigne, conclu à Turin le 24 Mars 1760* (Paris: Imprimerie Royale, 1762).

[72]   An account of the measurement of a base on Hounslow Heath: Major-General William Roy, read at the Royal Society, from April 21 to June 16, 1785 (London, 1785), 3. Quoted in Anderson, "State Imperatives," 21.

systematic surveys and producing military maps of each country, to the point of mapmaking becoming the very epitome of a military science.[73]

But the militarization of cartography was not confined to the European continent. Many of the cartographic practices later employed in Europe were first developed in a colonial context, reflecting a desire to facilitate colonial management by creating homogeneous spaces.[74] European expansion had long spurred a demand for maps that could be used to aid imperial expansion and settle territorial disputes between imperial powers; this is one reason why Spain and Portugal devoted much of their cartographic resources to their overseas possessions. And in North America, the making of the United States was premised on the possibility of creating a homogeneous and bounded political space that was amenable to republican forms of governance.[75] The American Revolutionary War added further impetus to its mapping. Since detailed and accurate maps still were lacking, the belligerents were compelled to develop mapmaking capabilities of their own in order to gain and maintain military advantage.[76]

The expansion of British military activities in South Asia increased the need for accurate maps, and by 1760, the first surveys of the Indian subcontinent were undertaken. Robert Orme – historian of the East India Company – made great efforts to communicate the military value of maps and geographic knowledge in general and collected large amounts of geographic information with the aim of facilitating future military operations of the Company.[77] As the awareness of the military importance of cartography grew, James Rennell was appointed Surveyor General of India. As we learn from the letter recommending

---

[73] See Matthew H. Edney, "British Military Education, Mapmaking, and Military 'Map-Mindedness' in the Later Enlightenment," *The Cartographic Journal* 31, no. 1 (1994): 14–20; Sven Widmalm, "Accuracy, Rhetoric, and Technology: The Paris-Greenwich Triangulation, 1784–88," in Tore Frängsmyr and John L. Heilbron (eds.), *The Quantifying Spirit in the 18th Century* (Berkeley: University of California Press, 1990), 179–206.

[74] Branch, *Cartographic State*, 100–19.

[75] Peter S. Onuf and Nicholas Greenwood Onuf, *Federal Union, Modern World: The Law of Nations in an Age of Revolutions, 1776–1814* (Madison, WI: Madison House, 1993).

[76] Buisseret, *Mapmakers' Quest*, 120.

[77] See Asoka SinhaRaja Tammita-Delgoda, "'Nabob, Historian and Orientalist': The Life and Writings of Robert Orme (1728–1801)," doctoral dissertation, King's College, London, 1991, 263ff.

his appointment, "so much depends upon accurate surveys both in military operations and in coming at a true knowledge of the value of your possessions, that we have employed everybody on this service who could be spared and were capable of it."[78] Based partly on maps previously drawn by Orme, Rennell published the *Bengal Atlas* in 1780 and a *General Map of All Hindostan* in 1782, both of which were to remain authoritative sources for some time.[79] Later, when prefacing an updated version of the latter work in 1788, he was pleased to note that the war against the notorious Tipo Sultan had "produced much new geographical matter, in various parts of the peninsula, by the marches of the different armies, and their detachments."[80] But since the Mogul empire now had been dismembered, its former provinces divided between different princes and its traditional boundaries dissolved, locating boundaries with any precision was no easy task for Rennell and his colleagues.[81] This posed a peculiar problem in the tumultuous south, where "north of the Cauvery ... boundaries are very ill defined, even by the governing powers themselves."[82] So, in contrast to European states, most of which by now were territorially bounded and unified, imperial possessions and colonial spaces displayed highly variegated geographies, often without any clear territorial demarcations or jurisdictions.[83]

Toward the end of the eighteenth century, the mapping of the European Continent had almost been completed. While large-scale surveys and mapping projects were now perceived as necessary precursors to the unification of state territories and the demarcation of national boundaries, they also informed the processes through which the congruence of authority and community within bounded territories gradually was realized. Consequently, maps and atlases produced

---

[78] Letter to the Court of Directors, March 30, 1767, in *The Journals of Major James Rennell, First Surveyor-General of India, Written for the Information of the Governors of Bengal during His Surveys of the Ganges and Brahmaputra Rivers 1764 to 1767* (Calcutta: Asiatic Society, 1910), 2.

[79] Tammita-Delgoda, "Nabob, Historian and Orientalist," 140; Matthew H. Edney, *Mapping an Empire: The Geographical Construction of British India, 1765–1843* (Chicago: University of Chicago Press, 1997).

[80] James Rennell, *Memoir of a Map of Hindoostan or the Mogul Empire* (London, 1788), iv.

[81] *Ibid.*, vi.   [82] *Ibid.*, 197.

[83] See Lauren Benton, *Law and Colonial Cultures: Legal Regimes in World History, 1400–1900* (Cambridge: Cambridge University Press, 2002).

during this period made consistent use of lines and colors to demarcate states from each other. Thus the *Atlas Universel* (1757) by Robert de Vaugondy and *Europe Divided into Its Kingdoms* (1772) by Robert Sayer both depicted the European continent divided into its principal states and their provinces and were followed by an outpouring of maps and atlases reflecting the changing political divisions in Europe in the aftermath of the Napoleonic Wars and the Congress of Vienna.[84] These changing political divisions were themselves fueled by advances in military geography and cartography. Both Napoleon and Wellington had gone to battle equipped with extensive map collections and their own cartographic staff, sometimes with decisive consequences for their campaigns. For example, after the battle of Buçaco in 1810, Wellington's troops could retreat to relative safety behind the Torres Vedras lines to the north of Lisbon, lines of defense that could not have been conceived and built without the detailed geographic knowledge that had been obtained well in advance of the peninsular war.[85]

Fortifying the State

In the preceding section, we saw how symbolic claims to territorial authority embodied in early modern maps were translated into a recognizably modern notion of territoriality through practices of cartographic demarcation. The next and no less important steps in translating such representations of territoriality into facts on the ground were taken by military engineers during roughly the same period. Military engineers were less interested in the contours of a landscape but all the more concerned with the possibility of exploiting its topography for the purposes of military defense and attack. Hence, in this section, I explore the connections between cartography and the art of fortification, arguing that their common indebtedness to geometric reasoning makes it possible to describe the process through which cartographic representations were implemented on the ground as a process of large-scale fortification. This does not imply that states were turned into fortresses other than in a metaphorical sense but that the fortress served as templates for territorial defense and domestic

[84] Biggs, "Putting the State on the Map," 398.
[85] See Richard H. P. Smith, "Peninsular War Cartography: A New Look at the Military Mapping of General Sir George Murray and the Quartermaster General's Department," *Imago Mundi* 65, no. 2 (2013): 234–52.

pacification, in similar way as the panopticon was to serve as a paradigm of surveillance.[86] The fact that fortification and cartography were indebted to the same epistemic framework and reflected similar concerns with state security warranted a partial confluence of methods and strategies. Both were based on geometric reasoning and on the assumption that state security would best be served by the application of scientific methods. Hence it was a widely shared belief that the construction of fortresses should be governed by geometric principles and that these should be adapted to the features of the terrain as rendered on maps and conveyed through observation.[87]

The early modern fortifications had originally developed in response to the use of gunpowder artillery in late fifteenth-century Italy. In their standard shape, with a pentagonal bastion protruding from a curtain wall, early modern fortifications betrayed strong influences from Roman military architecture and then especially from the recently rediscovered works of Vitruvius. Even if his defensive designs were no longer that useful in the age of gunpowder, this nevertheless corroborated the Vitruvian principle according to which any defensive countermeasures must be adapted to the offensive capabilities at hand.[88] Fortification was now an aspiring science of security whose ambitions were seemingly unlimited by any walls, and military architecture began to exercise a detectable influence on city planning to the point of turning towns into forts and forts into towns.[89]

Thus the pioneering military engineer, Errard Bar-le-Duc, felt it necessary to inform his intended audience of aristocratic readers that the art of fortification was based on "geometrical demonstrations that give infallible assurance to everybody," regardless of the fact that most of what he had to say on this topic was grounded in practical military experience rather than in anything resembling geometric proof.[90] With

---

[86] On the role of fortification in state making, see Charles S. Maier, *Once Within Borders: Territories of Power, Wealth and Belonging since 1500* (Cambridge, MA: Harvard University Press, 2016), 50–81.

[87] Janis Langins, *Conserving the Enlightenment: French Military Engineering from Vauban to the Revolution* (Cambridge, MA: MIT Press, 2004), 13–37.

[88] Vitruve, *Les Dix Livres d'Architecture* [reprint of the 1673 trans. by Claude Perrault] (Paris: Balland, 1979), vol. X: xvi, 336–40 (*De Repugnatoriis Rebus*).

[89] See Horst de la Croix, "Military Architecture and the Radial City Plan in Sixteenth Century Italy," *The Art Bulletin* 42, no. 4 (1960): 263–90.

[90] Jean Errard de Bar-le-Duc, *La Fortification Démontree et Reduicte en Art* [1600] (Paris, 1619), dedication to the nobility.

the importance of fortification increasing in proportion to the power of canons, attempts to put the art of fortification on a scientific footing continued unabated during the seventeenth century.[91] As White has described this, "it is doubtful whether the 'Cartesian' mentality, which assumed that mathematics is the key to reality, would have become dominant if Europe had not been assiduously bankrupting itself by building new military defenses in which assurance of safety was achieved less by tangible masses of masonry than by abstract geometrical patterns of lines of fire."[92] Such attempts to harness geometric knowledge for the purposes of security provide further clues to how the imagined congruence between political authority and territory was translated into facts on the ground. This was in effect a matter of drawing lines on the ground that aligned territories thus demarcated with their cartographic representations on maps rather than the other way around. Hence, and *pace* Branch, this was less a matter of replacing a series of discontinuous places with a singular and homogeneous space than it was largely a matter of turning states into places in their own right.[93]

While cartographic knowledge was considered necessary, it was not sufficient to guide efforts at territorial unification and demarcation. Geographic surveys often went hand in hand with statistical ones, reflecting the Enlightenment belief that numerical registration was a necessary precursor to domestic order and safety. Geography provided the basis of what Petty and Davenant had termed "political arithmetic" – the art of reasoning by figures on things relating to government – by delineating its units of analysis in space so that different places could be subjected to systematic comparison according to the size of their populations and their relative wealth.[94] This use of geography as a basis for statistics animated the work of the great military engineer Vauban, whose work was to be emulated by almost all European states during the seventeenth and eighteenth centuries. Although Vauban thought maps indispensable to military

---

[91] See Christopher Duffy, *The Fortress in the Age of Vauban and Frederick the Great: 1660–1789*, vol. 2 (London: Routledge Kegan & Paul, 1985).

[92] Lynn White, "Jacopo Aconcio as an Engineer," *American Historical Review* 72, no. 2 (1967): 425–44, at 425. Quoted in Langins, *Conserving the Enlightenment*, 45.

[93] Branch, *Cartographic State*, 142–64.

[94] Ted Mc Cormick, *William Petty and the Ambitions of Political Arithmetic* (Oxford: Oxford University Press, 2009); Withers, *Placing the Enlightenment*, 199–200.

planning and fortification, their lack of detailed information about different places prompted him to undertake survey missions to towns and
frontier areas to gather additional information about their populations
and wealth.[95] In his instructions for the conduct of such statistical surveys,
Vauban advised his colleague Caligny to first acquire a map on which to
mark the area to be surveyed with lines and colors. Caligny is then asked
to provide a detailed report on all the relevant characteristics of each area
in question, such as its topographic features, the presence of fortresses and
other military installations, the number of clergy and noblemen and their
possessions, the revenues to be extracted and the repairs to be made, the
number of acres and what is produced on them, the number of cattle and
poultry found in the area, the number of people in different age and status
groups, and so forth.[96]

Apart from commissioning such reports, Vauban himself undertook
several such missions, meticulously documenting the geographic and
topographic characteristics of border towns and their surroundings.[97]
In a detailed statistical analysis of Vézelay that was to become a template
for many subsequent surveys, Vauban provided an account of its tax
base, the customs of its inhabitants, their richness and poverty, and the
quality of the soil. All this information was then organized into tables
and analyzed, which resulted in recommendations on how to improve its
soils to alleviate a condition of chronic malnourishment among the
population.[98] Remarkable feats such as these earned Vauban a reputation – perhaps a bit anachronistically – as the father of modern statistics
and a pioneer in political economy fully on a par with Turgot.[99]

[95] Sebastién Prestre de Vauban, "Observations a Faire sur la Reconnaissance des
Places," in Eugène-Auguste-Albert de Rochas d'Aiglun (ed.), *Vauban. Sa famille
et ses écrits: ses "Oisivetés" et sa Correspondance, analyse et extraits*, vol. 1
(Paris: Berger-Levrault, 1910), 240–1.

[96] Vauban, "Lettre sur la Manière de Faire les Statistiques," in d'Aiglun, *Vauban*,
590–5.

[97] Vauban, "Relation du Voyage sur la Frontière Commence le 9 Avril 1698 et fini
le 12 Fevrier 1699," in d'Aiglun, *Vauban*, 603–12.

[98] Sébastien Le Prestre de Vauban, *Description Géographique de l'Élection de
Vézelay, contenant ses revenus, sa qualité, les moeurs de ses habitants, leur
pauvreté et richesse, la fertilité du pays et ce que l'on pourrait y faire pour en
corriger la stérilité et procurer l'augmentation des peuples et l'accroissement des
bestiaux*, Janvier 1696, Jean-Francois Pernot (ed.) (Paris: Association des amis
de la maison Vauban, 1986).

[99] See, for example, Bernard Buyer de Fontenelle, *Éloge de Monsieur le Maréchal
de Vauban, Histoire de l'Académie Royale des Sciences* (Paris: Compagnie des

Sometimes these reports resulted in pieces of concrete advice to Louis XIV. Much of this advice focused on what Vauban saw as necessary measures to create a unified and demarcated territory. His use of terminology in some of these reports indicates that he saw territory as a dueling ground on which it was necessary to impose order by creating infrastructure and developing economic resources.[100] As Vauban remarked in a letter to his superior, Louvois, "[t]he King ought to think a little about squaring the field. This confusion of friendly and enemy fortresses mixed together does not please me at all. You are compelled to maintain three for one; your people are tormented, your expenses greatly stretched and your forces diminished."[101] In regions where there were no natural frontiers, the vision of a unified territory resulted in the construction of what Vauban termed a *ceinture de fer* consisting in a double line of fortresses demarcating French territory from those of its neighbors.[102] Prompted by the porousness that the Peace of Nijmegen (1678) had brought to the northwestern frontier, this project was quickly initiated and completed toward the end of the century. Vauban expressed his worries in a memorandum to Louis XIV: "the frontier toward the Low Countries lies open and disordered as a consequence of the recent peace." What should be done to avert this threat is "to establish a new frontier and fortify it so well that it closes the approaches into our country to an enemy while giving us access to his." This was to be done by making the fortifications large enough "to contain not only the munitions required for their own defense but also the supplies needed if we invade enemy territory" and also by strengthening the line of defense with canals "along whose banks entrenchments could be dug in time of war ... while at the same time the canals would provide valuable assistance for the movement of goods, and

Libraires, 1752); Félix Cadet, *Histoire de l'économie politique: les précurseurs Boisguilbert, Vauban, Quesnay, Turgot* (Paris: H. Gérard, 1869).

[100] Langins, *Conserving the Enlightenment*, 70–1.

[101] Vauban to Louvois, January 20, 1673, in d'Aiglun, *Vauban*, vol. II, 89; also Gaston Zeller, *L'organisation défensive des frontières du Nord et de l'Est au XVIIe siècle: avec une carte hors texte* (Paris: Berger-Levrault, 1928), 60; Sahlins, "Natural Frontiers Revisited," 1434.

[102] Sahlins, "Natural Frontiers Revisited," 1434ff; Langins, *Conserving the Enlightenment*, 65.

commerce."[103] In order to prevent the Spaniards from posing a renewed threat from the Netherlands, Luxembourg and Strasbourg should be captured and duly fortified. In another *mémoir*, Vauban provides an assessment of the towns and frontier regions that could be sacrificed in the interest of peace but without weakening the state itself or its frontiers. These towns and their surroundings are evaluated according to their strategic importance, the revenues that can be extracted from their inhabitants in times of war, whether or not they are easily defended, and whether or not they can offer bridgeheads during offensive expeditions into neighboring countries. In towns that could be ceded without too much loss to the crown, he recommended demolishing existing fortifications before they could be handed over to the enemy.[104]

During the second half of the eighteenth century, when the process of fortification almost had been brought to completion, the French government started to demarcate its territory with boundary stones and entered into negotiations with its neighbors over the proper limits of its realm in order to purge it of enclaves and to eliminate remaining objects of dispute among frontier inhabitants.[105] As Vauban had argued, enclaves are good only for "causing quarrels and attracting disputes that are only decided with the sword."[106] In sum, "[b]y fortifying France's coastal and inland borders and by adopting a strategy of rapid, forward movement into the territory of a potential enemy, France achieved a level of security for its cities which was altogether unprecedented."[107] But these attempts to assert boundaries that were thought to be natural or historically rightful also found expression in a

---

[103] Sebastién Prestre de Vauban, *Memorandum on the Places on the Flanders Frontier which Must Be Fortified to Secure the Lands Owing Obedience to the King* (November 1678), in Eugène-Auguste-Albert de Rochas d'Aiglun, *Vauban. Sa famille et ses écrits: ses "Oisivetés" et sa Correspondance, analyse et extraits* (Paris: Berger-Levrault, 1910), 189–92.

[104] Vauban, "Places dont le Roi Pourrait se Défaire en Faveur d'un Traité de Paix Sans Faire Tort a l'État ni Affaiblir sa Frontière," in d'Aiglun, *Vauban*, vol. I, 192–207.

[105] Sahlins, "Natural Frontiers Revisited," 1438–40.

[106] Vauban, "Projet de Paix assez Raisonable Pour que Tous les Intéressez a La Guerre Présente, en deussent être contens, s'il avoit lieu et qu'il plut a Dieu d'y donner sa benediction" (1706), in d'Aiglun, *Vauban*, vol. I, 496–532, at 510.

[107] Konvitz, "The Nation-State, Paris and Cartography in Eighteenth- and Nineteenth-Century France," 11.

rather aggressive foreign policy. Although Vauban urged the king to exercise restraint by not expanding his territory beyond the natural frontiers of France, it turned out that properly establishing those "natural frontiers" nevertheless required swallowing a host of principalities and bishoprics.[108] By the time his successor, Cormontaigne, sketched a brief history of the art of fortification, it was obvious to him that the work of Vauban represented the culmination of a long development that had begun when humans first had erected primitive obstacles to ward off attacks by ferocious beasts. Those parts of France that did not enjoy natural protection by mountains and oceans were now protected by three lines of interconnected fortifications, with places of lesser strategic importance on the outer line for the defense of the more strategically important ones on the inner line.[109]

As Langins has summarized the role of the military engineering corps in this process of territorial unification and demarcation, the fortification of the French state "may have given them a distorted view of the national space of the country, [and] it was also a view that saw that space as becoming more coherent, more rational and more defensible."[110] And as we have seen, this process of territorial demarcation was carried out and justified with reference to the threats – real or imagined – of foreign invasion. But the imperative of external defense was also closely aligned with the desire for internal order, sometimes to the point of them being indistinguishable. The process of territorial demarcation was accompanied by infrastructural projects aimed at improving the internal circulation of people and commodities for the benefit of a unified and homogeneous political and economic space. The most ambitious of these projects – *Le Canal du Midi* – had been commissioned by Colbert in the hope of making the surrounding regions more governable and more profitable and was pursued relentlessly and ruthlessly by his contractor, Riquet, from 1661 to 1681. Realizing an ancient Roman dream of connecting the Mediterranean and the Atlantic through an extensive network of waterways, the canal was intended to facilitate trade between regions with different comparative advantages in the interest of increasing national economic

---

[108] Vauban, "Intérets Present des États de la Chrétienté," in d'Aiglun, *Vauban*, vol. I, 491–6.
[109] Louis de Cormontaigne, *Architecture Militaire, ou l'art de fortifier* (La Haye: Jean Neaulme & Adrien Moetjens, 1741), 1–8.
[110] Langins, *Conserving the Enligthenment*, 69.

integration. But by the time Vauban was commissioned to inspect and redesign it, the canal and its embankments had fallen into a state of severe disrepair. To the obvious economic advantages that were believed to ensue from its restoration, Vauban added some telling remarks on its military potentials. Although considerations of its military usefulness had figured preeminently in the original plans for the canal, the design features from which the navy was supposed to benefit had been abandoned because of technical difficulties.[111] But as we learn from his *Mémoire sur le Canal du Languedoc* (1691), a properly redesigned canal "will be very convenient for the transport of munitions, sealed and rigged according to need, promptly and safely from one ocean to the other ... to let galleys pass in less than ten to twelve days with a good number of Men of War is a sure way of inciting terror in the English, the Dutch and others."[112]

When seen in the broader context of state formation, the demarcation of territorial boundaries and the building of new infrastructure were two complementary processes. As Mukerji has argued, the making of the French state was not so much the result of centralization and rationalization as it was the outcome of improvement in logistics undertaken for both military and economic reasons. The lines of defense erected by military engineers under the guidance of Vauban and the many infrastructural projects initiated by Colbert and completed by civil engineers together reflect a coherent strategy designed to protect the country from foreign invasions as well as from domestic unrest, either by removing their underlying causes or by increasing the capacity to nip outbursts of domestic dissent in the bud.[113] Thus Cartesian dreams of a calculable order were fulfilled insofar as the *res* of the *respublica* was made identical with its *res extensa*, rather than with any of its abundant representations in *res cogitans*.

Given the widespread emulation of this model of territorial demarcation, with its emphasis on fortification as a method of establishing and protecting the natural frontiers of each state, it is not surprising

---

[111] Chandra Mukerji, *Impossible Engineering: Technology and Territoriality on the Canal du Midi* (Princeton, NJ: Princeton University Press, 2009).

[112] Vauban, *Mémoire sur le Canal du Languedoc*, in d'Aiglun, *Vauban*, 545–76, at 573.

[113] Chandra Mukerji, "The Territorial State as a Figured World of Power: Strategics, Logistics, and Impersonal Rule," *Sociological Theory* 28, no. 4 (2010): 402–24.

that military science should accept this outcome as a brute fact and a
baseline for strategic thinking. Even if military science reflected the
Enlightenment preoccupation with geometric reasoning, it could not
dispense altogether with the notion of natural frontiers. It is even
possible to argue that the notion of natural frontiers became essential
to the art of war precisely because of its salience to the art of fortification. As Lloyd argued in his *Reflections on the General Principles of
War* (1781), "[t]he march of armies cannot be calculated with any
degree of precision without the help of mathematics: because whatever
is not reduced to space and time, will in practice turn out very uncertain."[114] And if the conduct of war indeed is a matter of mastering time
and space, it follows that "the most important object ... to those who
aspire to the command of armies, is geography; not only that which
consists in a general knowledge of a country, but a local one: a man
must be thoroughly acquainted with the face of the country ... and
particularly with those objects which are immediately connected with
military operations."[115] Lloyd then applies the principles of geography
to practical warfare by describing in detail the frontier lines of different
European states. Knowledge of these lines shall "enable the sovereign,
ministers, and generals to form their plans of war."[116] As a matter of
principle, "however extensive such a line may be, the points on which it
can be attacked are determined by the number and quality of the roads
that lead to it, and by the position and distance of the respective
capitals, and other strong places within a hundred miles of it."[117]
Thus the "the absolute force of a frontier consists in natural obstacles,
which an enemy would find in approaching and attacking it."[118] But
apart from capitalizing on natural barriers to attack provided by
mountain ranges and rivers, "the relative force of a frontier line
depends on the distance of the capitals and fortresses, where the depots
are lodged, of those who attack and defend it."[119] Although advances
in surveying and cartography now allowed for a precise demarcation of
boundaries without any reference to the concept of natural frontiers,

[114] Henry Lloyd, "Reflections on the General Principles of War; and on the
Composition and Characters of the Different Armies in Europe," in
*Continuation of the History of the Late War in Germany between the King of
Prussia and the Empress of Germany and Her Allies* (London: Hooper, 1781),
xx.
[115] *Ibid.*, xxiv.   [116] *Ibid.*, 153.   [117] *Ibid.*, 151.   [118] *Ibid.*, 153.
[119] *Ibid.*, 154.

military engineers remained convinced that states should stick to their natural frontiers as defined by rivers and mountains because the latter made it easier to organize attacks and mount defense.[120]

Geographies of Violence

In Chapter 2, we saw how the early modern historians held that each state had a territorial extension that could vary over time as a consequence of wars and invasions. In this chapter, we have seen how early modern geographers and cartographers assumed that states enjoyed temporal continuity within their mutable and often porous boundaries. Early modern historiography and geography thereby provided the basic coordinates for the creation of states and an international system by making their temporal limits and spatial boundaries appear natural as a consequence of being co-constitutive. But geography and cartography not only provided new methods of territorial demarcation and unification but also furnished new ways of understanding mankind as a whole. The discoveries had revealed new evidence of human diversity that was hard to reconcile with received views of the unity of mankind, and colonial encounters with peoples in remote corners of the earth yielded additional information about different cultures, their customs, and their habits. All these differences stood in need of scientific explanation. While the causes of these differences were hotly contested in the early human sciences, a first step toward understanding them was to study the distribution of human difference across time and space.[121]

Doing this would bring a gradual convergence of history and geography. Although history and geography had been closely aligned during the early modern period, they were distinct branches of knowledge with different epistemic foundations. Historical writing continued to be informed by the precepts of renaissance humanism into the eighteenth century and beyond, and as we have seen, geography had been heavily indebted to the ideals of geometric reasoning from its inception. The earliest attempts to make sense of the distribution of human differences in time and space were largely conjectural in character, and although they did distinguish between different stages of human development and often related these to variations in climate and

---

[120] Sahlins, "Natural Frontiers Revisited," 1442.
[121] Withers, *Placing the Enlightenment*, 136–63.

habitat, it was not until Turgot that stadial theories of human development were systematically aligned with the study of geography. The task that Turgot had set for himself was to describe the "distribution of peoples on the globe and the division into states."[122]

The attempt to fuse geography and history together was to some extent motivated by the need to reconcile the concept of the territorially bounded state with the last wave of imperial expansion that had started in 1870s. When the evolutionary perspective began to make its presence felt within almost all scientific fields during the latter half of the nineteenth century, this offered an opportunity to bring history and geography closer by arguing that both disciplines were concerned with aspects of human evolution, albeit from different vantage points and with various methods. Yet their shared preoccupation with the mechanisms of evolution broadly conceived made it possible to fuse geography and history into a single field of investigation and to argue that this would yield a more comprehensive and coherent account of human evolution that any of these disciplines could claim to convey in isolation.[123] Since Darwinism brought the concept of natural selection to bear on both fields, this made it easier for historians and geographers to cast earlier differences aside and join forces by claiming to share the same scientific foundation and basic assumptions.[124] But as we shall see in this section, it also made it possible to explain territorial demarcation and unification as outcomes of natural selection, this selection resulting from an ongoing struggle between nations and races for space. Hence the idea that war was a productive force in human affairs found new support in what was widely regarded as the main scientific achievement of the day and which made it possible to reconcile the territorially bounded state with claims to imperial authority now being asserted with renewed vigor.

[122] Anne-Robert-Jacques Turgot, "Plan d'un Ouvrage sur la Géographie Politique" [1751], in Gustave Schelle (ed.), *Oeuvres de Turgot* (Paris: Félix Alcan, 1913), 255–74, at 255. For an analysis, see Michael Heffernan, "On Geography and Progress: Turgot's Plan d'un ouvrage sur la géographie politique (1751) and the Origins of Modern Progressive Thought," *Political Geography* 13, no. 4 (1994): 328–43.

[123] See Henry Clifford Darby and Michael Williams. *The Relations of History and Geography: Studies in England, France and the United States* (Exeter: University of Exeter Press, 2002).

[124] See David R. Stoddart, "Darwin's Impact on Geography," *Annals of the Association of American Geographers* 56, no. 4 (1966): 683–98.

One early example of Darwinian influence on geography was *Die Darwin'sche Theorie und das Migrationsgesetz der Organismen* (1868) by Moritz Wagner, in which he sought to explain the geographic distribution of living beings in terms of natural selection. Although the law according to which the struggle for survival prompted migration was applied mainly to plants and animals, its application to the development of the human race "is certainly capable of much greater amplification than is aimed at in this treatise."[125] And such amplification was certainly in the coming. Within this nascent field that only decades later would transmute into geopolitics proper, existing territorial boundaries were seen as the result of struggles between different races over territory. The principles of natural selection were invoked not only to explain the existence of boundaries between states but also to justify the fine lines of demarcation separating the civilized from the uncivilized parts of the world. Yet it was an open question whether such boundaries were fixed or should be understood as mutable. To those adhering to the former view, states should stick to the boundaries bestowed upon them by a historical accident. To those who subscribed to the latter view, it was obvious that states and entire civilizations expanded and contracted according to the logic of natural selection, so the stronger and most vigorous human communities necessarily would conquer weaker ones.

As Bryce summarized the starting point for bringing geography closer to the human sciences, "geography is as a meeting-point between the sciences of Nature and the sciences of Man."[126] And he went on to add, "it is in discovering the carrying effects produced on the growth of man as a social and political, a wealth-acquiring and State-forming creature, by the geographical surroundings in which he is placed, that we find the meeting point of geography and history."[127] Thus the configuration of the Earth's surface will "determine the directions in which races move, the spots in which civilization first develops . . . [and] the frequency and ease with which communication takes place between two races or political communities."[128] As Bryce further explains, among the branches of geography with the most influence of the course

---

[125] Moritz Wagner, *The Darwinian Theory and the Law of the Migration of Organisms*, trans. James L. Laird (London: Edward Stanford, 1873), 5.
[126] James Bryce, "The Relations of History and Geography," *Contemporary Review* 69 (1887): 426–43, at 426.
[127] Bryce, "Relations of History and Geography," 427. [128] *Ibid.*, 427.

of history we find political and military geography, being concerned with the "relations of the artificial boundaries of States to the natural boundaries which Nature has tried to draw, and which have become of later years more important by the consolidation of small States into large ones."[129] For example, the history and national sentiments of France and Spain are conditioned by the simple fact that they are separated by the Pyrenees rather than by any notable racial differences between them.[130] But in an increasingly interconnected world, race struggle will produce an inevitable outcome, that is, "when nearly all its habitable parts have been surveyed, when the great races, the great languages, the great religions, spreading swiftly over its surface, are swallowing up the lesser."[131]

To some extent this desire to make history and geography converge was determined by the effort to establish geography as an autonomous discipline at this point in time. As the young Mackinder argued, geography proper ought to be separated from physical geography narrowly defined because the latter had become unduly subsumed under geology. Rather than merely describing the geographic features of a given country, the main function of geography "is to trace the interaction of man in society and so much of his environment as varies locally."[132] Although he envisioned no close connection between the disciplines of history and geography, he held that geographic features were important in the development of civilizations, such as waterways facilitating commerce and natural barriers protecting against foreign invasions.[133]

To Freeman, the main task of historical geography was to understand the causes and effects of boundaries between states. The first step in this inquiry was "draw the map of the countries with which we are concerned as it appeared after each of the different changes which they have gone through, and then to point out the historical causes which have led to the changes on the map."[134] An assumption commonly made within this field was that the differentiation into distinct and bounded communities in Europe and elsewhere had resulted from the

---

[129] *Ibid.*, 430.   [130] *Ibid.*, 438.   [131] *Ibid.*, 443.
[132] Halford J. Mackinder, "On the Scope and Methods of Geography," *Proceedings of the Royal Geographical Society*, 3 (1887): 141–74, at 143.
[133] Mackinder, "On the Scope and Methods of Geography," 158–9.
[134] Edward A. Freeman, *A Historical Geography of Europe*, vol. 1 (London: Longmans, Green, 1881), 2–3.

gradual fission of primordial races and language groups into smaller units. Although history certainly is shaped by national character, geographic position had something to do with forming the national character, and in all cases it has had an influence on it, by giving it a better or a worse field for working and showing itself."[135] To Freeman, it was obvious that "[w]hether we look at Europe now, or whether we look at it at the earliest times of which we have any glimmerings, it is preeminently an Aryan continent."[136] But the Aryan predominance was but the result of a series of struggles through which they had established themselves as masters by driving off or successfully assimilating inferior racial elements. As he proceeded to argue, "Sicilian history is chiefly made up of struggles for the mastery between Carthage and the Greek cities. This was in truth a struggle between the Aryan and the Semitic race."[137] But after having warded off such undesirable influences, Europeans had to confront barbarism in a new and more potent guise when Cyprus "shared the fate, not of Sicily but of Crete, and became the solid prize of the Ottoman."[138] But at the time Freeman was writing, the destiny of Europe seemed manifest, "having spread herself beyond her geographical limits in the foundation of new European states beyond the Ocean."[139]

Although Freeman was among the first to develop what could be described as a historical geography of race struggle, attempts in a similar direction were made by military historians and geographers. To Maguire, for example, it was important that citizens should have a clear conception of the art of war and its relationship to geography because "in battles the highest faculties of the race are exerted in their most intense energy. The struggles of embattled men are perennially interesting to all men, and the history of mankind is the history of armies."[140] And as George argued in his curious effort to combine military history and geography, "[h]istory is not intelligible without geography. This is obviously true in the sense that the reader of history must learn where are the frontiers of states, where wars were fought out, whither colonies were dispatched."[141] From this George inferred a

---

[135] *Ibid.*, 11. [136] *Ibid.*, 12. [137] *Ibid.*, 48–9. [138] *Ibid.*, 404.
[139] *Ibid.*, 569.
[140] T. Miller Maguire, *Outlines of Military Geography* (Cambridge: Cambridge University Press, 1899), 13.
[141] Hereford B. George, *The Relations of Geography and History* (Oxford: Clarendon Press, 1901), 1.

guiding principle of his entire work, namely, that "[a]ll external relations, hostile and peaceful, are based largely on geography."[142] This
assumption is particularly interesting in the present context because
George then presents an explanation of the relative fixity of boundaries. "As men grew less savage and more settled, and learned to live
within reach of one another without perpetual war, there would arise a
need for recognized boundaries between tribes, or between aggregates
of tribes that were making, the first steps towards a larger union.
Geographical facts doubtless in most cases determined these."[143]
Thus, all seemingly natural frontiers had resulted from the prehistorical
movement of races because "[i]n process of time mankind settled down
to permanent occupation of territory; and then the mountains, which
had been obstacles dividing races, tended to become permanent frontiers."[144] Whereas rivers first had provided the means for interconnec-
tion between different groups and races, they owe their importance as
frontiers to the modern art of war.[145]

As Maguire pointed out, "no frontier, however massive, or however
strengthened by nature and art, can prevent a luxurious, inert or
corrupt race from ruin."[146] But to George, the relationship between
race and geography was not that straightforward. Geographic and
racial boundaries do not necessarily coincide, and on those occasions
when they do not, "[g]eography may well despair of drawing any
frontier that will honestly satisfy ethnology, and must therefore let
politics settle the question."[147] In fact, race struggle is only likely to
occur where races live separated in sparsely populated areas, but as
soon as "tribes come to be in more or less close contact, instead of being
surrounded by large unpeopled lands, intermixture of race begins ...
Thus in the modern world there is no such thing as a really pure race, at
any rate among civilized mankind."[148] Admittedly, as Dann argued
when the heydays of historical geography were drawing to a close, "[m]
ost of the cosmos of nations has been created out of the chaos of
barbarism or social revolution by fighting; and the landmarks of the
world's annals are battles and treaties."[149] In the final analysis, civilization was but an accidental offspring of barbarism and a happy end

---

[142] *Ibid.*, 1.   [143] *Ibid.*, 12–13.   [144] *Ibid.*, 21.   [145] *Ibid.*, 29, 31.
[146] Maguire, *Outlines of Military Geography*, 178.
[147] George, *Relations of Geography and History*, 32.   [148] *Ibid.*, 120.
[149] Ernest W. Dann, *Historical Geography on a Regional Basis, vol. II: Europe*
(London: Dent, 1908), 10.

product of race struggles, events that now were believed to be things of the past, at least in Europe.

As Benton has shown, whereas the European states system was structured according to the principle of territorial sovereignty, the methods of rule used by imperial powers outside Europe gave rise to multilayered and variegated geographies composed of semiautonomous spaces where sovereignty was divided among local actors and colonial powers.[150] With the spatial limits of the European state being settled in theory and practice, the contrasts between the European system of states and its non-European and supposedly uncivilized outside became increasingly apparent to historical geographers. Some set out to explain the absence of civilization and sovereign statehood outside Europe with reference to the geographic features of foreign lands and the backwardness of their inhabitants. To Bryce, for example, it was obvious that in northern and central Asia, "[Y]ou will see that the highest European races would, if placed there, find it almost impossible to develop a high type of civilization for want as well of fuel as of the sources of commercial wealth."[151] To others, it was obvious that the geographic lines of demarcation that separated Europe from its outside coincided with the distinction between civilization and its others. As Ramsay pointed out in the introduction to his magisterial *Historical Geography of Asia Minor* (1890), "the peninsula of Asia Minor has been from the beginning of history a battlefield between the East and the West ... the very character of the country has marked it out as a battleground between the Oriental and the European spirit."[152] But despite repeated efforts to bring civilization to this part of the world, "[t]he Oriental element does not retreat, it is not driven back by open war: it dies out on the coast by a slow yet sure decay."[153]

The perhaps most influential attempt to transpose the study of historical geography to the global level was made by Friedrich Ratzel in his *Völkerkunde* (1885–8). Criticizing his contemporaries for their narrow focus on European civilization, Ratzel saw it as "the duty of ethnography to apply itself all the more faithfully to the neglected lower strata of humanity."[154] In the ensuing study of all the known races of

---

[150] Lauren Benton, *A Search for Sovereignty*.
[151] Bryce, "Relations of History and Geography," 429.
[152] W. M. Ramsay, *The Historical Geography of Asia Minor* (London: John Murray, 1890), 23.
[153] *Ibid.*, 25.

the world, he argued, "[t]he geographical conception of their surroundings, and the historical consideration of their development, will thus go
hand in hand."[155] Applying the principles of natural selection to the
intercourse between different races across global space, Ratzel was
bound to conclude that "[t]he greater bulk, quicker growth, and superiority in all conquering arts, which mark the more highly civilized races,
give them ... the advantage in this process, and we can speak of an
absorption of the lower by the higher even where the latter for the
present are not in the majority."[156] Ratzel then set out to explain why
non-European peoples had failed to become civilized and to create
anything resembling modern states and hence why they were condemned to foreign rule by their colonial masters. Unsurprisingly, this
failure was due to the violent disposition of the "natural races" because
"[m]ost of what we know of the history of natural races is the history of
their wars."[157] But in contrast to the Europeans who had entered civil
society and formed governments, barbarous peoples were stuck in a
perpetual state of war from which they could not escape by their own,
even if it "must be pointed out that among barbarians also there are
peaceful races and peace-loving rulers."[158] And should barbarous
peoples ever succeed in establishing political authority, their states
were bound to fail as a consequence of being territorially unbounded.
"Want of defined frontiers is in the essence of the formation of barbarous states. The line is intentionally not drawn, but kept open as a clear
space of varying breadth."[159] To Ratzel, this lack of clearly defined
boundaries corresponded to another sharp line of demarcation
between the civilized and the uncivilized parts of the world because
"[t]he case in which sharp frontiers are soonest formed is where the two
fundamentally different modes of civilization and life, nomadism and
agriculture, come into contact."[160]

This also made it possible to reconcile the concept of the territorially
bounded state with the realities of imperial expansion.[161] Generalizing
these insights in his later works, Ratzel tried to explain how territorial

[154] Friedrich Ratzel, *The History of Mankind*, vol. 1 [1885], trans. A. J. Butler (London: Macmillan 1896), 3.
[155] *Ibid.*, 3.   [156] *Ibid.*, 12.   [157] *Ibid.*, 130.   [158] *Ibid.* 131.
[159] *Ibid.*, 136.   [160] *Ibid.*, 137.
[161] See Mark Bassin, "Imperialism and the Nation State in Friedrich Ratzel's Political Geography," *Progress in Human Geography* 11, no. 4 (1987): 473–95.

boundaries changed in response to the growth of states and the geographic expansion of civilizations. Such explanations formed the basis of his notorious concept of *Lebensraum*, a concept that became the cornerstone of various imperial ideologies during the early twentieth century.[162] In his *Politische Geographie* (1897), parts of which were translated into English, Ratzel emphasized the territorial basis of all politics, arguing that all politics is in essence a quest for space. One cause of the progress of mankind, he maintained, was that "as more states and larger states grow up, the nearer do they edge together, and so much the more intimately must they act and react upon one another; history, therefore, means mutual approach and compression."[163] But since the space of the globe is finite, this means that only a few states can expand and rise to great power status at a time and that European civilization is compelled to expand on other continents in its quest for more space. The quest for finite space led Ratzel to formulate a central axiom of geopolitics: "Geographical space in general ... is estimated according to the power which must be expended for its conquest, and this power, in turn, is measured in terms of this space, and will always grow with the expansion of the same from age to age."[164] Since conceptions of space condition the political possibilities of states in each age, he argued, space is an independent political force rather than a mere substratum of politics. Hence, "[t]he capacity for territorial conquest, which forms one element in 'the qualities of a ruler,' or in 'talent for organization,' must meet a similar endowment in the people, if it is to lead to an enduring extension of political area."[165] Since this applies to every state and every people equally, geopolitical conflict is an inescapable part of the human condition. "Just as the struggle for existence in the plant and animal world always centers about a matter of space, so the conflicts of nations are in great part only struggles for

---

[162] See Woodruff D. Smith, "Friedrich Ratzel and the Origins of Lebensraum," *German Studies Review* 3, no. 1 (1980): 51–68; Matus Halas, "Searching for the Perfect Footnote: Friedrich Ratzel and the Others at the Roots of Lebensraum," *Geopolitics* 19, no. 1 (2014): 1–18.

[163] Friedrich Ratzel, "Studies in Political Areas I: The Political Territory in Relation to Earth and Continent," *American Journal of Sociology* 3, no. 3 (1897): 297–313, at 297.

[164] Friedrich Ratzel, "Studies in Political Areas II: Intellectual, Political, and Economic Effects of Large Areas," *American Journal of Sociology* 3, no. 4 (1898): 449–63, at 449–50.

[165] *Ibid.*, 452.

territory."[166] When seen in the context of imperial expansion, it was obvious to Ratzel that the encounter between European civilization and non-European peoples not only was a clash between different conceptions of space where those with the most expansive view were likely to prevail but also that European expansion on other continents would imply that territorial rivalries within Europe would become less pronounced and that the foreign relations of European states therefore would be greatly simplified and less bellicose.[167]

As a mature Mackinder summarized what the happy marriage between history and geography had delivered in terms of scientific insights, "we are for the first time in a position to attempt, with some degree of completeness, a correlation between the larger geographical and the larger historical generalizations."[168] Among these generalizations, it was now obvious that violent conflict had been responsible both for bringing the world together and for dividing it into distinct communities because "[t]he ideas which go to form a nation, as opposed to a mere crowd of human animals, have usually been accepted under the pressure of a common tribulation, and under a common necessity of resistance to external force."[169] This meant that "it was under the pressure of external barbarism that Europe achieved its civilization."[170] Hence, in a world system structured by mutual antagonism and perennial discord, the fate of nations and races was decided by their relative power, and that power was "the product, one the one hand, of geographical conditions, both economic and strategic, and, on the other hand, of the relative number, virility, equipment, and organization of the competing peoples."[171]

So when we reach the beginning of the twentieth century, the imagined congruence between authority and territory had been established as a social fact and was taken to be an indisputable foundation of modern political order. It was now obvious that states were defined by their territorial extension and were demarcated by boundaries and that territory long had constituted an apple of discord over which numerous and constitutive wars had been fought. Consequently, it was accepted as true that territoriality was a defining characteristic of the international system and that the territorial extent of states was

---

[166] *Ibid.*, 458.   [167] *Ibid.*, 460–2.
[168] Halford Mackinder, "The Geographical Pivot of History," *The Geographical Journal* 23, no. 4 (1904): 421–44, at 422.
[169] *Ibid.* 422–3.   [170] *Ibid.*, 423.   [171] *Ibid.*, 437.

grounded in the brute facts of geography rather than in acts of human volition. Yet none of this was the result of a rationalization of space through which claims to sovereign authority embodied in early modern maps were projected onto the surface of the Earth and directly translated into political practice and embodied in legal agreements. The process of conversion was much less uniform and much more complex, involving the gradual militarization of cartography and weaponization of maps in the hands of political elites. Translating the claims to sovereignty represented on maps to actual facts on the ground such as demarcated boundaries and unified territories took a concerted effort of generations of surveyors and military engineers who supplemented what they took to be insufficient cartographic and geographic information with population statistics, blended it with considerations of strategy and political prudence, and proceeded with large-scale fortifications and infrastructural improvements to bring state territories in conformity with the claims to sovereign authority that long had been represented on maps. By and large, this process of conversion was sometimes motivated by and very often justified with reference to the imperatives of state security. Fears of foreign invasions, threats of domestic unrest, and the desire to promote the wealth of populations were all consistently invoked by those who sought to realize visions of territorial sovereignty.

With political authority firmly grounded and bounded, it was left to historical geographers to trace the spatial trajectory of individual states in time and, by implication, to naturalize the outcome of territorialization. Although historical geographers saw boundaries as contingent, they took the overall congruence between political authority and territory largely for granted and accounted for the mutability of boundaries and territories by invoking the productive force of race struggle and natural selection. The actual territorial extent of individual states and the nature of their boundaries were seen as outcomes of prior disputes fueled by the quest for power in space as well as over space. What was open to dispute, however, was the extent to which territorial boundaries reflected the natural circumstances of each state or whether they were but temporary stopping points on an endless road of European expansion. Although historical geographers did not dispute that authority and territory ought to be congruent in principle, evolutionary theory made it possible to argue that since boundaries were outcomes of natural selection, they were bound to be mutable and to reflect the relative vigorousness of races in their perpetual struggle for space. Thus notions of natural selection made it possible to reconcile the concept of the territorially bounded state with schemes of boundless imperial expansion, thereby legitimizing European rule of foreign lands defined by their lack of proper boundaries and unified territories. Yet all of this stood in need of legal justification in order to get off the ground. It is to these justifications that we now must turn.

4 | *Wars of Law, Laws of War*

Introduction

In previous chapters we have seen how the temporal limits and spatial boundaries of the modern state and the international system were drawn by means of a consistent appeal to the productive force of war in the emerging fields of historiography and geography from the early modern period onward. International war was thereby constituted as a natural correlate of the modern political order, and the meaningful use of this concept came to presuppose the existence of bounded political communities characterized by domestic peace and order. In this chapter, I describe how attempts to regulate the use of force by means of law have depended on similar, albeit slightly more subdued, assumptions about the productive force of hostility and violence in human affairs. To this end, I engage some canonical texts in international law from the early seventeenth to the late nineteenth century.

The regulative force of international law presupposes that it can transcend the contingencies of history and geography by virtue of its universalistic aspirations. Yet, as I show, many attempts to justify the existence of an international legal order and international legal norms share many of the assumptions made by historians and geographers in their endeavor to make sense of the sovereign state and the international system. Notions of human hostility and war appear to be as crucial to the explanation and justification of international legal order as they were to understanding of the origins of the sovereign state and the international system. As Carl Schmitt once remarked, "the history of international law is a history of the concept of war."[1]

Yet my argument must be distinguished from reductionist views of international law. First, according to a quintessentially realist view,

---

[1] Carl Schmitt, "The Turn to the Discriminating Concept of War" [1937], in Carl Schmitt, *Writings on War*, trans. Timothy Nunan (Cambridge: Polity Press, 2011), 31.

international law is nothing but an expression of the will of the most powerful states, its main function being to legitimize the use of force by them.[2] In contrast to its realist critics, however, I would like to maintain that the habit of harnessing legal principles for the purposes of power politics did not originate in any sudden sacrifice of the autonomy of international law on the altar of state power. Rather, I believe that the embarrassing congruence between the concerns of international law and those of secular statecraft is an unintended consequence of sustained attempts to preserve the autonomy of the former in a world gradually being structured according to the principles of the latter. Thus – and *pace* Skinner – I will not treat the natural law tradition as distinct from that of secular statecraft, but instead assume that these traditions have in fact long been confluent.[3]

Second, according to its postcolonial critics, one main function of international law has been to impose Western standards of civilization on the rest of the world, excluding non-European peoples from membership in international society on the grounds that they lack the marks of sovereignty and other essential characteristics of civilized nations.[4] By contrast, I maintain that these tendencies did not arise from any deep-seated cultural prejudices against non-European peoples but from the inner logic of international law itself. While the exclusion of non-European peoples from the pale of international law was often justified with reference to cultural differences, that exclusion was a consequence of attempts to come to terms with the primitive forms of violence and hostility that already had been posited at the very foundation of international law. From the seventeenth to the early nineteenth century, many international lawyers were simply not that concerned with what took place outside European states. But by differentiating between

[2] For a recent restatement of this view, see Jack L. Goldsmith and Eric A. Posner, "Moral and Legal Rhetoric in International Relations: A Rational Choice Perspective," *Journal of Legal Studies* 31, no. 1 (2002): 115–39; Jack L. Goldsmith and Eric A. Posner, *The Limits of International Law* (Oxford: Oxford University Press, 2005).

[3] For this contention, see Quentin Skinner, *The Foundations of Modern Political Thought*, Vol. 2, (Cambridge: Cambridge University Press, 1978), 172.

[4] Antony Anghie, *Imperialism, Sovereignty and the Making of International Law* (Cambridge: Cambridge University Press, 2007); Brett Bowden, "The Colonial Origins of International Law: European Expansion and the Classical Standard of Civilization," *Journal of the History of International Law* 7, no. 1 (2005): 1–23; Edward Keene, *Beyond the Anarchical Society: Grotius, Colonialism, and Order in World Politics* (Cambridge: Cambridge University Press, 2002).

different kinds of hostility and violence – normalizing some while rendering others pathologic – international lawyers made certain practices of exclusion indispensable to the coherence of international law itself. By defining some forms of violence as natural parts of the human condition and as normal features of state intercourse while identifying other forms with those found in the dark past of European states, international law thereby created the preconditions of its own identity and disciplinary integrity.

Third, it is important to distinguish the present argument from the view according to which law is altogether contingent on power and violence. As we learn from Nietzsche's *Zur Genealogie der Moral* (1887), "states of legality can never be anything but *exceptional states*, as partial restrictions of the true will to life, which seeks power and to whose overall purpose they subordinate themselves as individual measures, that is to say, as a means of creating greater units of power."[5] In a similar vein, Schmitt later maintained that law cannot determine what goes on in the political sphere because law is but the offspring a sovereign decision that constitutes the political community on the basis of a distinction between friends and enemies.[6] During the twentieth century, this kind of argument was twisted into a critique of the state and its reliance on violence for its smooth functioning. As Benjamin argued, if law indeed originates in violence, "it follows ... that all violence as a means, even in the most favorable case, is implicated in the problematic nature of law itself."[7] And as he went on to explain, "lawmaking is power making, and, to that extent an immediate manifestation of violence."[8] Expanding on this account, Derrida has argued that although law does not necessarily originate in raw power, the making and justification of law nevertheless depend on "a performative and therefore interpretative violence that in itself is neither just nor unjust." Hence both the founding authority and the law itself "are themselves a violence without

[5] Friedrich Nietzsche, *On the Genealogy of Morality*, trans. Carol Diethe (Cambridge: Cambridge University Press, 2006), II, § 11, 50.
[6] Carl Schmitt, *The Concept of the Political* [1927] (Chicago: University of Chicago Press, 2008).
[7] Walter Benjamin, "Critique of Violence," in Walter Benjamin, *Reflections: Essays, Aphorisms, Anthropological Writings*, ed. Peter Demetz (New York: Schocken Books, 1978), 277–300, at 287.
[8] Benjamin, "Critique of Violence," 295.

ground."[9] A curious blend of these views has recently found favor with those who take the violent origins of law to be indicative of its utter lack of legitimacy and who therefore are inclined to argue that we are stuck in a permanent state of exception and lawlessness.[10]

These accounts assume that some kind of primordial violence lies at the heart of all law because otherwise there would be nothing there for law to regulate and nothing there that would prompt its emergence in the first place. Yet, to my mind, what matters to the emergence of law is not whether some actual violence was present in the beginning but rather the curious fact that the possibility and necessity of violence are *imagined by law itself as a condition of itself*. Thus there is an inescapable circularity in those accounts of law that both take violence to be foundational *and* purport to present an antidote to its excesses or otherwise undesirable manifestations. I therefore think that international law and its history will start to make much more sense once we are willing to realize that there is no "war" apart from that constructed by lawyers in order to provide international law with its ultimate justification. This implies that the reductionist accounts discussed earlier – whether realist, postcolonial, or critical – perhaps should be seen as late modern manifestations of a long tradition of thought that has insisted on a symbiotic relationship between violence and law. Instead of taking these accounts at face value and using them as field guides in the present, I think they should best be read as examples of a form of legal reasoning that was initiated long ago and thus fit into a more encompassing account of the role of violent imaginaries in the constitution of sociopolitical order.[11]

When it comes to making sense of the symbiotic relationship of war and law, historians of international law are generally more helpful than political philosophers. As Koskenniemi has argued, early modern

[9] Jacques Derrida, "Force of Law: The 'Mystical Foundation of Authority,'" in Drucilla Cornell, Michael Rosenfield, and David G. Carlson (eds.), *Deconstruction and the Possibility of Justice* (London: Routledge, 1992), 3–67, at 14–15.

[10] Giorgio Agamben, *State of Exception* (Chicago: University of Chicago Press, 2005); Giorgio Agamben, *Homo Sacer: Sovereign Power and Bare Life* (Redwood City, CA: Stanford University Press, 1998).

[11] See, for example, Ronald C. Jennings, "Sovereignty and Political Modernity: A Genealogy of Agamben's Critique of Sovereignty," *Anthropological Theory* 11, no. 1 (2011): 23–61.

natural jurisprudence was not primarily concerned with restricting the use of force by an appeal to a universal normative order but was more a matter of harnessing it for the purposes of secular statecraft given the limits posed by nascent conceptions of sovereignty.[12] And, as Berman has noted, "throughout its history, the contours of the legal construction of war have been contested, defended, transformed, and reconstructed through myriad discursive and practical activities."[13] This implies that the distinction between war and not-war is open to what Berman has called "strategic instrumentalization," that is, the deployment of this "distinction itself for partisan advantage – seeking to achieve practical or discursive gains through shifting back and forth between war and not-war."[14] Pursuing this argument further, Kennedy has argued that war is best understood as a legal institution. Hence the rules of war should not be viewed primarily as attempts to impose limits on the use of force but rather as constitutive of that very institution. Since "the changing nature of warfare is also a function of changing ideas about law," international law is not distinct from the practices of war.[15] Rather, conversely, "law now offers an institutional and doctrinal space for transforming the boundaries of war into strategic assets, as well as a vernacular for legitimating and denouncing what happens in war."[16] So, ultimately, "we make war in the shadow of law, and law in the shadow of force."[17]

Yet, as I propose, the symbiosis between law and war runs even deeper than this, thanks to its long historical pedigree. While many of the authors in the canon of international law subscribed to

---

[12] Martti Koskenniemi, "International Law and Raison d'État: Rethinking the Prehistory of International Law," in Benedict Kingsbury and Benjamin Straumann (eds.), *The Roman Foundations of the Law of Nations: Alberico Gentili and the Justice of Empire* (Oxford: Oxford University Press, 2010), 297–339.

[13] Nathaniel Berman, "Privileging Combat?: Contemporary Conflict and the Legal Construction of War," *Columbia Journal of Transnational Law* 43, no. 1 (2004): 1–71, at 6. See also Roger Normand and Chris af Jochnick, "The Legitimation of Violence: A Critical History of the Laws of War," *Harvard International Law Journal* 35, no. 1 (1994): 49–95.

[14] Berman, "Privileging Combat?," 7.

[15] David Kennedy, *Of Law and War* (Princeton, NJ: Princeton University Press, 2006), 8. Also David Kennedy, *A World of Struggle: How Power, Law and Expertise Shape the Global Political Economy* (Princeton, NJ: Princeton University Press, 2016), 256–76.

[16] Kennedy, *Of Law and War*, 116.   [17] *Ibid.*, 165.

ontogenetic views of war similar to those detailed in the preceding chapters, I believe that the preoccupation with war is indicative of the extent to which international law has tried to legitimize itself by appealing to what would likely happen if violence were left uncategorized and hence also un-naturalized and unregulated. Thus we are confronted with a double bind between law and the use of force than runs parallel to the history of the relationship between war and the sovereign state. War appears as the evil twin of both: as much as war needs international law to exist as a meaningful category of thought and action, international law needs war in order to maintain its autonomy as a field of inquiry.

So, while Benjamin might have been right in insisting that military violence is "primordial and paradigmatic of all violence used for natural ends" and hence that "there is in all such violence a lawmaking character,"[18] this equation would not be possible to uphold unless that peculiar form of violence already had been defined and delimited by means of legal concepts distinguishing it from its less instrumental and more destructive forms. Conversely, while international lawyers might be right in pointing out that these legal categories have been socially constructed and constantly contested across time and space, they have been able to make this point against the backdrop of a widespread conviction that war has been around in a similar form long enough to constitute a perennial problem to which commensurable solutions could be proposed, compared, validated, or disqualified.

But war and law can only be made to appear co-constitutive to the extent that international law presupposes that hostility and enmity among political communities is a natural or at least a customary condition while suggesting that this hostility and enmity also are amenable to some regulation and perhaps even to eventual abolition in some distant future. Hence we should also guard against the tendency to project notions of international law back onto a past in which such notions would have made little or no sense.[19] So, rather than assuming that international law in some recognizably modern form has been present from the early modern period onward, it is imperative that we should try to reconstruct its emergence and institutionalization in

---

[18] Benjamin, "Critique of Violence," 283.
[19] On the perils of anachronism in the historiography of international law, see David Kennedy, "Primitive Legal Scholarship," *Harvard Journal of International Law* 27, no. 1 (1986): 1–98.

terms of its imagined symbiotic relationship with war and how this relationship has evolved in tandem with the constitution of the sovereign state and the modern international system.[20]

Catering to these desiderata, the rest of this chapter is organized as follows. In the next section, I describe how theorists of natural law made foundational assumptions about human hostility and how these assumptions shaped their outlook on the law of nations. I then dwell on those who made the first attempts to supplement the naturalist framework with voluntary and positive law, arguing that this resulted in a further naturalization and reification of war as a productive force in human affairs. In the final section, I analyze the nineteenth-century transition to legal positivism, arguing that this resulted in an outward projection of the forms of hostility and violence that long had been imagined at the very foundations of international law.

Natural Law and Natural Hostility

As Schmitt has famously argued, the decisive step from medieval to modern international law lies in the separation of questions of just cause grounded in moral arguments from the idea of legal equality of belligerents.[21] I have already described how this transition from war as law enforcement to war as a duel between equals made it possible to attribute ontogenetic capacities to war and to impose temporal limits and spatial boundaries on those still nebulous entities that were in the process of becoming sovereign states. In this and the following sections, I will analyze how this new understanding of war affected attempts to regulate the intercourse of sovereign states by means of law and how these efforts were premised on the hostility and violence posited at the very foundation of that law.

But first let me add some complication to this transition. As Neff has described the just-war tradition, it "was notably lacking in any idea of moral equivalence, or equality of rights, between a just and an unjust belligerent. The unjust side, by definition, had no right whatever to use force against the just side, any more than a criminal

---

[20] For recent attempts in this direction, see Olaf Asbach and Peter Schröder (eds.), *War, The State, and International Law in the Seventeenth Century* (Farnham: Ashgate, 2010).

[21] Carl Schmitt, *The Nomos of the Earth in the International Law of the Jus Publicum Europaeum* (New York: Telos Press, 2006), 110.

has a 'right' to use violence against a magistrate."[22] This view of war as punishment by some rightful authority remained central to the scholastic tradition well into the sixteenth century. As Vitoria stated in his *De Iure Belli* (1539), "the sole and only just cause for waging war is when harm has been inflicted," adding that "not every or any injury gives sufficient grounds for waging war." This being so, because a "prince cannot have greater authority over foreigners than he has over his own subjects; but he may not draw the sword against his own subjects unless they have done some wrong; therefore he cannot do the same against foreigners except in the same circumstances."[23] To Vitoria, the fact that humanity was divided into distinct political communities did not entail that war against foreigners was more easily justified than war against inner enemies of each such community. Yet, as I shall try to show, the transition from medieval doctrines of just war to the modern understanding of war never was as smooth and straightforward as Schmitt and Neff would like us to believe because the very ambition to regulate war between legal equals depended precisely on the endurance of irregular forms of violence – real or imagined – that could be invoked as the defining characteristic of those who stood outside the law and whose lingering presence made legal regulation of the use of force seem both necessary and desirable.

Since the task of this chapter is to inquire into how different conceptions of war and enmity have shaped international law from the seventeenth to the nineteenth century, a focus on the humanist tradition is a natural starting point not only because of its preoccupation with war but also because of its substantial influence on the subsequent development of international law. Although legal scholasticism remained important throughout the early modern period, it was mainly influential in the development of the private rights of dominium that were crucial to commercial and imperial pursuits.[24] Drawing on recently rediscovered Roman sources, the humanist tradition was based on the

---

[22] Stephen C. Neff, *War and the Law of Nations: A General History* (Cambridge: Cambridge University Press, 2005), 62.

[23] Francisco de Vitoria, "On the Law of War," in *Vitoria: Political Writings*, ed. Anthony Pagden and Jeremy Lawrance (Cambridge: Cambridge University Press, 1991), § 13–14, 303–4.

[24] See Martti Koskenniemi, "Empire and International Law: The Real Spanish Contribution," *University of Toronto Law Journal* 61, no. 1 (2011): 1–36.

assumption that self-preservation is the most fundamental principle of natural law. This principle was equally applicable to individuals and political communities and especially so in the absence of a common political or legal authority. As a result, most humanists felt little or no contradiction between the precepts of secular statecraft and the principles of natural law because safeguarding political communities from external threats was seen as necessary to their independence and thus also to the possibility of maintaining individual rights within them.[25]

Although early modern natural law theorists differed on the meaning of sovereignty, they had inherited the assumption that only wars waged by some legitimate authority are justifiable. And although their understandings of what constituted such legitimate authority did differ markedly, this implied that political authority and the right to wage war came to be defined in terms of each other right from the start. As a consequence, war is at the foundation of political authority and law because "the legitimacy of the state could now be understood as a function of the logic driving its own formation, rather than in terms of its historical appearance."[26] Early theorists of natural law therefore typically start by presupposing that hostility and violence are natural or at least customary features of the human condition, partly because human beings are predisposed to violence and partly because there is no common authority there to check those predispositions. They then proceed to differentiate war proper from irregular forms of violence. Whereas proper war is the prerogative of legitimate authorities, the existence of irregular forms of violence is invoked to explain the emergence of sovereignty and law with reference to the disorder and violence that are likely to ensue in their absence. Such irregular forms of violence can only be justifiably employed by legitimate authorities

---

[25] See Richard Tuck, *The Rights of War and Peace: Political Thought and the International Order from Grotius to Kant* (Oxford: Oxford University Press, 1999), 16–50; also Ryan Greenwood, "War and Sovereignty in Medieval Roman Law," *Law and History Review* 32, no. 1 (2014): 31–63. The contrast between the scholastic and humanist traditions should not be overstated, however. See Randall Lesaffer, "The Classical Law of Nations (1500–1800)," in Alexander Orakhelashvili (ed.), *Research Handbook on the Theory and History of International Law* (Cheltenham: Elgar, 2011), 408–40; Diego Panizza, "Political Theory and Jurisprudence in Gentili's *De Iure Belli*: The Great Debate between 'Theological' and 'Humanist' Perspectives from Vitoria to Grotius," *International Law and Justice Working Papers* 15/5 (2005).

[26] David William Bates, *States of War: Enlightenment Origins of the Political* (New York: Columbia University Press, 2012), 51.

against actors who are deemed illegitimate precisely with reference to
their own propensity to resort to irregular forms of violence.

That war is nothing but a duel between moral equals stuck in a
condition devoid of common authority is a core assumption of
Gentili's *De Jure Belli* (1588/1598), a book that proclaimed to be
nothing less than a first philosophy of war. As Gentili states in the
first chapter, "it does not appear to be the function either of the moral
or of the political philosopher to give an account of the laws which we
have in common with our enemies and with foreigners ... This philosophy of war belongs to that great community formed by the entire
world and the whole human race."[27] That great community of all
humankind is bound together by the law of nations, which is "that
which is in use among all the nations of men, which native reason has
established among all human beings, and which is equally observed by
all mankind."[28] Yet the presence of such a world community is not
itself sufficient to establish any binding norms that could restrain the
use of force because it does not have any corresponding authority to
enforce such norms.[29]

Gentili then sets out to define the concept of war and discuss its role
within this universal legal order. Proceeding from a definition according to which "war is a just and public contest of arms," Gentili stipulates that "the arms on both sides should be public, for *bellum*, 'war,'
derives its name from the fact there is a contest for victory between
equal parties, and for that reason it was first called *duellum*, a contest of
two ... The term *hostis* was applied to a foreigner who had equal rights
with the Romans. In fact *hostire* means 'to make equal' ... Therefore
hostis is a person with whom war is made and who is the equal of his
opponent."[30] Thus, in contrast to scholastics such as Vitoria, Gentili
emphasizes that war properly understood can only take place between
legal equals, and whatever violence that takes place between *unequal*

---

[27] Alberico Gentili, *De Jure Belli Libri Tres*, trans. John C. Rolfe (Oxford:
Carnegie Endowment for International Peace, 1933), I.I.3. For a recent and
illuminating discussion, see Peter Schröder, "Taming the Fox and the Lion:
Some Aspects of the Sixteenth Century's Debate on Inter-State Relations," in
Asbach and Schröder, *War, the State, and International Law*, 83–102.

[28] Gentili, *De Jure Belli*, I.I.8.

[29] See Andreas Wagner, "Francisco de Vitoria and Alberico Gentili on the Legal
Character of the Global Commonwealth," *Oxford Journal of Legal Studies* 31,
no. 3 (2011): 565–82.

[30] Gentili, *De Jure Belli*, I.II.12.

parties must take on a different form, such as brigandage, or as warfare undertaken to punish those who threaten the integrity or existence of the universal community of humankind.[31]

That justice could lie with both parties also meant that "war has its origin in necessity; and this necessity arises because there cannot be judicial processes between supreme sovereigns or free peoples unless they themselves consent, since they acknowledge no judge or superior. Consequently they are only supreme and they alone merit the title of public, while all others are inferior and are rated as private individuals ... Therefore it was inevitable that the decision between sovereigns should be made by arms."[32] So although Gentili holds that war should be the resorted to only when all attempts at arbitration have failed, he is adamant that war is a method of dispute settlement, "for we are inquiring into the method of settling a case, not into that of taking vengeance and inflicting punishment."[33] From this definition of war as a contest between equals that recognize no superior authority also follows that "private individuals, subject peoples, and petty sovereigns are never confronted with the necessity of resorting to the arbitrament of Mars, since they can obtain their legal rights before their superiors' tribunal."[34] Thus the key concepts of the laws of war are defined in terms of each other: war is defined in terms of the formal equality of the belligerents; equality is defined in terms of their mutual hostility, mutual hostility, in turn, being a consequence of their refusal to recognize any supreme authority and their refusal to recognize any supreme authority being a corollary of their claims to sovereignty, claims to sovereignty being but a consequence of the kind of primitive hostility that otherwise would reign unobstructed within as well as between political communities.

Now, equivocations like this could easily be taken to indicate that Gentili foreshadowed a recognizably modern account of the relationship between the sovereign state and war by making the latter the exclusive prerogative of the former. Against this it could be objected that Gentili had a rather vague notion of the meaning, locus, and scope of sovereignty, thus making such inferences anachronistic and

[31] For a similar argument, see Wouter G. Werner, "From Justus Hostis to Rogue State the Concept of the Enemy in International Legal Thinking," *International Journal for the Semiotics of Law* 17, no. 2 (2004): 155–68.
[32] Gentili, *De Jure Belli*, I.III.15. [33] *Ibid.*, I.III.19. [34] *Ibid.*, I.III.20.

unwarranted.[35] But, by drawing extensively on the writings of
Bodin, the meaning he imputed to sovereignty seems sufficiently
precise for the task at hand, namely, to distinguish between those
who are subject to the laws of war and those who are not.[36] Hence, as
Gentili goes on to explain with a little help from Cicero, "he is an
enemy who has a state, a senate, a treasury, united and harmonious
citizens, and some basis for a treaty of peace, should matters so shape
themselves." Yet, although the term *hostis* implies equality, this term
is "sometimes extended to cover those that are not equal, namely, to
pirates, proscribed persons, and rebels; nevertheless, it cannot confer
the rights due to enemies ... and the privileges of regular warfare."[37]
War is thus a category applicable to formal equals only, whereas
those who are "the common enemies of all mankind ... do not enjoy
the privileges of a law to which they are foes."[38] By virtue of not
being enemies in any proper sense, and hence not subject to the laws
of war, all nonsovereign malefactors are fair game for punishment at
the hands of legitimate sovereigns. So, although this is necessary in
order to carry out a clear-cut transition from a unilateral to a bilateral conception of war, the former remains essential to the coherence
of the latter.

Even among actors of equal standing, we find a rather licentious
view of the right to wage war. The right to wage war derives from its
very nature. While Gentili disagrees with the view that hostility is a
natural condition of all men, he maintains that the distinction
between friend and enemy is made by custom. Yet custom is second
nature to us, firmly rooted in the unruly passions of men. Thus "it is
through the fault of the human race that dissensions arise, since
mankind is uneasy and untamed, and always engaged in a struggle
for freedom or glory or dominion."[39] No war is therefore ever natural, but wars can nevertheless arise out of natural causes. Self-
defense is a case in point because "this is the most generally accepted
of all rights. All laws and all codes allow the repelling of force by

[35] See Benedict Kingsbury, "Confronting Difference: The Puzzling Durability of
Gentili's Combination of Pragmatic Pluralism and Normative Judgment,"
American Journal of International Law 92, no. 1 (1998): 713–23, at 715.
[36] See Peter Schröder, "Vitoria, Gentili, Bodin: Sovereignty and the Law of
Nations," in Benedict Kingsbury and Benjamin Straumann (eds.), *The Roman
Foundations of the Law of Nations: Alberico Gentili and the Justice of Empire*
(Oxford: Oxford University Press, 2010), 163–86.
[37] Gentili, *De Jure Belli*, I.IV.25.   [38] *Ibid.*, I.IV.23.   [39] *Ibid.*, I.XII.54.

force. There is one rule which endures forever, to maintain one's safety by any and every means."[40] Apart from self-defense in the more narrow sense of preventive war, wars of expediency may be also waged justly as long as they serve the broader aim of self-preservation.[41] This being so, "no one ought to wait to be struck, unless he is a fool. One ought to provide not only against an offence which is being committed, but also against one which may possibly be committed."[42] Thus conceived, the right of self-defense entails an obligation to resist those who attempt to aggrandize themselves at the expense of others because it "is better to provide that men should not acquire too great power, than to be obliged to seek a remedy later, when they have already become too powerful."[43] As one perceptive commentator has pointed out, Gentili thereby "decoupled the notion of just war from the concept of punishment and described all just wars as defensive in character."[44]

Yet the definition of war implies that both belligerents are equally likely to maintain that their cause is just and that there are few, if any, reliable methods available to ascertain the validity of their respective claims. Only in the rare cases where one party is "contending without any adequate reason [is] ... that party surely practising brigandage and not waging war."[45] But those who do have adequate, if not always valid, reasons for going to war have to be prepared that the law that "grants the rights of war to both contestants makes what is taken on each side the property of the captors, and regards the prisoners of both parties as slaves."[46] In a predicament devoid of superior

---

[40] *Ibid.*, I.XIII.59. On this point, see Gregory M. Reichberg, "Preventive War in Classical Just War Theory," *Journal of the History of International Law* 9, no. 1 (2007): 5–34.

[41] Gentili, *De Jure Belli*, I.V.30.

[42] *Ibid.*, I.XIV.62. For a detailed account of how such permissive views of self-defense played themselves out in practice, see Randall Lesaffer, "Defensive Warfare, Prevention and Hegemony: The Justifications for the Franco-Spanish War of 1635," Parts I and II, *Journal of the History of International Law* 8, nos. 1 and 2 (2006): 91–123, 141–79.

[43] Gentili, *De Jure Belli*, I.XIV.65.

[44] Pärtel Piirimäe, "Alberico Gentili's Doctrine of Defensive War and Its Impact on Seventeenth-Century Normative Views," in Benedict Kingsbury and Benjamin Straumann (eds.), *The Roman Foundations of the Law of Nations: Alberico Gentili and the Justice of Empire* (Oxford: Oxford University Press, 2010), 187–209.

[45] Gentili, *De Jure Belli*, I.VI.31–2.   [46] *Ibid.*, I.VI.33.

moral or legal authority, religious differences can never be a just cause of war "since the laws of religion do not properly exist between man and man, therefore no man's rights are violated by a difference in religion, nor is it lawful to make war because of religion."[47] Yet the very absence of religion constitutes a valid exception to this rule because "we are not now speaking of those who, living rather like beasts than like men, are wholly without religious belief; for I should hold that such men, being the common foes of all mankind, as pirates are, ought to be assailed in war and forced to adopt the usages of humanity."[48] Likewise, while it may not always be necessary to wage war against barbarians and infidels, *their* hostility is a valid reason for going to war against them. "[W]e have war with the Turks because they act as our enemies, plot against us, and threaten us. With the greatest treachery they always seize our possessions, whenever they can. Thus we constantly have a legitimate reason for war against the Turks."[49] As Malcolm has pointed out, friendly relations with infidels were ruled out by Gentili on a variety of grounds, some pragmatic and others theological in character.[50]

By carefully constructing a chain of inferential connections between his core concepts, and by using those concepts to determine the content of the laws of war as well as the conditions of their applicability, Gentili seems to be saying the following: while hostility may not be part of the natural condition of humankind, the passions of men will inevitably give rise to enmity as long as those passions remain untamed by sovereign authority and law. Yet human hostility is also what makes law possible and indeed necessary, insofar as it compels men to submit to sovereign authority in the interest of self-preservation and to avoid the random violence that would otherwise ensue in its absence. Customary hostility is thus a great equalizer of political communities coexisting in a condition devoid of supreme authority and that which makes it possible to distinguish between war proper and war as law enforcement. While war in the former sense is necessary for the law of nations to emerge and solidify, war in the latter sense is necessary to protect the law of nations from the evil acts of those who out of choice

---

[47] *Ibid.*, I.IX.41.   [48] *Ibid.*, I.IX.41.   [49] *Ibid.*, I.XII.56–7.
[50] Noel Malcolm, "Alberico Gentili and the Ottomans," in Benedict Kingsbury and Benjamin Straumann (eds.), *The Roman Foundations of the Law of Nations: Alberico Gentili and the Justice of Empire* (Oxford: Oxford University Press, 2010), 127–45.

or disposition stand outside law altogether and therefore constitute enemies of all humankind.

Similar connections between the concepts of war, law, and sovereignty run through the many pages of *De Iure Belli ac Pacis Libri Tres* (1625) by Hugo Grotius. Although Grotius incorporated more strands from the scholastic tradition than did Gentili and consequently held more restrictive views on the use of force, he subscribed to an ontogenetic view of war that is not very different from that of his predecessor. He starts by noting that "all the Differences of those who do not acknowledge one common Civil Right . . . relate either to the Affairs of War, or Peace."[51] That civil right issues from civil power that "is that which governs the State. The State is a compleat Body of free Persons, associated together to enjoy peaceably their Rights, and for their common Benefit."[52]

In contrast to the medieval conception of war as an instrument of law enforcement, Grotius stipulates that "war is the State or Situation of those . . . who dispute by Force of Arms."[53] Noting that *bellum* derives from *duellum*, this implies "a Difference between two Persons, in the same Sense as we term Peace Unity (from *Unitas*) for a contrary Reason."[54] Thus war and peace are defined as mutually exclusive states of affairs that cannot coexist within the same slice of time and space and whose distinctness is closely connected to the presence of law and legitimate authority within the state and their absence outside the state. While Grotius held that war is a condition in which both individuals and states easily could find themselves in the absence of overarching authority, the resort to violent means is justified with reference to the right to self-preservation: "'tis the first Duty of every one to preserve himself in his natural State, to seek after those Things which are agreeable to Nature, and to avert those which are repugnant."[55] Furthermore, since "that it is a Law of Nature, fixed in all living Creatures, to be desirous of Life; and that we therefore look on them as our Enemies, who would openly deprive us of it, it follows that 'by the Law of Nature' then, which may also be called the Law of Nations, it is plain, that every Kind of War is not to be condemned."[56]

---

[51] Hugo Grotius, *The Rights of War and Peace*, ed. Richard Tuck (Indianapolis: Liberty Fund, 2005), I.I.133.
[52] Grotius, *Rights of War and Peace*, I.I.162.   [53] *Ibid.*, I.I.134.
[54] *Ibid.*, I.I.135.   [55] *Ibid.*, I.II.180.   [56] *Ibid.*, I.II.188–9.

From these more general considerations of war as the ultimate tool
of justice and peace, Grotius proceeds to distinguish between different forms of war and on what grounds they might be justified.
Leaving aside his definition of private war for the moment, Grotius
distinguishes between public wars that are solemn and those that are
not. The former, he informs us, is a war that is lawful in the sense
"that it be made on both Sides, by the Authority of those that have
the Sovereign Power in the State."[57] This being so, since by "War the
whole State is endangered, therefore it is provided, by the Laws of
almost all Nations, that it be undertaken only by the Order or with
the Approbation of the Sovereign."[58]

The requirement that wars must be declared and waged by some
sovereign authority prompts Grotius to consider the meaning of
this latter term in some detail.[59] Equating sovereignty with supreme
authority within a given polity, we learn that "the common Subject
of Supreme Power is the State; which I have before called a perfect
Society of Men."[60] Thus public wars occur "only between those
that acknowledge no common Judge" since in the absence of such
superior legal authority, the right of self-defense "arises directly
and immediately from the Care of our own Preservation, which
Nature recommends to every one, and not from the Injustice or
Crime of the Aggressor."[61] But, in contrast to Gentili, the right of
self-defense does not imply the right to take up arms in order to
curb the rising power of another state or on sheer suspicion of
aggressive intentions. As Grotius states, "to justify taking up
Arms in our own Defence, there ought to be a Necessity for so
doing, which there is not, unless we are sure, with a moral
Certainty, that he has not only Forces sufficient, but a full
Intention to injure us."[62] This and similar passages have been
interpreted as evidence that Grotius took a more restrictive view
on the use of force and that he thereby laid the foundations of a
distinct tradition of international thought that takes legal norms to

---

[57] *Ibid.*, I.III.250.   [58] *Ibid.*, I.III.251.

[59] Although Grotius uses the term *imperium* to describe supreme authority, he
does so invoking distinctively Bodinian connotations of indivisibility; see Knud
Haakonssen, "Hugo Grotius and the History of Political Thought," *Political
Theory* 13, no. 2 (1985): 239–65.

[60] Grotius, *Rights of War and Peace*, I.III.259.   [61] *Ibid.*, II.I.416, 397.

[62] *Ibid.*, II.XXII.1102.

be valid and applicable beyond the boundaries of individual states.[63]

But wars could also be fought lawfully by private actors, sometimes on their own initiative and sometimes at the behest of their sovereigns. Grotius starts his discussion of private war by noting that this is the most ancient form of war, yet the "[l]iberty allowed before is now much restrained."[64] Thus private war is now permissible only where legal authority is absent and the road to formal justice closed, such as "in Places not inhabited, as on the Seas, in a Wilderness, in desert Islands; and any other Places where there is no Civil Government."[65] Given this definition, whether a war is public or private depends on whether it is waged by sovereign authorities or not.

As Keene has shown, although Grotius held sovereignty to be indivisible in principle, he readily admitted that it was often divided in practice. But even if Grotius did not exclude non-European peoples from international law and considered them capable of entering into and honoring legally binding agreements, the fact that their political institutions did not fulfill the formal requirements of sovereignty meant that they were fair game for different forms of interference.[66] Yet none of this seems to have been motivated by any cultural prejudices on his behalf, however. Grotius had published a dissertation on the origin of the American Indians that provided few, if any,

---

[63] For some statements, see Hersch Lauterpacht, "The Grotian Tradition in International Law," *British Yearbook of International Law* 23 (1946): 1–53; Hedley Bull, "The Importance of Grotius and International Relations," in Hedley Bull, Benedict Kingsbury, and Adam Roberts (eds.), *Hugo Grotius and International Relations* (Oxford: Oxford University Press 1992), 65–93; Martin Wight, *International Theory: The Three Traditions*, ed. Gabriele Wight and Brian Porter (Leicester: Leicester University Press, 1991); Benedict Kingsbury, "Grotian Tradition of Theory and Practice: Grotius, Law, and Moral Skepticism in the Thought of Hedley Bull," *Quinnipiac Law Review* 17, no. 3 (1997): 3–33; Benedict Kingsbury and Benjamin Straumann, "The State of Nature and Commercial Sociability in Early Modern International Legal Thought," *Grotiana* 31, no. 1 (2010): 22–43. For critical discussions, see Jens Bartelson, "Short Circuits: Society and Tradition in International Relations Theory," *Review of International Studies* 22, no. 4 (1996): 339–60; John T. Parry, "What Is the Grotian Tradition in International Law?," *University of Pennsylvania Journal of International Law* 35, no. 2 (2014): 299–377; Randall Lesaffer, "The Grotian Tradition Revisited: Change and Continuity in the History of International Law," *British Yearbook of International Law* 73, no. 1 (2003): 103–39.

[64] Grotius, *Rights of War and Peace*, I.III.240.   [65] *Ibid.*, I.III.241.

[66] Keene, *Beyond the Anarchical Society*, 40–59.

reasons for their dispossession and subjugation, all while his naturalism predisposed him to regard them and other non-European peoples
as default members of the great community of humankind.[67] Hence
he tells us that "the Indians of the orient are neither insane nor
irrational, but clever and sagacious, so that not even in this respect
can a pretext for their subjugation be found."[68] It rather seems that
the differential treatment of non-European peoples finds justification
in his distinction between public and private wars. This implies that
any act of hostility between fully sovereign states and those whose
sovereignty is weak, absent, or divided will automatically fail to meet
the criteria of public war and instead be subsumed under the more
nebulous and permissive category of private war. Grotius had thereby
created two distinct spheres of war, each with its own rules of engagement. Among sovereign states, the use of force could be subjected to
restrictions according to the law of nations. On those parts of the
non-European world outside where there was no sovereignty and
hence no law worthy of the name, actors were constrained by the
principle of self-defense only.

To Grotius, the perennial presence of violence in human affairs is
not only what motivates his inquiry but also that which determines
its conceptual and logical structure. While war takes on a recognizably modern meaning by being defined as a contest between
sovereign equals, what motivates this exercise in definition and
classification is the underlying assumption that war is always
already present in some primitive and unregulated form so that
defining the meaning of this concept is a necessary precursor to its
eventual regulation. While war in its crude, unregulated, and private form antedated and conditioned the emergence of sovereign
authority and law in Europe, that kind of war is now found outside
Europe and thus beyond the scope of legal regulation.

While much intellectual effort has gone into contrasting the
Grotian view of international law with that of Hobbes, the fact
that Hobbes had little to say about interstate relations has greatly
complicated such comparisons and has probably also facilitated the

---

[67] See Joan-Pau Rubiés, "Hugo Grotius's Dissertation on the Origin of the
      American Peoples and the Use of Comparative Methods," *Journal of the History
      of Ideas* 52, no. 2 (1991): 221–44.
[68] Hugo Grotius, *Commentary on the Law of Prize and Booty*, trans. Gwladys L.
      Williams and W. H. Zeydel (Oxford: Clarendon Press, 1950), 220–2.

co-optation of his work by modern political realists.[69] But, as Tuck has argued, "Hobbes need not to be seen as differing from Grotius over ethical matters, strictly understood, *at all.*"[70] Although Hobbes differed from Grotius in that he equated the state of nature with a state of war and thus imputed little innate sociability to human beings, both saw self-preservation as the most fundamental right of both individuals and states and also equated international law with the law of nature as applied to the latter.

In the present context, however, a more interesting difference between Grotius and Hobbes lies in the fact that the latter much more explicitly invokes hostility and enmity to explain how the sovereign state and law are possible in the first place. This move is made possible by Hobbes's clear definition of war as a state of affairs with a definite spatiotemporal extension rather than as an indefinite sequence of violent actions. As Hobbes tells us in the *Elements of Law* (1640), "[w]ar is nothing else but that time where the will and intention of contending by force is either by words or actions sufficiently declared; and the time which is not war is Peace."[71] Parts of this definition are reiterated in *Leviathan* (1651), but with the important addition that war is now defined with reference to the absence of supreme authority so that "during the time men live without a common power to keep them all in awe, they are in that condition which is called Warre ... Warre consisteth not in Battell onely, or the act of fighting; but in a tract of time Wherein the will to contend by Battell is sufficiently known."[72] What matters here is thus not the presence of overt hostilities between the parties, but the fact that they happen to coexist and interact in the absence of a common authority. That is, even if they should fail to recognize that there is no one there to keep them in awe or fail to interpret such an absence as a license to do battle, they are nevertheless stuck in a state of war because war

[69] See David Armitage, *Foundations of Modern International Thought* (Cambridge: Cambridge University Press, 2013), 59; David Boucher, "Hobbes's Contribution to International Thought, and the Contribution of International Thought to Hobbes," *History of European Ideas* 41, no. 1 (2015): 29–48.

[70] Tuck, *Rights of War and Peace*, 135; Tuck, *Philosophy and Government*, 279–348.

[71] Thomas Hobbes, *The Elements of Law Natural and Politic*, ed. Maurice Goldsmith (London: Frank Cass, 1969), 73.

[72] Thomas Hobbes, *Leviathan*, ed. Richard Tuck (Cambridge University Press, 1991), I.XIII.88.

"consisteth not in actuall fighting; but in the known disposition thereto, during all the time there is no assurance to the contrary."[73]

But why must the absence of common authority necessarily lead to war? In *De Cive* (1642), we learn that the state of nature is nothing but a state of war because "it cannot be denied but that the natural state of men, before they entered into society, was a mere war, but a war of all men against all men."[74] This question has long puzzled political theorists and scholars of international relations. If it cannot be shown that the state of nature *necessarily* is also a state of war, it cannot be shown why men should voluntarily submit to sovereign authority in the interest of self-preservation, and if that cannot be shown, the Hobbesian justification of sovereignty crumbles. Some authors have responded to this problem by focusing on the dispositions that according to Hobbes may compel human beings to violence. The dispositions invoked by him to this end – competition, diffidence, and glory – have somewhat anachronistically been taken to mean that background conditions such as a scarcity of resources, a lack of security, and a desire for recognition, either alone or taken together, are sufficient conditions of war.[75] Others have argued that the uncertainty about the intentions of others that comes naturally with anarchy, coupled with the corresponding lack of a common moral vocabulary, is sufficient to explain why hostilities are likely to break out in the absence of sovereign authority.[76]

While the preceding accounts have focused on the inferential connections between the concepts of war and sovereign authority, they have failed to notice that Hobbes also takes the state of war to be *productive* of sovereign authority and law in a more sociological and historical sense.[77] This omission is hardly surprising given that much of what he has to say

---

[73] Hobbes, *Leviathan*, I.XIII.88.

[74] Thomas Hobbes, *De Cive or the Citizen* (New York: Appleton-Century-Crofts, 1949), I.29.

[75] See, for example, Arash Abizadeh, "Hobbes on the Causes of War: A Disagreement Theory," *American Political Science Review* 105, no. 2 (2011): 298–315; Jean Hampton, "Hobbes's State of War," *Topoi* 4, no. 1 (1985): 47–60; Gregory S. Kavka, "Hobbes's War of All Against All," *Ethics* 93, no. 2 (1983): 291–310.

[76] Richard Tuck, *Hobbes* (Oxford: Oxford University Press, 1989); Jonathan Havercroft, *Captives of Sovereignty* (Cambridge: Cambridge University Press, 2011).

[77] For a recent analysis of the sociological dimensions of Hobbes's thought, see Hans Joas and Wolfgang Knöbl, *War in Social Thought: Hobbes to the Present* (Princeton, NJ: Princeton University Press, 2013), 16–21.

about the state of war could be taken to indicate that this is a purely analytical concept: "there was never such a time, nor condition of warre as this; and I believe it was never generally so, over all the world." Hence it is tempting to interpret the state of war as a convenient fiction construed to provide sovereign authority with a good, if not logically watertight, justification. Yet, later in the same infamous paragraph, the state of war is exemplified with "Kings and Persons of Soveraigne Authority,' who by virtue of their indepen-dence, find themselves "in the state and posture of Gladiators."[78] But this analogy merely raises the obvious question of how such an international state of war ever could have emerged had not sovereign states been present beforehand. But since the state of war is invoked to explain why human beings are compelled by their fear of death to relinquish their natural freedom and settle for relative security within the state, such recourse to an international state of war fails to provide the desired justification for the simple reason that it presupposes precisely what it purports to explain.

But Hobbes was arguably less concerned with the actual foundation of states and more with the threat that subversion posed to states was already in existence. To avoid dissension and civil war, Hobbes proposed that the sovereign should propagate an ideology designated to curb subversive ideas and replace them with doctrines conducive to peace and order. He states this point in *De Cive*: "It follows therefore that this one ... to whom the city hath committed the supreme power, have also this right; that he both judge what opinions and doctrines re enemies unto peace, and also that he forbid them to be taught."[79] This point is repeated in a more condensed form in *Leviathan*, where Hobbes holds that it is annexed to sovereignty "to be Judge of what Opinions and Doctrines are averse, and what conducive to Peace."[80] Given the importance Hobbes attaches to matters of doctrine and opinion in *Leviathan* and elsewhere, the answer to the question of why he posited a state of war as the very foundation of his *own* doctrine should perhaps be sought in the rhetorical functions that this assumption performs rather than in its inferential connections – or lack thereof – with other core assumptions.[81] Although Hobbes was mainly

---

[78] Hobbes, *Leviathan*, I.XIII.90. [79] Hobbes, *De Cive*, VI.76.
[80] Hobbes, *Leviathan*, XVIII.124.
[81] On the rhetorical aspects of his work, see David Johnston, *The Rhetoric of Leviathan: Thomas Hobbes and the Politics of Cultural Transformation* (Princeton, NJ: Princeton University Press, 1986); Quentin Skinner, *Reason and*

concerned with the adverse effects of various religious doctrines, what he said about religious beliefs could perhaps be extended to false beliefs in general. As Malcolm has pointed out, while Hobbes recognized that ancient kingdoms sometimes had been founded on myth, a state ought ideally to rest on true beliefs about the nature and necessity of sovereignty of the kind that Hobbes himself sought to establish.[82] The fact that Hobbes sought to justify sovereign authority with reference to the violence and disorder that would ensue in its absence would thus entail that the purposes of domestic peace would be best served if members of society were well aware of the fearful consequences such an absence would bring.

But, as Waldron has cautioned us, this does not imply that Hobbes tailored his view of the truth to the ends of the commonwealth, either by saying that what is true is that which is conducive to peace and order or by saying that what is true is that which serves the interests of the sovereign.[83] But even if Hobbes was opposed to backing sovereign authority up with myths and falsehoods and also held that false doctrines were potent sources of civil discord, he hoped that his civil science would bring truth and authority to converge and reinforce each other. Hobbes thus recognized the need to legitimize the sovereign state by harnessing all available resources of reason and eloquence to this end. For this reason, he also invoked a state of war to explain how states are formed and then projects this state onto the stateless past of European societies, as well as onto the primitive peoples of the New World. As Boucher has pointed out, Hobbes's choice of examples illustrates that he took hostility among groups of men rather than among individuals to be the paradigmatic case of violent conflict and that the kind of group he mostly had in mind was a family headed by a patriarch.[84] For example, in the *Elements of Law*, we are informed that the state of hostility is what we know "by the experience of savage nations that live at this day, and by the histories of our ancestors, the old inhabitants of Germany and other now civil countries, where we find the people few and short lived, and without the ornaments and

Rhetoric in the Philosophy of Hobbes (Cambridge: Cambridge University Press, 1996), 296–325.

[82] Noel Malcolm, *Reason of State, Propaganda, and the Thirty Years' War: An Unknown Translation by Thomas Hobbes* (Oxford: Clarendon Press, 2007), 121–2.

[83] Jeremy Waldron, "Hobbes and the Principle of Publicity," *Pacific Philosophical Quarterly* 82, nos. 3–4 (2001): 447–74.

[84] Boucher, "Hobbes's Contribution to International Thought," 12–13.

comforts of life, which by peace and society are usually invented and procured."[85] So when Hobbes sets out to explain how states have been formed out of a state of nature, he describes a process essentially driven by war:

[I]t is sufficiently showed, in what manner, and by what degrees, many natural persons, through desire of preserving themselves, and by mutual fear, have grown together into a civil person, whom we have called a city. But they who submit themselves to another for fear, either submit to him whom they fear, so some other whom they confide in for protection. They act according in the first manner who are vanquished in war, that they may not be slain; they according to the second, who are not yet overcome, that they may be not overcome.[86]

In ancient times, such a state of war was mitigated by custom, however, so that those who were living by rapine "taking away the rest, to spare life, and abstain from oxen fit for plough, and every instrument service-able to husbandry," since "lest by too much cruelty, they might be suspected guilty of fear."[87] A similar explanation of the origin of the state recurs in *Leviathan*, where we learn that the successful institution of government depends on outside enemies, so "the Multitude suffi-cient to confide in for our security, is not determined by any certain number, but by comparison with the enemy we feare."[88] But when the risk of war has faded and fear subsided, that is, "when either thy have no common enemy, or he that by one part is held for an enemy, is by another held for a friend, they must needs by the difference of their interests dissolve, and fall again into a Warre amongst themselves."[89] To the same extent that states are formed out of war between rivaling groups, a state will depend on the presence of external enemies for its continuity and cohesion; hence "the state of cities among themselves is natural and hostile."[90]

But what was part of the past of European states was also to be found *outside* the confines of the emergent European system. It is no coincidence that *libertas* is represented by a Native American in the frontispiece to *De Cive*. To Hobbes, practices of rapine and piracy were as rampant among the savage peoples of the New World as they once had been among the German tribes of antiquity. Here Hobbes

---

[85] Hobbes, *Elements of Law*, XIV.73.   [86] Hobbes, *De Cive*, V.68–9.
[87] *Ibid.*, V.64.   [88] Hobbes, *Leviathan*, 118.   [89] *Ibid.*, 119.
[90] Hobbes, *De Cive*, 150.

exemplifies the state of war with the natural condition of the American Indians: "For the savage people in many places of *America*, except the government of small Families, the concord whereof dependenth on natural lust, have no government at all; and live at this day in that brutish manner."[91] As a number of scholars have pointed out, the contrast between a condition of natural liberty and that of security produced by sovereign authority was reinforced by letting this contrast coincide with a geographic divide between the New World and the Old. The fictitious state of nature had its empirical counterpart in the savage anarchy thought to be characteristic of the New World, whereas peoples in the Old World could enjoy the fruits of civilization brought about by their voluntary subjection to sovereign authority. Not only did this help Hobbes to substantiate the assumption that the state of nature was a state of war, but it also made it possible to locate savage peoples beyond the scope of international law. His account of sovereign authority presupposed that such authority was absent or weak in non-European societies and that the savagery of primitive societies represented a condition that European societies had long ago left behind thanks to the sovereign state.[92] While the Europeans had escaped that condition by subjecting themselves to a common political authority, non-Europeans were stuck in this state of affairs and with little hope of escaping it without the aid of the Europeans. From this followed a right, if not a duty, on behalf of Europeans to subject those peoples to sovereign authority, and this well before anything like a modern standard of civilization had been articulated.

By virtue of the same logic according to which European peoples had successfully escaped the state of war by entering into the civil state, they now found themselves in a condition of hostility not only toward each other but also toward those who had not yet escaped the primordial state of war. Hence the state of war cannot but duplicate itself because overcoming this state at one level amounts to nothing but its

---

[91] Hobbes, *Leviathan*, XIII.89.

[92] See Tuck, *Rights of War and Peace*, 135–9; Beate Jahn, "IR and the State of Nature: The Cultural Origins of a Ruling Ideology," *Review of International Studies* 25, no. 3 (1999): 411–34; Pat Moloney, "Hobbes, Savagery, and International Anarchy," *American Political Science Review* 105, no. 1 (2011): 189–204; Robert Lee Nichols, "Realizing the Social Contract: The Case of Colonialism and Indigenous Peoples," *Contemporary Political Theory* 4, no. 1 (2005): 42–62.

reproduction at another. To the same extent as European states had been able to overcome internal discord and consolidate themselves, this could only accentuate their superiority in relation to those peoples who had not been able to enter into civil societies of their own and hence justify their subjugation at the hand of the Europeans in exactly those terms. Thus the state of war is not only productive of sovereignty and law but also of the separation of European and non-European peoples that later would make international law *inapplicable* outside the society of sovereign states. Yet none of this was made possible by cultural prejudices but rather followed from the attribution of ontogenetic capacities to the state of war.

At this point, it is worth noting that Locke – who shared the view that the law of nations derived from the law of nature – drew different conclusions when it came to the role of hostility and war in human affairs. In his view, the law of nature does not entail that humans are inflamed by hatred to such an extent that that they must be divided into mutually hostile states. Rather, the division of mankind into distinct communities was the result of positive agreements and the reciprocal recognition of exclusive territorial rights between peoples.[93] But, by equating the law of nations with natural law as applied to sovereign states, Hobbes also invited attempts to distinguish more firmly between the *ius gentium* and the *ius inter gentes*. Whereas the former contained elements of laws that were common to all peoples, the latter comprised laws that regulated the intercourse *between* different peoples and nothing else.[94] Insisting on this distinction meant that the law of nations could be divorced from natural law and be equated more squarely with positive agreements between states. Thus Zouche, in his *Juris et Judiciis fecialis, sive Juris inter Gentes* (1650), defined the law between peoples as "the law which is recognized in the community of different princes or peoples who hold sovereign power – that is to say, the law which has been accepted among most nations by customs in harmony with reason, and that upon which single nations agree with one another, and which is observed by nations at peace and by those at war."[95] Although Zouche had almost nothing to say about the

[93] Armitage, *Foundations of Modern International Thought*, 75–89.
[94] For this point, see *ibid.*, 68.
[95] Richard Zouche, *An Exposition of Fecial Law and Procedure, or of Law between Nations, and Questions Concerning the Same*, trans. J. L. Brierly (Washington, DC: Carnegie Endowment for International Peace, 1911), I.I.1.

historical origins of war, except when he noted that "men, from a depraved reason and corrupted customs, have become ill-affected one towards another," he – like Hobbes – equated the condition of peace with the subjection to civil government. But he also added that peace might well also obtain between states to the extent that they recognize each other as friends and allies by virtue of having entered into various contractual agreements.[96] War, however, is that "condition of princes or peoples who are at strife or contention with others" and "is that which causes some to be regarded as unfriendly persons and others as enemies."[97] Zouche goes on to argue that "those are unfriendly with whom there is no friendship or legal intercourse, as aliens and adversaries. Aliens were called by the Greeks barbarians, and by the Romans *peregrini*, and if injury or damage was done them they had no legal remedy; so that, as regards some of the effects of war, they appeared to be in the position of enemies."[98] Here Zouche makes the important, if neglected, point that the state of war produces enmity among states rather than the other way around.

War effectively turns those who otherwise would be but strangers into enemies, and this stratification of the world into friends and enemies constitutes the baseline for the rights of war and peace between nations. Drawing on Livy, Zouche then divides enemies into two distinct categories. In the first were all those who pose a threat to the sovereign state: "enemies proper are those whom it is lawful to offend and destroy utterly," for example "those who have taken up arms against their prince or commonwealth with hostile intent" and "rebels and deserters, who have revolted from the prince to whose government they were subject. Robbers are those who go about in the manner of enemies without the authority of a state, as brigands on land, and pirates at sea."[99] Now echoing both Cicero and Gentili, the second category consists of lawful enemies, which are those who have "a State, Senate, Treasury, citizens consenting and agreeing, and some method of making peace or war, if occasion requires."[100] Whereas Zouche is relatively unbothered by the emergence of the sovereign state and its relationship to various forms of violence, he is perhaps the first to argue that war is productive of enmity rather than the other way around and that such enmity between states is constitutive of the international realm quite irrespective of whether states themselves are born out of

[96] *Ibid.*, I.I.3–4.   [97] *Ibid.*, I.VI.37.   [98] *Ibid.*   [99] *Ibid.*, I.VI.38.   [100] *Ibid.*

hostility or not. This is a point that would continue to resonate all the way into modern political realism.

Whether states are born out of war or not has been a main sticking point in the interpretations of von Pufendorf. As Hont has argued, von Pufendorf was among the first to dispute the quintessentially Hobbesian contention that the state had originated from a state of war.[101] According to this interpretation, human intercourse in the state of nature was tempered by the natural sociability of men, which *first* led them to enter society in order to fulfill their most basic needs and only *later* compelled them to voluntarily relinquish some of their liberty to sovereign authority in order to protect themselves from internal and external enemies. This reading is not without textual support, since von Pufendorf is adamant that a state of war of the kind described by Hobbes never existed: "A common or universal War engaging all Mankind at the same time, is an impossible Supposition; this being a direct Consequence of the State of Beasts."[102] Hence the state of nature is not a state of war because "those who live in a State of Nature both may, and ought, and frequently do, consent to live Socially."[103] The natural condition of men is therefore one of peace, being instituted by "bare Nature, without the Intervention of any human Deed ... and doth not owe its first Introduction to the Agreement and Covenant of Men."[104] In contrast to Hobbes, therefore, it would follow that states simply cannot have emerged out of wars between small groups of people subjected to some form of paternal government, since such wars would presuppose that some rudimentary sovereign authority already had been established *within* these groups:

[T]he notorious violence of many Persons, and their Desire of oppressing others, might possibly give occasion to the Fathers or Families, living independent and scattered up and down, to unite in political Bodies. It is moreover evident, that most Empires, which have made a Noise and Figure in the World, if not all in general, have owed their Growth and Progress to War. And yet this is no reason why we should pitch upon War for the Original and Fountain of Government. For at least, that Band of Men, which first

---

[101] Istvan Hont, *Jealousy of Trade: International Competition and the Nation-State in Historical Perspective* (Cambridge, MA: Harvard University Press, 2005), 159–84.

[102] Samuel von Pufendorf, *Of the Law of Nature and Nations*, trans. Basil Kennet (London, 1749), I.I.viii.

[103] *Ibid.*, II.II.v.　　[104] *Ibid.*, II.II.xi.

conspired to invade their Neighbours, voluntarily engaged in Subjection to a common Leader. And as for those who were invaded, no lawful Sovereignty could be established over them, till by giving their Covenant and Faith, they had promised Obedience to the Conquerour.[105]

But once we start to uncover the meaning attributed to the concept of sociability in this context, the contrast between Hobbes and von Pufendorf wears thin. As one leading scholar has argued, to von Pufendorf, sociability is not so much a natural human predisposition as it is a legal and political institution.[106] This view finds ample support in what von Pufendorf had to say about the formation of civil societies, both in *De Iure Naturae et Gentium* (1672) and in his historical writings discussed in Chapter 2. In fact, much of what he has to say about the history of European nations is consistent with his views on the origins of civil society set forth in his magnum opus and can even be read as an attempt to substantiate this view empirically. As von Pufendorf describes the reasons why human beings enter civil society, they "first embraced civil Society, not as led to it by the Biass of Nature, but as driven by the Fear of greater Evils." The greater evils from which man must seek protection stem from his own depraved nature "so that Nothing, besides the Fear of Punishment, could keep the greater Number in any tolerable Order." Since "Competition for Riches, Honour, Command, or any Prerogative and Power above others, inclines to Contention, Enmity, and War ... civil Societies are absolutely necessary to their Safety."[107] Thus the formation of civil societies is only possible through their voluntary subjection to a common authority because "the malicious Inclinations of Men, and their ready Disposition to their Neighbour's Hurt, cannot [in] any way be more effectually kept under, than by setting before their Eyes some present Danger."[108]

Now, that present danger can come from within as well as from without. In the final analysis, therefore, "the true and leading Cause why the Fathers of Families would consent to resign up their natural Liberty, and to form a Commonwealth, was thereby to guard themselves against those Injuries, which one man was in Danger of

---

[105] *Ibid.*, VII.II.v.

[106] See Fiammetta Palladini, "Pufendorf Disciple of Hobbes: The Nature of Man and the State of Nature – The Doctrine of *Socialitas*," *History of European Ideas* 34, no. 1 (2008): 26–60.

[107] von Pufendorf, *Law of Nature and Nations*, VII.I.iv.   [108] *Ibid.*, VII.II.i

sustaining from another."[109] And given his definition of war as a "[s]tate of Men mutually engaged in offering and repelling Injuries," it is hard to see how his appeal to sociability could make any big difference between his account of the emergence of the state and that of Hobbes.[110] And once communities have been formed in order to protect men from the wickedness of others, the same condition inevitably recurs between states. As von Pufendorf describes their mutual relations, "Civil Communities, even in the times of profoundest Peace, do yet fortify their Towns, guard their Frontiers with Troops, and fill their Granaries with warlike Stores; all which would be an unnecessary Expence, did not they apprehend some Danger from their Neighbours."[111] None of this is very far from the view of Hobbes.

In this section, I have tried to show that early modern legal theorists understood human hostility as a natural or at least a customary condition rooted in the violent predispositions of men. Although tempered in varying degrees by human reason and sociability, overcoming this hostility and its destructive consequences necessitated the creation of civil government and law. To make sense of the genesis of government and law, *ius naturalists* distinguished between forms of hostility and violence that served to create or preserve sovereign authority and legal order and forms that were believed to be destructive of that order. Such distinctions were then used to structure conjectural accounts of the origin of political authority and civil society, as well as ordering the political world into distinct spheres of violence with different rules of conduct. In as much as the law of nations derived its existence from natural hostility and the fear of death, it was based on a systematic suppression of forms of hostility and violence that were deemed incompatible with its existence, such as brigandage, rapine, and piracy. The enemies of legal order responsible for such irregular forms of violence were found in the conjectural prehistory of law, and although infidels and Indians were sometimes saddled with such savagery, the differentiation of the political world into distinct spheres of violence was not primarily justified with reference to cultural differences. Underlying universalistic assumptions made such differences legally irrelevant, and the scant knowledge available about non-European peoples did not provide solid enough justifications for their dispossession and

---

[109] *Ibid.*, VII.I.vii   [110] *Ibid.*, I.I.viii.   [111] *Ibid.*, VII.I.vii.

subjugation. Yet the very lines of demarcation that excluded non-European peoples from the scope of international law were drawn long before appeals to their apparent lack of civilization were made. But those lines of demarcation were less a result of systematic prejudices against non-European peoples and more a reflection of the symbiotic connection between war and legitimate authority that had been forged within the humanist tradition.

From Natural Law to the Modern Law of Nations

While most *ius naturalists* equated the law of nations with the laws of nature being applied to states, it would be misleading to regard them as founders of international law in any recognizably modern sense of this term. Struggling to supersede the universalistic framework of their scholastic predecessors, humanists had articulated conceptions of sovereignty that became foundational to modern international law. But to the same extent as natural lawyers had assumed that hostility and a general state of war were productive of domestic order, their modern successors assumed that an *international* state of war must necessarily give rise to constraints on the use of force in order to preserve a modicum of international order. From this followed a shared ambition to distinguish sharply between legitimate and illegitimate forms of violence and a corresponding quest to regulate and formalize the former while stigmatizing the latter. While legitimate war now was widely understood as a method of dispute settlement in the absence of any superior authority, illegitimate war was understood as a threat to the existence of international order and hence something that required exceptional measures and an extraordinary use of force to protect that order. Fire was to be fought by fire.

All of this presupposed that a firm line of demarcation could be drawn between what was inside states and what was outside them and what was inside the international system and what was outside and thus foreign to it. Since the early *ius naturalists* had equated the law of nations with the laws of nature, the savagery found outside the international realm was not very different from the savagery found in the prehistory of states: the demons the Europeans had invented to justify the sovereign state had merely migrated outward as a consequence of its success. Yet, in *Le Droit des Gens* (1758) by Emer de Vattel, this order of things appears to have been reversed. Like

Montesquieu before him, Vattel does not assume that a state of nature among individuals necessarily must be a state of war but nevertheless held that the formation of states had produced an international state of war. While the traces of hostility still found inside states were remnants of a distant and more violent past, those traces could not lend legitimacy to the sovereign state. Instead, that legitimacy appears to derive from the *external* sovereignty of the state, that is, from the international realm in which states enjoy exclusive authority and independence.[112]

Thus, to Vattel, there is no longer any necessity to appeal to the conjectural prehistory of the state to justify its existence in terms of the violence and disorder that had antedated it and again would reappear in its absence. The state is already there as a legal and political fact and is instead justified with reference to its inner purpose and the prospects of its perfection in the context of international competition and cooperation. "Nations or states are bodies politic, societies of men united together for the purpose of promoting their mutual safety and advantage by the joint efforts of their combined strength."[113] As such, "the state ... remains absolutely free and independent with respect to all other men, all other nations, as long as it has not voluntarily submitted to them."[114] States, being externally sovereign by virtue of their independence from any superior authority, are subject to the law of nations, which "is originally no other than the law of nature applied to nations."[115] While sovereignty entails rights of self-preservation and self-perfection, the first general law of nations dictates that the natural society of all humankind brings an obligation to assist other states in their endeavor at preservation and perfection, but only on condition "that each nation should be left in the peaceable enjoyment of that liberty which she inherits from nature. The natural society of nations cannot subsist, unless the natural rights of each be duly respected."[116] Such natural liberty and independence implied that all states are equals when it

---

[112] See Stéphane Beaulac, "Emer de Vattel and the Externalization of Sovereignty," *Journal of the History of International Law* 5, no. 2 (2003): 237–92.

[113] Emer de Vattel, *The Law of Nations, Or, Principles of the Law of Nature, Applied to the Conduct and Affairs of Nations and Sovereigns, with Three Early Essays on the Origin and Nature of Natural Law and on Luxury* [1758/1797], edited and with an introduction by Béla Kapossy and Richard Whatmore (Indianapolis: Liberty Fund, 2008), prel. § 1, 67.

[114] *Ibid.*, prel. § 4, 68.   [115] *Ibid.*, prel. § 6, 68–9.   [116] *Ibid.*, prel. § 15, 74.

comes to their rights and obligations toward each other because "[p]ower or weakness does not in this respect produce any difference. A dwarf is as much a man as a giant; a small republic is no less a sovereign state than the most powerful kingdom."[117]

The fact that sovereign states can constitute a society of their own by virtue of their formal equality implied that it was possible to speak of an international system having been formed in Europe. "Europe forms a political system, an integral body, closely connected by the relations and different interests of the nations inhabiting this part of the world. It is not, as formerly, a confused heap of detached pieces, each of which thought herself very little concerned in the fate of the others, and seldom regarded things which did not immediately concern her."[118] As several commentators have pointed out, however, in order to make sense of the emergent international system, and in order to be able to offer useful precepts for political action within it, Vattel adapted the principles of natural law to the demands of "Reason of State" and then tried to strike a balance between the universalism of the former and the particularism of the latter.[119] This led him to emphasize balance of power as a source of liberty and international order and to place his bets on diplomacy as the chief instrument of maintaining it. So what ultimately held the European system together was not any shared legal norms or moral values, but a common interest in maintaining the liberty of individual states. "Hence arose that famous scheme of the political balance, or the equilibrium of power; by which is understood such a disposition of things, as that no one potentate be able absolutely to predominate, and prescribe laws to the others."[120] In order to preserve the balance of power, states have a right to anticipate attacks from those who might be suspected of entertaining designs of oppression and conquest and are "justifiable in taking advantage of this happy opportunity to weaken and reduce a power too contrary to the equilibrium, and

[117] *Ibid.*, prel. § 18, 75.   [118] *Ibid.*, III.III. § 47, 496.

[119] See, for example, Tuck, *Rights of War and Peace*, 191–6; Isaac Nakhimovsky, "Vattel's Theory of the International Order: Commerce and the Balance of Power in the Law of Nations," *History of European Ideas* 33, no. 2 (2007): 157–73; Ian Hunter, "Vattel's Law of Nations: Diplomatic Casuistry for the Protestant Nation," *Grotiana* 31, no. 1 (2010): 108–40; Richard Devetak, "Law of Nations as Reason of State: Diplomacy and the Balance of Power in Vattel's Law of Nations," *Parergon* 28, no. 2 (2011): 105–28.

[120] Vattel, *Law of Nations*, III.III. § 47, 496.

dangerous to the common liberty."[121] Although Vattel produces a number of examples of such mischievous designs, unsurprisingly, the paradigm case was provided by the Ottoman Empire. "[W]hen the Turks were successfully pursuing their victorious career, and rapidly advancing to the zenith of power, all Christian nations ought ... to have considered them as enemies."[122]

But what, more precisely, is the role of hostility and violence in this theory? Although Vattel does not explain the emergence of sovereign states and the international system with reference to human hostility and warfare, he nevertheless implies that the existence and legitimacy of both depend on their ability to contain and regulate more primitive manifestations of violence. Inside states, the abolition of private war between individuals marks the monopolization of power in the hands of the sovereign to the effect that "[l]aws and the authority of the magistrates having been substituted in the room of private war, the conductor of a nation ought not to suffer individuals to attempt to do themselves justice, when they can have recourse to the magistrates."[123] The only remaining instance of private war is the practice of dueling, which "is a manifest disorder, repugnant to the ends of civil society."[124] Until men have got rid of this "Gothic idea," the only antidote is "to make a total distinction between the offended and the aggressor" and then to mercilessly punish the latter while acquitting the former.[125] Thus the right of punishment no longer belongs to private individuals but only to the moral person of the state, "who has a right to provide for its own safety, by punishing those that trespass against it."[126]

The same right applies in relations between states. Since "[o]ne of the ends of political society is to defend itself with its combined strength against all external insult or violence," it follows that each state also enjoys a fundamental right to self-preservation. "Every nation, as well as every man, has therefore a right to prevent other nations from obstructing her preservation, her perfection, and happiness ... It is this right to preserve herself from all injury that is called the right to security."[127] As Vattel goes on to explain, the right to employ force for the preservation of the state and the maintenance of its right is

---

[121] *Ibid.*, III.III. § 49, 498.   [122] *Ibid.*, II.I. § 16, 270.
[123] *Ibid.*, I.XIII. § 175, 194.   [124] *Ibid.*   [125] *Ibid.*, I.XIII. § 176, 195.
[126] *Ibid.*, I.XIII. § 169, 190–1.   [127] *Ibid.*, I.XIV. § 177, 198, II.V. § 49, 288.

constitutive of proper government. This right to redress injuries by means of force derives from the fact that there is no authority to settle disputes among sovereign states. "Each nation in fact maintains that she has justice on her side in every dispute that happens to arise: and it does not belong to either of the parties interested, or to other nations, to pronounce a judgment on the contested question."[128] As such, the right to war "can belong only to the body of the nation, or to the sovereign, her representative. It is doubtless one of those rights, without which there can be no salutary government, and which are therefore called rights of majesty ... Thus the sovereign power alone is possessed of authority to make war."[129]

In order to fulfill the requirements of legitimate war, wars undertaken by sovereign authorities must be preceded by a formal declaration of war in the hope of settling differences without bloodshed. Wars undertaken for motives other than those of self-preservation and the maintenance of rights are condemned by Vattel on the grounds that they threaten not only the existence of individual states but also the existence and well-being of international society as a whole.

[T]hose who seem to delight in the ravages of war, who spread it on all sides, without reasons or pretexts, and even without any other motive than their own ferocity, are monsters, unworthy the name of men. They should be considered as enemies to the human race, in the same manner as, in civil society, professed assassins and incendiaries are guilty, not only towards the particular victims of their nefarious deeds, but also towards the state, which therefore proclaims them public enemies. All nations have a right to join in a confederacy for the purpose of punishing and even exterminating those savage nations.[130]

But, as Silvestrini has pointed out, the idea of a just war against the enemies outside international society is a precondition of the concept of formalized war between sovereign equals inside international society.[131] So just as the state must be purged of practices inimical to its perfection – such as dueling – international society must be purged of those enemies whose violent practices violate the spirit of the law of nations either by

---

[128] *Ibid.*, prel. § 21, 76.   [129] *Ibid.*, III.I. § 4, 470.
[130] *Ibid.*, III.III. § 34, 487.
[131] Gabriella Silvestrini, "Justice, War and Inequality: The Unjust Aggressor and the Enemy of the Human Race in Vattel's Theory of the Law of Nations," *Grotiana* 31, no. 1 (2010): 44–68.

representing illegitimate forms of authority or by resorting to illegitimate forms of warfare or both.[132] Such wars are "undertaken, either without lawful authority, or without apparent cause, as likewise without the usual formalities, and solely with a view to plunder . . . A nation attacked by such sort of enemies is not under any obligation to observe towards them the rules prescribed in formal warfare. She may treat them as robbers."[133]

Vattel then goes on to list the entities deserving of such treatment. Apart from pirates of all denominations, we learn that since the Duke of Savoy committed an act of brigandage when he attacked Geneva in 1602, this provided a perfectly legitimate ground for all the prisoners taken from the Savoyards to be hanged as robbers. Thus, although Vattel made few, if any, explicit assumptions about hostility and war being foundational to the law of nations, the logic of his account nevertheless implies the existence of a host of others that alone and together constitute a potent threat to the coherence and cohesion of *any* legal order. In a world without the usual suspects of duelists, pirates, brigands, and Turks, there would be no need for international law beyond the customary principles that already have been codified through the intercourse of sovereigns.

From Natural Law to the Positive Law of Nations

The tendency to downplay the violent foundations of the law of nations becomes even more pronounced during the transition to legal positivism. Whereas the *ius naturalists* explained and justified the existence and necessity of law with reference to the primitive hostility that would reign unobstructed in its absence, most legal positivists have little to say about the historical or philosophical origins of law. Although they remain preoccupied with containing or abolishing irregular forms violence, the constant possibility of war remains a background condition inherent in the international system to be reckoned with rather than lamented or subjected to internationalist reform. But this underlying agreement raises the question of how and why war was increasingly taken for granted as a natural condition of the international system in an age so obsessed with progressive reform in other areas of human affairs. This, in turn, makes it

---

[132] Vattel, *Laws of Nations*, prel. § 22, 77.   [133] *Ibid.*, III.IV. § 67–8, 507.

imperative to understand what was really at stake in the transition from natural law to positive law.

While legal positivism sometimes has been seen as opposed to natural law, I think it makes more sense to view the former as an offspring of the latter. As Koskenniemi has pointed out, rather than being opposed to natural law, positivism was a logical response to many of the practical questions left unresolved by the naturalists. Natural law still provided the underlying theoretical framework of the law of nations, but it was left to positivism to elaborate its practical implications.[134] Yet, in Britain, there was no sustained university tradition of teaching in law and a decline in the belief in the living force of natural law, which prompted lawyers to create such a tradition more or less from scratch.[135] Thus it has been argued that in British nineteenth-century legal thought it is hard to detect any sharp distinction between legal naturalism and legal positivism because they coexisted and blended with little apparent contradiction.[136] Still those early attempts to build a positive law of nations on such foundations remained premised on the existence of hostility and the constant possibility of violence. Even though early positivist writers rarely made explicit references to the violent origins of states, their basic assumptions about sovereignty and the international system indicate that war and hostility were perceived as natural facts of the legal and political world.

This is nowhere clearer than in the work of von Martens, which is widely believed to mark an important phase in the transition from natural law to positivism. He begins by stating in his *Precis du droit des gens modernes de l'Europe* (1789) that while each nation should be considered a moral being living in the state of nature, "[t]heir common interest obliges them to soften the rigour of the law of

---

[134] Martti Koskenniemi, "Into Positivism: Georg Friedrich von Martens (1756–1821) and Modern International Law," *Constellations* 15, no. 2 (2008): 189–207, at 190; see also Martti Koskenniemi, *The Gentle Civilizer of Nations: The Rise and Fall of International Law 1870–1960* (Cambridge: Cambridge University Press, 2001), 19–20.

[135] James Crawford, "Public International Law in Twentieth Century England," in Jack Beatson and Reinhard Zimmermann (eds.), *Jurists Uprooted German-Speaking Emigré Lawyers in Twentieth Century Britain* (Oxford: Oxford University Press, 2004), 681–701, at 689.

[136] Casper Sylvest, "International Law in Nineteenth-Century Britain," *British Yearbook of International Law* 75, no. 1 (2005): 9–70.

nature, to render it more determinate, and to depart from that
perfect equality of rights, which must ever, according to the law of
nature, be considered as extending itself even to the weakest."[137]
Thus, although natural law constitutes the foundation of the law of
nations, its assumptions of perfect equality must be open to modification in light of the treaties and conventions that actually govern
the intercourse between states and that must take differences in
power and standing into consideration. One of von Martens' main
contributions to the development of international law was to have
collected treaties made between European states into a series of
volumes entitled *Recueil de Traités*. Thus it is "the aggregate of the
rights and obligations established among the nations of Europe (or
the majority of them), whether by particular but uniform treaties, by
tacit convention, or by custom, which form the general positive law
of nations."[138] From this it follows that the laws governing the
intercourse of European states cannot be deduced from the principles of natural law alone but must be sought in the history of
European states. Excluding the Turks, "one may consider Europe
as a society of nations and states, each which has its laws, its
customs, and its maxims, but which it cannot put in execution without observing a great deal of delicacy towards the rest of the
society."[139] Before identifying the laws governing European states,
Martens classifies them according to whether they are fully sovereign
or not, according to how much power they possess, and according to
their form of rule, carefully distinguishing between monarchies and
republics. While fully sovereign states are nominally equal and
therefore equally subject to the law of nations, differences in relative
power and forms of rule imply that they may enter treaties and
conventions from positions of unequal strength and with different
intentions.

In the society of states envisioned by Martens, secular statecraft is a
natural fact of political life that inevitably will be reflected in the
cumulated historical experience that constitutes the depository of positive laws. This follows from his conception of sovereignty because "[a]
natural consequence of the liberty and independence of nations is, that

---

[137] Georg Friedrich von Martens, *A Compendium of the Law of Nations Founded
on the Treatises and Customs of the Modern Nations of Europe*, trans. William
Cobbett (London: Cobbett & Morgan, 1802), introduction, II.II.
[138] *Ibid.*, introduction, IV.V.   [139] *Ibid.*, introduction, I.I.II, 27.

every sovereign has a right to make, in his own dominions, whatever arrangements he may judge proper for the internal security of the state."[140] In order to maintain their security, states have a right to augment their power not only by improvement of their inner resources but also by external aggrandizement. Since aggrandizement may sooner or later endanger the liberty and security of neighboring states, "[i]n such [a] case there arises a collision of rights, which authorizes the latter to oppose by alliances, and even by force of arms, so dangerous an aggrandizement, without the least regard to its lawfulness. This right is still more essential to states which form a sort of general society, than to such situated at a great distance from each other."[141] Martens here echoes the contemporary obsession with the balance of power as the key to maintaining order and stability in the society of states but is remarkably unwilling to place any restraints on this practice on the grounds that this would risk contravening the sovereignty and liberty of individual states.

War is therefore likely to be endemic in such a society of states. If differences between sovereigns are to be settled by forcible means only as a last resort, and if nothing "short of the violation of a perfect right, either committed, committing, or with which a nation is threated in the future, can justify the undertaking of a war," war between states remains a constant possibility and an important rationale for legal regulation of interstate affairs.[142] Not only are states stuck in a quest for security and liberty that makes it very likely that their rights will collide in ways that provide them with justifications of war, but the fact that the scope of domestic sovereignty also is virtually unlimited means that the ensuing wars are likely to involve the entire social body in the effort. As Martens argues with respect to the rights of war, "[f]rom the moment a sovereign is in a state of war, he has a right, strictly speaking, to act as an enemy, not only with respect to the persons and property found in the territory of the enemy, but also with respect to his enemy's subjects and their property, which may happen to be situated in his own territory at the breaking out of the war."[143] As Martens goes on to explain with reference to the *ius in bello*, "war gives a nation an *unlimited* right of exercising violence, against its enemy. But, the civilized nations of Europe, animated by a desire of diminishing the horrors

[140] *Ibid.*, IV.I.II, 123–4.   [141] *Ibid.*, IV.I.III, 125–6.   [142] *Ibid.*, VIII.II.III, 280.
[143] *Ibid.*, VIII.II.V, 282.

of war, now acknowledge certain violences which are as destructive to both parties, as contrary to sound policy, as unlawful, though not entirely forbidden by the rigour of the law of nations."[144] Thus the restriction on the excessive use of force does not derive from natural law or from positive law in a strict sense but from the latter in the rather vague sense as that which is being embodied in convention and upheld by the civilized nations of Europe only. But in relation to non-European political communities, other conventions kick in. "The ancient custom of making slaves of the conquered is no longer practiced by the powers of Europe, except by way of retaliation towards the barbarians."[145]

To those who wanted to reform international law in a more liberal and humanist direction, Martens' view of the law of nations appeared far too static to accommodate any real progress. To others, its rationalist underpinnings meant that it was unable to make sense of the historical origins of law and its subsequent development.[146] This view gained more traction because during the first decades of the nineteenth century, the tide of evolutionism and historicism had already found its way into legal scholarship, with authors such as Savigny taking on himself to explain "how law has actually developed itself amongst nations of the nobler races." In his account of the origin of positive law, all law is ultimately an expression of the popular spirit of a nation, so "law will be found to have already attained a fixed character, peculiar to the people, like their language, manners and constitution."[147] While such national tendencies may become more and more pronounced with the progress of civilization, this did not rule out the possibility of a law of nations as long as one was willing to admit that European nations formed a community of their own as a consequence of their long historical interconnections and common cultural heritage.[148]

---

[144]　*Ibid.*, VIII.III.I, 286.　　[145]　*Ibid.*, VIII.III.V, 291.

[146]　See, for example, Harold Berman, "The Historical Foundation of Law," *Emory Law Journal* 54, no. 1 (2005): 13–24; Koskenniemi, *Gentle Civilizer of Nations*, 42–7.

[147]　Friedrich Karl von Savigny, *Vom Beruf unserer Zeit für Gesetzgebung und Rechtswissenschaft* [1814] [*Of the Vocation of Our Age for Legislation and Jurisprudence*], trans. Abraham Hayward (London: Littlewood, 1831), 24. For a background, see John E. Toews, "The Immanent Genesis and Transcendent Goal of Law: Savigny, Stahl, and the Ideology of the Christian German State," *American Journal of Comparative Law* 37, no. 1 (1989): 139–69.

[148]　For a reinterpretation of Savigny's work, see Andreas Rahmatian, "Friedrich Carl von Savigny's *Beruf* and *Volksgeistlehre*," *Journal of Legal History* 28, no. 1 (2007): 1–29.

But taking history seriously could equally well lead to a profound skepticism concerning the ability of international law to restrain the use of force. The turn to history made it possible to view the law of nations as little but the outcome of a perpetual struggle for power in which war was the final arbiter. Thus, to Hegel, "war should not be regarded as an absolute evil and as a purely external contingency whose cause is therefore itself contingent." Instead, now paraphrasing Turgot, Hegel held that "the ethical health of nations is preserved in their indifference towards the permanence of finite determinacies, just as the movement of the wind preserves the sea from that stagnation which a lasting calm would produce – a stagnation which a lasting, not to say perpetual, peace would also produce among nations."[149] Since there cannot be any real and viable legal order above the state, it is not possible to speak coherently about a society of states. Rather the kind of order that exists between states is completely lawless and characterized by a constant struggle for security and survival. As his follower, Lasson, argued in his *Princip und Zukunft des Völkerrechts* (1871), since the plurality of states cannot be transcended by any means, and since the sovereign and moral personality of states effectively rules out the formation of any real sense of community between them, constant contest is their natural form of intercourse. What we call international law is wholly contingent on the shifting self-interest of states, treaties between them being but expressions of their relative power in the international system. Within this view, war is a means of negotiation among states and therefore also an important source of order and progress in its own right.[150]

The horrors of the Franco-Prussian War were soon to invalidate any idea that the European mode of warfare was that civilized and prompted renewed attempts to reform the law of nations in a liberal and humanist direction. Koskenniemi has described this concerted effort as a matter of articulating "the legal conscience of the civilized world," to provide it with a firm scientific footing and finding ways to translate its liberal and humanist principles into legal and political practice. Yet this posed some difficulties. Publication of *The Province of Jurisprudence Determined* in 1832 by John Austin had confronted

---

[149] Georg Wilhelm Friedrich Hegel, *Philosophy of Right* [1821], trans. H. B. Nisbet (Cambridge: Cambridge University Press, 1991), § 324, 361.

[150] Adolf Lasson, *Princip und Zukunft des Völkerrechts* (Berlin: Wilhelm Hertz, 1871), 9–76.

international lawyers with the challenge to explain to what extent international law qualified as law proper. If positive law indeed derives from sovereign command only and depends on the presence of a political hierarchy for its enforcement, it was hard to see that something equivalent could be said to exist in the international sphere. To Austin, international law was a prime example of law improperly so called and was in fact nothing but a set of moral rules imposed and possibly enforced by the weak authority of public opinion.[151] To counter this objection and rescue international law, international lawyers sought the sources of international law not in any supreme authority but in the piecemeal evolution of legal consciousness among European states. European states now formed a family or community whose customs and conscience were the foundations of international law.[152] As Lieber stated in 1868, "[t]he civilized nations have come to constitute a community, and are daily forming more and more a commonwealth of nations, under the restraint and protection of the law of nations."[153] From such a viewpoint, the latter "may be regarded as a living organism, which grows with the growth of experience, and is shaped in the last resort by the ideas and aspirations current among civilized mankind."[154]

Although the greatest scholar of legal evolution – Henry Maine – had been mostly concerned with domestic legal institutions, he also gave a series of lectures in Cambridge that addressed the origins and nature of international law. Contrary to what had been believed, he argued, "[i]t is not peace which was natural and primitive and old, but rather war. War appears to be as old as mankind, but peace is a modern invention."[155] The first effective bridle on incessant warfare had been provided by the great empires of antiquity. "No doubt they were a result rather of man's rapacity than of his humanity . . . but nevertheless no one could say how much war they extinguished by the prohibition, which they undoubtedly

---

[151] John Austin, *The Province of Jurisprudence Determined* (Cambridge: Cambridge University Press, 1995).

[152] Koskenniemi, *Gentle Civilizer of Nations*, 47–51.

[153] Francis Lieber, *Fragments of Political Science on Nationalism and Inter-Nationalism* (New York: Schribner, 1868), 22. Quoted in Koskenniemi, *Gentle Civilizer of Nations*, 67.

[154] Thomas Joseph Lawrence, *The Principles of International Law* [1894] (Boston: D.C. Heath, 1900), preface, v.

[155] Henry Sumner Maine, *International Law: A Series of Lectures Delivered before the University of Cambridge* (London: John Murray, 1888), 8.

carried out, of hostilities among the various sub-divisions of their sub-jects."[156] This meant that modern international law owed its existence to Roman law, and Roman law to the authority of the Roman Empire. From this it followed that if empire had been an effective antidote against primitive warfare in the past, so would its revival and extension in the present. Thus the evolutionary view of law provided a new and potent justification for European imperialism.[157]

The gradual acceptance of the evolutionary view of law compelled international lawyers to dig deep into the cultural heritage of interna-tional society in search for principles that had governed the intercourse of civilized peoples. This was deemed necessary because international law is "an inquiry into what is, not into what ought to be. And its method must of necessity be historical, since statesmen discover what rules to apply to particular cases by an inquiry into the history of previous cases."[158] In this context, civilization was conceived of as both process and outcome, and in this dual sense, the concept of civiliza-tion provided international law with a way of explaining how interna-tional law had developed from is primitive origins to a more advanced stage without invoking any notion of supreme authority, whether divine or human.[159] Evolutionary theories of international law thereby made it possible to project primitive hostility and irregular forms of violence outward, if only to justify the spread of civilization through conquest and colonial rule. Again, the barbarian of the past reappeared on the outside of the present.

Much of this is evident in the use of the concepts of sovereignty and civilization. As Anghie and Koskenniemi have shown in great detail, the increased emphasis on state sovereignty brought by positivism restricted the scope of international law to sovereign states while excluding forms of human association that lacked centralized authority structures or were territorially unbounded.[160] But it was precisely by

---

[156] *Ibid.*, 9–10.
[157] For an analysis, Karuna Mantena, *Alibis of Empire: Henry Maine and the Ends of Liberal Imperialism* (Princeton, NJ: Princeton University Press, 2010).
[158] Lawrence, *Principles of International Law*, § 16, 20–1.
[159] See Sylvest, "International Law in Nineteenth-Century Britain," 40–1. For a background, see John W. Burrow, *Evolution and Society: A Study in Victorian Social Theory* (Cambridge: Cambridge University Press, 1966).
[160] Antony Anghie "Finding the Peripheries: Sovereignty and Colonialism in Nineteenth-Century International Law," *Harvard International Law Journal*, 40, no. 1 (1999): 1–71; Koskenniemi, *Gentle Civilizer of Nations*, 98–179.

taking sovereignty for granted that it became possible to project its violent origins outward. While many authors were content to argue that the origins of the state were irrelevant to the elaboration of international law, they sometimes made revealing assumptions about the role of human hostility in its creation. As Lawrence put it rather bluntly in his *Principles of International Law* (1894), "[t]he methods by which central authority is created are outside our present subject."[161] But a decade before publishing his *Principles*, Lawrence had traced the origin of the state to the evolutionary pressure generated by private warfare so that "before law as we understand it now had come into being, before any central authority existed to enforce obedience to the rules it imposed ... the rough justice of revenge impelled the injured party and his kinsfolk to retaliate as best they were able upon those who had done them wrong."[162] Following a series of progressive steps, "[a]t last civilization banishes the vendetta altogether, and civilized man regards it as a mark of barbarism, when he observes it in less advanced communities."[163] In a similar vein, Holland held that "[e]ven were the theory of an original contract within the scope of the present treatise, it would be unnecessary to repeat here the arguments by which its untenableness has been almost superfluously demonstrated."[164] Yet Holland could not refrain from quoting Hobbes when defining the object of law. Laws were brought into the world to "limit the natural liberty of particular men" so that they could "joyne together against a common enemy."[165]

An interesting exception in this regard is Whewell, whose *Elements of Morality* (1845) made references to the desire for safety and security when explaining the genesis of society and the state. While the latter is "the necessary Origin of all the Rights which exist within itself," it was the outcome of a long process of evolution from "a condition in which men are in a perpetual state of war and violence, like hostile beasts of prey." But, as he was quick to add, "the desires of man, when his irascible affections are not inflamed by conflict, tend towards a state of

---

[161] Lawrence, *Principles of International Law*, § 43, 56.
[162] Thomas Joseph Lawrence, "The Evolution of Peace," in *Essays on Some Disputed Questions of International Law* (Cambridge: Deighton, Bel, 1885), 234–77, at 249.
[163] *Ibid.*, 256.
[164] Thomas Erskine Holland, *The Elements of Jurisprudence* [1880] (Oxford: Clarendon Press, 1916), IV, 49.
[165] *Ibid.*, VI, 79.

things the opposite of this."[166] So well before the springs of human action had made society possible, that is, "[i]n rude and half-savage tribes, in which clansmen assist each other with unbounded zeal, the stranger is looked upon as naturally an object of enmity."[167] So what was found at the beginnings of the sovereign state and law could now be conveniently relocated to the barbarous outside the European family of states, where the gentleness of the civilizer decreased in direct proportion to the cultural distance from its targets.

The law of nations consisted of the rules that had evolved among sovereign states so as to regulate their intercourse and temper their use of regularized violence. As Wildman defined the subject matter, "[i]nternational law is the customary law, which determines the rights and regulates the intercourse of independent states in peace and in war."[168] Yet this focus on the state created another problem because many states in Asia and Africa indeed displayed some of the defining characteristics of sovereignty, such as centralized authority structures and de facto control over their territories. In response to such embarrassing facts, positivist international lawyers shifted focus away from formal requirements of sovereignty to the question of whether their *societies* were civilized or not. By doing so, legal positivists created a sharp distinction between civilized and uncivilized societies, a distinction that was sometimes thought to imply that the relations between the former and the latter were outside the realm of law altogether.[169]

Whereas early modern naturalists had assumed that the law of nations was equally applicable to all communities irrespective of any cultural differences, positivists argued that international law was applicable to civilized states only. Thus Wheaton could maintain that there is no such thing as a universal and uniform law of nations but that

---

[166] William Whewell, *The Elements of Morality, Including Polity* (London: John W. Parker, 1845), I.471, 39. On Whewell's influence on the discipline, see Anne Orford, "Scientific Reason and the Discipline of International Law," *European Journal of International Law* 25, no. 2 (2014): 369–85.

[167] *Ibid.*, I. 511.

[168] Richard Wildman, *Institutes of International Law* (London: William Benning, 1849), I. i.

[169] Anghie, *Finding the Peripheries*, 23–30; Brett Bowden, "The Colonial Origins of International Law: European Expansion and the Classical Standard of Civilization," *Journal of the History of International Law* 7, no.1 (2005): 1–23; Gerrit W. Gong, *The Standard of Civilization in International Society* (Oxford: Oxford University Press, 1984).

"public law, with slight exceptions, has always been, and still is, limited to the civilized and Christian people of Europe or those of European origin."[170] Savages were explicitly excluded from statehood because a "[s]tate is also distinguishable from an unsettled horde of wandering savages not yet formed into a civil society."[171] It would, Lawrence argued, "be absurd to expect the Sultan of Morocco to establish a Prize Court, or to require the dwarfs of the central African forest to receive a permanent diplomatic mission."[172] Other international lawyers formulated similar arguments in favor of exclusion. To Hall, it was evident that "international law is a product of the special civilization of modern Europe, and forms a highly artificial system of which the principles cannot be supposed to be understood or recognized by countries differently civilized; such states can only be subject to it as are inheritors of that civilization."[173] In order to be admitted into the family of civilized states, uncivilized nations must "do something ... which amounts to an acceptance of the law in its entirety beyond all possibility of misconstruction."[174]

That something often amounted to little more than yielding to the superior military force of European powers and accepting the terms imposed. Thus, although the European society of states appeared internally fragmented as a consequence of the emphasis on sovereignty and resurgence of nationalism, Europe was understood as a political and cultural unity in its dealings with the rest of the world. As Europe advances, "it will be her duty to aid in the development of the more backward quarters of the globe, and to exercise police authority over barbarous races."[175]

It was during this period that the doctrine of international recognition was reformulated for the purpose of excluding non-European peoples from membership in international society. Having emerged during the Age of Revolutions, the modern doctrine of recognition had been devised to accommodate newborn states in the Americas. But during the nineteenth century, the requirements of international

---

[170] Henry Wheaton, *Elements of International Law* (London: Sampson Low, 1864), 16–17.
[171] *Ibid.*, 30.   [172] Lawrence, *Principles of International Law*, § 44, 58.
[173] W. E. Hall, *Treatise on International Law* (Oxford: Clarendon Press, 1890), 42.
[174] *Ibid.*, 43.   [175] Lawrence, "The Evolution of Peace," 277.

recognition were modified in accordance with the standard of civilization.[176] Taking important steps toward to this end, Lorimer suggested
that law should incorporate insights from the nascent discipline of
ethnology – from the "science of races" as he had it – in order to
distinguish between states according to the degree of civilization they
had attained. This led him to divide political communities into civilized, barbarous, and savage ones and to propose that only European
states should be granted full recognition by international law, while
uncivilized ones might be granted partial recognition but denied full
membership in international society on racial and religious grounds.[177]

   This crucial distinction between civilized and uncivilized peoples
also had profound consequences for the laws of war and their
applicability. On the one hand, and as Koskenniemi has pointed
out, liberal lawyers of the late nineteenth century were generally
opposed to war, which they regarded as a manifestation of destructive impulses that had reigned unobstructed in the past but now
had gradually been brought under control by means of international law. It was widely agreed by liberal and positivist lawyers
that the ultimate desideratum was to abolish warfare from the life
of civilized nations and, should that fail, at least to temper its
excesses in the hope of making warfare less brutal and more
humane. To the extent that the resort to force was at all permissible by international law during this period, it was for the vindication of rights and self-defense only. And in the case that war
broke out, international lawyers insisted that it should be waged in
accordance with humanitarian principles such as those laid down
in the Lieber Code during the American Civil War and in the 1864
Geneva and 1868 St. Petersburg declarations.[178] As Lawrence
argued in his essay, "The Evolution of Peace" (1885), since we
should not expect to attain perpetual peace immediately, "we must
be content to give our aid in strengthening all the healthy

---

[176] Jens Bartelson, "Recognition: A Short History," *Ethics & International Affairs*
       30, no. 3 (2016): 303–21.
[177] James Lorimer, "La Doctrine de la Reconnaissance, Fondement du Droit
       International," *Revue de Droit International et de Législation Comparée* 16
       (1884): 335–59. On the role of international legal recognition in the expansion
       of international society, see Hedley Bull, "The Emergence of a Universal
       International Society," in Hedley Bull and Adam Watson (eds.), *The Expansion
       of International Society* (Oxford: Clarendon Press, 1984), 117–26.
[178] Koskenniemi, *Gentle Civilizer of Nations*, 83–90.

sentiments and popularizing all the practical proposals that tend to make wars less frequent in our own time."[179] To Westlake, it was obvious that the improvement of the laws of war among European states represented a major achievement of international law, made possible by the fact that these states had come to identify themselves as members of a common civilization in which warfare was increasingly understood to be a thing of the past.[180]

On the other hand, such restraint applied to civilized nations only, not between them and nations for various reasons deemed uncivilized, savage, or barbarous. Instead, the latter were fair game for those practices of conquest and occupation that civilized states were proud of having made illegal among themselves, since it followed from this doctrine that "[a]ll territory not in the possession of states who are members of the family of nations and subjects of international law must be considered *res nullius* and therefore open to occupation."[181] Since war now was narrowly defined in interstate terms, whatever kind of violence that was inflicted on nonsovereign communities or uncivilized nations was not war properly understood but fully legitimate means of creating and maintaining the conditions of civilized government where it was found lacking or judged necessary to compel uncivilized peoples to enter into unequal treaties. For example, while reprisals had run their course in civilized warfare, "in cases where a strong state or group of states finds itself obliged to undertake what are practically measures of police against weak or barbarous powers, one or other of the means above described may be a useful alternative to war."[182] Finally, although Lawrence affirmed that natives stand outside international law, "[j]ustice demands that the inhabitants of occupied districts should be treated with fairness." Yet, as he was cautious to add, "when representatives of superior and inferior races come into contact, the former must prevail."[183]

When discussing the position of uncivilized natives with regard to international law, Westlake maintained that any principle that would make the free consent of an uncivilized population "necessary to the establishment over it of a government possessing international

[179] Lawrence, "The Evolution of Peace," 234–77, at 248.
[180] John Westlake, *Chapters on the Principles of International Law* (Cambridge: Cambridge University Press, 1894), X.264–75.
[181] Lawrence, *Principles of International Law*, § 93, 146.
[182] *Ibid.*, § 160, 299.   [183] *Ibid.*, § 96, 155–6.

validity" merely would invite questions "too obscure among uncivilized populations" and give rise to unnecessary controversies among colonial powers "whether the irregular violence to which savages are prone amounted to aggression justifying conquest."[184] To Westlake, the real test of civilization – and the only thing that would protect a nation from conquest and occupation under international law – was the possession of *government*. Apart from protection from arbitrary violence under the rule of law, a crude form of government is present when natives observe the laws of war and expect their enemies to do the same.[185] While this had been the case in the old Asian empires, whenever native inhabitants had failed to furnish such government for themselves, it was necessary that others should do that for them: "international law has to treat such natives as uncivilized. It regulates, for the benefit of civilised states, the claims which they make to sovereignty over the region, and leaves the treatment of the natives to the conscience of the state to which sovereignty is awarded."[186] Consequently, the title to occupied territories comes with certain duties that "consist in establishing in the country occupied an authority which may protect the natives with whom contact has become inevitable, and under which the civil rights essential to European life can be enjoyed in tranquility."[187] Westlake thereby saddled those seemingly uncivilized natives with the same propensity for irregular violence that once had been posited as the very origin of law in Europe.

The use of force against uncivilized peoples could thereby be further justified by arguing that since those peoples were prone to uncontrolled violence, they could therefore not be expected to understand or respect the laws of war. As Hall argued in the aftermath of the Opium Wars, "it cannot be hoped that China, for a considerable time to come, would be able, if she tried, to secure obedience by her officers and soldiers even to the elementary rules of war."[188] Lamenting the mistreatment of natives, Lawrence nevertheless observed that "[i]t is commonly supposed that a vast impression is made upon the minds of savages by driving off their cattle, destroying their crops, and setting fire to the thatch of their mud huts."[189] As Oppenheim helped to explain to a lay audience in the 1914 edition of the *Manual of Military Law*,

[184] Westlake, *Chapters on the Principles of International Law*, VIII, 139–40.
[185] *Ibid.*, IX, 142.   [186] *Ibid.*, IX, 143.   [187] *Ibid.*, IX, 159.
[188] Hall, *Treatise on International Law*, 44.
[189] Lawrence, *Principles of International Law*, § 229, 441.

the rules of International Law apply only to warfare between civilized nations, where both parties understand them and are prepared to carry them out. They do not apply in wars with uncivilized States and tribes, where their place is taken by the descretion of the commander and such rules of justice and humanity as recommend themselves in the particular circumstances of the case.[190]

As Mégret has shown, the exclusion of the uncivilized, the savage, and the barbarian from the protection of humanitarian law was very much part and parcel of the constitution of that law. During the formative moments of humanitarian law, European states were simultaneously engaged in a scramble for colonies in Africa. While the treatment of native populations was subject to considerable debate among international lawyers, it was never doubted that these populations were uncivilized. Those who argued that natives should be excluded from the protection offered by the laws of war also sanctioned methods of warfare against native populations that had been banned among European states, such as the use of dum-dum bullets and the burning of villages. The use of irregular methods of warfare against uncivilized peoples was justified on two different but interconnected grounds. First, since native populations did not constitute sovereign states according to prevailing standards, they could not have ratified the relevant humanitarian conventions and were therefore excluded from their scope. Second, by virtue of being uncivilized or savage, native populations could not be expected to respect the laws of war and honor the notions of civilized warfare. Their ways of war lacked all legal and moral restraint and recognized no distinction between combatants and noncombatants. According to an impeccable but twisted logic, since uncivilized peoples were uncivilized partly because they waged war in uncivilized ways, and since the laws of war apply to civilized states only, the latter needed not to be restrained by those laws when waging war against the former.[191]

Yet, by focusing on the transition to positivism during the late nineteenth century, postcolonial historians of international law such as Anghie and Mégret have failed to note the extent to which the notions of barbarism and savagery attributed to non-European peoples had

[190] *Manual of Military Law* (London: War Office, 1914), 235.
[191] Frédéric Mégret, "From 'Savages' to 'Unlawful Combatants': A Postcolonial Look at International Law's Other," in Anne Orford (ed.), *International Law and Its Others* (Cambridge: Cambridge University Press, 2006), 265–317.

been foundational to the enterprise of international law all the way from its crude naturalist beginnings onward. As I have argued in this chapter, assumptions about natural hostility and the violent dispositions of men were constitutive of early modern attempts to explain why law was possible and indeed necessary by pointing to what would the world would look like in its absence. When the notions of divine command and a preordained order of things had ceased to convince as sources of legal authority, such assumptions were invoked to explain how and why law had emerged in the first place and why it was necessary to the orderly conduct of human affairs within as well as between political communities. Early modern *ius naturalism* was thus the handmaiden of secular statecraft insofar as it provided the philosophical justifications for sovereignty and law by distinguishing between different forms of violence and different subjects of violence. While the forms of violence that could be harnessed for the purposes of secular statecraft were deemed legitimate and subjected to systematic attempts at regulation, other forms of violence – such as piracy and brigandage – were judged to be profoundly destructive of all attempts to create political and legal order. While certain subjects were vested with the prerogative of using violence to create and maintain order, others were seen as inherently threatening by virtue of their propensity for irregular violence and thus made legitimate targets for an equally unrestricted use of force. While the Others of international law can be found in many different times and places, their distinguishing attributes have displayed a remarkable continuity across both time and space, making it possible to lump pirates, brigands, duelists, boors, Indians, Ottomans, and African natives together into one single family of lawless outcasts lingering in the constitutive shadow of legality and legitimacy.

This means that there never was any smooth transition from unilateral to bilateral conceptions of war. Rather, as I have tried to make plain in this chapter, the modern conception of war as a contest between moral and legal equals has only been possible to uphold as a consequence of a consistent exclusion and othering of all subjects thought *not* to be morally or legally equal. To the extent that the law of nations has depended on the existence of natural hostility and irregular violence, it also owed much of its coherence and persuasiveness to the existence of such others, whether located in the prehistory of the state or relegated to the non-European outside of the modern international system. Thus the savages and barbarians invented by legal positivists were relative latecomers in this regard, with a rich ancestry in the history of legal theory. The paradigmatic Other of international law is not found in the colonies but in the dark past of European statehood, where barbarians had dwelled undisturbed and exercised their hidden creative powers at least since the reappropriation of Roman law during the sixteenth century. Rather than sensitizing themselves to cultural differences and basing their exclusions on these differences, positivists merely reactivated a legacy that long had been buried in the same naturalist past they were struggling so hard to either absorb or shake off and ended up unwittingly projecting what was still dormant in that legacy onto non-European peoples found outside the international system.

So perhaps it was never simply the case that the oppressive operation of the West against the rest was founded on any prejudices among the Europeans against non-Europeans. Ignorance, nascent Orientalism, and scanty reports from foreign shores certainly fueled cultural prejudice that made everyone else on this planet fair game for a vast array of practices of othering, exclusion, and discrimination. Yet none of this would have been possible without first having a veritable cauldron of hostility simmering inside European political and legal culture, much as a consequence of the sustained attempts to put political authority on a secular footing by conceptualizing hostility and violence as the ultimate sources of law and then reinforcing claims to secular authority with recurrent appeals to social, religious, and cultural differences between *European* peoples while upholding these claims with reference to the ever-present possibility of war between them.

Conclusion

The Return of the Repressed?

Making War, Making Sense

In the previous chapters we have seen how war has been consistently invoked to explain the genesis of modern political order and to legitimize the identities and boundaries on which this order was built. As a consequence, the concept of war took on its modern connotations in the context of an emerging tradition of international thought, a tradition to which war was a productive force in human affairs. Rather than reflecting a transition from the medieval conception of war as law enforcement between unequal parties to a modern conception of war as an armed contest among legal equals, this was made possible by the revival of the Roman notion that war is a productive force in human affairs that ought to be harnessed for political purposes, such as the creation of a peaceful political and legal order. As I have argued, this conception is distinct both from the view war as law enforcement and from war as a contest of equals insofar as both these latter views presuppose that some political and legal order already exists in order for war to be a meaningful category of thought and action. The notion of enforcement only makes sense if there is a law there to enforce, and this, in turn, presupposes some claim to jurisdiction and some claim to political authority with which to back law enforcement up. By the same token, the notion of war as a contest of equals makes sense only on condition that the belligerents are readily identifiable independently of the hostilities taking place between them, which requires them to be at peace with themselves.

Although the purposes of war could range from the creation of tiny principalities to grand schemes of imperial expansion, many early modern writings on war came to converge on the assumption that the main purpose of warfare was the creation of territorial states and their protection from internal and external enemies. Prompted by a felt necessity to put political and legal authority on a secular footing in an

180

age beset by profound epistemic doubt and religious discord, war and its many cognates were invoked when explaining the emergence of individual states and justifying their existence as the sole locus of legitimate political authority in the modern world. From there it was but a short step to account for the nascent international system in similar terms by construing its emergence as a tragic but inevitable consequence of the successful escape out of a domestic state of war: if war had once made states possible, then states now had made war necessary. In this concluding chapter, I elaborate some implications of this analysis for how we can understand the phenomenon of war in general and contemporary warfare in particular. I end with a few reflections on the possibility and limits of a critical study of war.

But let me start by summarizing some of my main findings. In early modern historiography, a primordial state of war was postulated in order to make sense of the historical trajectory of individual states and to distinguish their present from a past characterized by warfare between patrimonial groups. Early modern cartographers and geographers drew on similar imaginaries when making sense of and justifying practices of territorial demarcation, while military geographers consistently invoked the possibility of foreign invasion and threats of domestic unrest when they translated cartographic representations of sovereignty to facts on the ground by embarking on large-scale projects of statistical surveying and fortification of frontier areas that were typical of early modern state making. The early modern law of nations – which has been seen as an antidote to the excessive use of force within this emergent order – nevertheless posited hostility and violence at the very foundation of international legal order and then proceeded to explain how irregular forms of warfare should be harnessed for the purpose of maintaining a modicum of order among what was in the process of becoming a community of sovereign equals in the eyes of international lawyers.

Enlightenment historians, geographers, and lawyers continued to build on those foundations. Having accepted that the sovereign state originated in war, historians and philosophers were busy coming to terms with the international state of war that had emerged as a consequence of state formation and the gradual abolition of irregular forms of warfare in Europe. Apart from placing some confidence in the balance of power as a means of preserving the liberty of states while maintaining international order in a context of intensifying rivalries between European states, many Enlightenment historians and philosophers saw war as a source of human progress that would contribute to the spread of civilization and perhaps eventually issue in perpetual peace. While Enlightenment cartographers now turned territoriality into a natural fact by representing states as territorially unified and bounded, geographers continued unabated to chart frontier areas and colonial spaces in a relentless quest for strategic advantages over a range of real and imagined enemies. And although Enlightenment lawyers sought to supplement the inherited naturalist framework through a more systematic appeal to customs and treaties, this could but reinforce the impression that war was a natural companion to the international system, all the while positing the suppression of irregular forms of warfare as its sine qua non.

During the latter part of the nineteenth century, what had largely been an internal European affair got literally globalized. To the extent that assumptions of natural hostility and enmity had animated explanations and justifications of political order in Europe, these accounts tended to locate the sources of hostility and war in the dark prehistory of statehood, in the lower strata of society, in the rude populations of foreign nations, or on the barbarous fringes of the European continent. Although the sources of hostility were thereby skillfully disowned, they were still very much alive in European historical consciousness. But, with the rise of historicism and evolutionism in the human and legal sciences, it became possible to project those disowned parts of European experience outward onto non-European peoples. When statist historiography was challenged by cultural history, it coincided not only with the emergence of a recognizably modern and rationalist conception of war as an instrument of state policy but also with the transposition of notions of race struggle to the stage of world history. To early sociologists such as Sumner and Ward, international politics was not primarily a struggle for security and power among states but essentially a struggle for survival between races that would be carried out across global space until the superior white race had achieved conclusive mastery over all others. Simultaneously, within the field of historical geography, bounded territoriality was seen both as a natural fact and as a historically contingent outcome of a struggle between races for limited space, a struggle that eventually must result in some form of empire, if only to defuse territorial disputes within Europe. Finally, in what was about to become modern international law, the confluence of legal positivism and evolutionism made it possible to distinguish between an international community of civilized and sovereign states and an undifferentiated outside composed of peoples lacking the characteristics essential to self-determination. The latter were therefore fair game for conquest and control by the former, who were guided by the conviction that the predisposition to unrestrained violence of the outsiders justified a response in kind.

Thus it was assumed across different intellectual fields that war – whether between European states or between them and uncivilized peoples – was not only inevitable given its firm basis in the doctrines of race struggle and power politics but also desirable from an evolutionary perspective because it would render the superiority of certain nations unquestionable and their right to govern the world unassailable. Although there was an agreement to the effect that European peoples were superior to non-European peoples, however, there was no agreement as to *which* European nation could legitimately claim to best represent the superior race, just a conviction that this question could be decided only by an armed contest among states sharing the same kind of superiority complex. Given that this background understanding of war was widely shared among the political and military elites of the day, the outbreak of the First World War seems less surprising, as do the genocidal schemes that were implemented simultaneously in Africa and elsewhere in what appears as dress rehearsals of what was to come later in Europe.[1]

It was this background understanding of war that was superficially challenged in the interwar period and then downplayed and forgotten after the end of the Second World War. Although the productive view of war became unfashionable among the liberal intelligentsia and was either blamed on the Germans and their obsession with power or attributed to an accidental confluence of nasty currents in fin de siècle social thought, it nevertheless survived in military circles during the interwar period.[2] Quite regardless of the pacifism that was widely professed by liberals during this period, the underlying belief in the ontogenetic powers of war had hardly been shaken by the experiences of the First World War. Instead, it was the invention of nuclear

[1] See Beatrice Heuser, *The Evolution of Strategy: Thinking War from Antiquity to the Present* (Cambridge: Cambridge University Press, 2010), 113–36.
[2] See, for example, Wilkinson Dent Bird, *The Direction of War: A Study and Illustration of Strategy* (Cambridge: Cambridge University Press, 1925), 6.

weapons that eventually convinced Western elites that war could no longer serve any constructive purposes whatsoever. As Brodie then argued, "[t]he minimum destruction and disorganization that one could expect from an unrestricted thermonuclear attack in the future is likely to be too high to permit further meaningful mobilization of war-making capabilities." Assessing the damage of such an attack, "we should also recognize once and for all when it comes to predicting human casualties [that] we are talking about a catastrophe for which it impossible to set upper limits appreciably short of the entire population of a nation."[3]

Making Sense of War

But to what extent does a historical ontology of war such as the preceding help us to understand war? While a historical ontology cannot provide a general explanation of why wars occur, it can contribute some potentially valuable insights into how conceptions of war condition the range of motivations and justifications available to actors. Conceptions of war imply different answers to the basic question of what war *is*, and those basic commitments make it possible for actors to make sense of war in terms of its social meaning and political purpose, and from attributions of meaning and purpose will follow distinct possibilities of legitimizing war and warfare. Those who believe that war is a means of law enforcement will go to war for reasons distinct from those who hold the belief that war is an armed contest between legal and moral equals, but those who subscribe to an ontogenetic view of war will go to war to create preconditions for the kind of political order within which law enforcement and armed contest would make sense in the first place. While we might well think that the idea of ontogenetic war is flawed because it presupposes that war makes sense in the absence of identifiable belligerents, it remains a social and historical fact that war has long been conceived of as a productive force in human affairs and that this understanding has at times informed legitimizations of war as well as actual practices of warfare. Investing creative powers in war seems to have been an important part of the process of state-making in Europe insofar as

---

[3] Bernard Brodie, *Strategy in the Missile Age* (Santa Monica, CA: RAND Corporation, 1959), 167.

such conceptions were invoked not only by those contemplating its outcomes from a safe distance but also and more importantly by those who were in the business of selling it to their contemporaries. To them, the dictum that "war made the state, and the state made war" would not only have appeared self-evident but would most likely have commanded a very literal interpretation of what such making entailed. The productive powers attributed to war in the process of state-making were later reinvested in the international system and conveniently buried in the constitutive belief that wars occur because there is nothing there to prevent them. There international anarchy became nothing but another avatar of Mars, equally impersonal and compelling yet equally removed from the scope of human volition and intervention. But to what extent are we today experiencing a return of the ontogenetic view of war? In this section, I describe what I take to be some important preconditions of this return, such as the rise and spread of notions of state failure and the changing norms of military intervention.

During the past decades, there has been a growing conviction that the international system has come under pressure from another set of impersonal forces subsumed under the concept of globalization. As noted in Chapter 1, some of those who argued that international wars were becoming obsolete pointed to the simultaneous proliferation of domestic conflicts and argued that these had taken on a new and transnational character as a consequence of globalization. Many theorists have been inclined to blame this on unrestricted flows of capital and people believed to be corrosive of governmental authority and national identity, thereby increasing the likelihood of domestic conflicts along ethnic and religious lines in already weak states.[4] Yet these accounts are based on the assumption that state weakness or failure was both a cause and a consequence of violent conflicts. Violent conflicts between domestic groups were caused by a lack of state control over territories and populations, and whenever such conflict remained unresolved, they could not but erode the authority and legitimacy of the state further. Yet such notions of state fragility and failure had evolved well before the forces of globalization were invoked to explain patterns of domestic conflicts. In fact, it is fully possible to argue that most of the

---

[4] See, for example, Martin Van Creveld, *Transformation of War* (New York: Free Press, 1991); Mary Kaldor, *New and Old Wars: Organized Violence in a Global Era* (Oxford: Polity Press, 1999).

phenomena that have been lumped together under the label of state failure were in fact little but the combined consequences of decolonization and superpower rivalry in the preceding decades. As Jackson and Rosberg argued already in 1982, while many African states enjoyed statehood only by virtue of their membership in international society, "most of the national governments exercise only tenuous control over the people, organizations, and activities within their territorial jurisdictions. In almost all of these countries, the populations are divided along ethnic lines; in some, there has been a threat of political disorder stemming from such divisions; in a few, disorder has deteriorated into civil warfare."[5] These civil wars lacked the productive character of those that had propelled state formation forward in Europe, where "statesmen created jurisdictions over the course of several centuries in Machiavellian fashion – by dominating internal rivals and competing with external rivals – until the international system had attained its present-day jurisdictions."[6]

Such conclusions were further reinforced by another influential study of Third World states from this period, in which Migdal argued that despite appearances to the contrary, many states in the Third World lacked the core capabilities of statehood, such as the capacity to penetrate society and regulate social relations, as well as the ability to extract and appropriate resources in an effective way. Since postcolonial patterns of conflict had failed to produce both strong states and domestic peace and order, anything like the European experience of state formation was unlikely to repeat itself on other continents, thus condemning many postcolonial states to a condition of perpetual weakness and internal discord unless exposed to exogenous shocks.[7] When insights such as these began to penetrate international relations theory and were assimilated to traditional concerns with international security, this resulted in the contention that weak states were a threat not only to themselves and their own populations but also to

---

[5] Robert H. Jackson and Carl G. Rosberg, "Why Africa's Weak States Persist: The Empirical and the Juridical in Statehood," *World Politics* 35, no. 1 (1982): 1–24, at 1. See also Robert H. Jackson, "Quasi-States, Dual Regimes, and Neoclassical Theory: International Jurisprudence and the Third World," *International Organization* 41, no. 4 (1987): 519–49.

[6] Jackson and Rosberg, "Why Africa's Weak States Persist," 23.

[7] Joel S. Migdal, *Strong Societies and Weak States: State-Society Relations and State Capabilities in the Third World* (Princeton, NJ: Princeton University Press, 1988).

neighboring states as well and to international order and peace more generally.[8]

Soon enough notions of state fragility and failure were followed by pleas for intervention and the restoration of state capacities by external actors. In an article that set the tone for much of the subsequent debate, Helman and Ratner argued that "[a]s those states descend into violence and anarchy – imperiling their own citizens and threatening their neighbors through refugee flows, political instability, and random warfare – it is becoming clear that something must be done."[9] Since traditional ways of promoting economic and political development by means of aid were believed to have had failed in this regard, the international community was now faced with the task of creating an altogether new political environment for states riven by war, yet it was prevented from taking constructive action by the "extreme view that all the internal affairs of a state are beyond the scrutiny of the international community."[10] Thus, in response to what was perceived as widespread state failure in the Third World, the international community should adopt a stance of conservatorship, ranging from governance assistance to more intrusive forms such as the delegation of governmental author-ity to the United Nations, which in effect amounted to subjecting many failed states to a regime of trusteeship. The basic idea underwriting this proposal, namely, that failed states had to relinquish some of their external sovereignty and give up on their claims to self-determination in order to be saved from themselves, would continue to resonate with academics and policymakers in the coming decade.[11]

---

[8] Most notably, Barry Buzan, *People, State and Fear: An Agenda for International Security Studies in the Post–Cold War Era* (Boulder, CO: Lynne Rienner, 1991); Mohammed Ayoob, *The Third World Security Predicament: State Making, Regional Conflict, and the International System* (Boulder, CO: Lynne Rienner, 1995).

[9] Gerald B. Helman and Steven R. Ratner, "Saving Failed States," *Foreign Policy* 89 (1992): 3–20, at 3.

[10] *Ibid.*, 9.

[11] See, for example, Jennifer Milliken and Keith Krause, "State Failure, State Collapse, and State Reconstruction: Concepts, Lessons and Strategies," *Development and Change* 33, no. 5 (2002): 753–74; Robert O. Keohane, "Political Authority after Interventions: Gradations in Sovereignty," in Jeff L. Holzgrefe and Robert O. Keohane (eds.), *Humanitarian Intervention: Ethical, Legal and Political Dilemmas* (Cambridge: Cambridge University Press, 2003), 275–98; Stephen D. Krasner, "Sharing Sovereignty: New Institutions for Collapsed and Failing States," *International Security* 29, no. 2 (2004): 85–120.

Partly in response to this predicament, the norms of military intervention began to change. As we saw in Chapter 4, many early modern and modern lawyers took a quite permissive view on preventive and preemptive warfare, either in order to nip foreign aggression in the bud or in order to maintain political order by punishing or eliminating its imagined enemies. The stronger the belief that the maintenance of political order depended on the successful taming of irregular forms of violence, the more permissive the use of force to those ends was bound to appear. So, although the norm of nonintervention had long been seen as a corollary of state sovereignty, many scholars of international law now maintained that sovereignty entailed the right to intervene in the affairs of other states for a variety of reasons beyond the imperative of mere self-defense. For example, during the heydays of colonialism, intervention in non-European states was a prerogative of imperial powers that extended even to entities granted formal autonomy under colonial rule.[12] But after decolonization had been more or less completed, foreign intervention was largely understood as infringement on sovereignty and exception from the right of non-intervention that require careful moral and legal justification to be regarded as legitimate by members of the international community.[13] Hence it can be argued that the connection between norms of sovereignty and nonintervention is a rather recent invention, dating no further back than to the United Nations Charter and the Cold War.[14]

After the end of the Cold War, a much more permissive attitude toward military intervention in response to humanitarian catastrophes and state failure began to emerge among lawyers and policymakers. As summarized by a leading expert on humanitarian

[12] Lauren Benton, "From International Law to Imperial Constitutions: The Problem of Quasi-Sovereignty, 1870–1900," *Law and History Review* 26, no. 3 (2008): 595–620.

[13] See, for example, Neta Crawford, *Argument and Change in World Politics: Ethics, Decolonization, and Humanitarian Intervention* (Cambridge: Cambridge University Press, 2002); Cynthia Weber, *Simulating Sovereignty: Intervention, the State and Symbolic Exchange* (Cambridge: Cambridge University Press, 1994); Helle Malmvig, *State Sovereignty and Intervention: A Discourse Analysis of Interventionary and Non-Interventionary Practices in Kosovo and Algeria* (London: Routledge, 2006).

[14] See Luke Glanville, *Sovereignty and the Responsibility to Protect: A New History* (Chicago: University of Chicago Press, 2013); Martha Finnemore, *The Purpose of Intervention: Changing Beliefs about the Use of Force* (Ithaca, NY: Cornell University Press, 2004).

interventions, "[m]ilitary interventions in the name of humanity must be understood in the normative context in which they occur. The post-cold war normative context gives purpose and meaning to actions that were politically inconceivable not long ago."[15] Part of this normative context was provided by the international theorists who attempted to redefine the concept of sovereignty to entail the responsibility of states to protect their citizens from severe suffering while arguing that the right to self-determination and nonintervention was contingent on their ability to fulfill these responsibilities.[16] Should states fail to fulfill their responsibilities in this regard, and should the international community have exhausted all other options to assist the target state, military intervention should be considered legitimate to the extent that it could be expected to be effective in alleviating human suffering. Although the purpose of humanitarian interventions is thus limited, "it has far more meaning and legitimacy when it is accompanied by a long-term commitment to conflict resolution and reconstruction of the political, economic and social systems of the war-torn country." Disputes over humanitarian interventions and their legality and legitimacy eventually resulted in the development of the responsibility-to-protect doctrine. According to this doctrine, states have a responsibility to protect their populations from atrocities such as genocide, war crimes, ethnic cleansing, and crimes against humanity, and the doctrine stipulates that in the event that states fail to meet this obligation, the international community has a duty to assist them in a variety of ways. Should such assistance fail, the international community has a right to intervene – with military means if deemed absolutely necessary.[17]

---

[15] Taylor B. Seybolt, *Humanitarian Military Intervention: The Conditions of Success and Failure* (Oxford: Oxford University Press, 2008), 7.

[16] For important statements, see Fernando Tesón, *Humanitarian Intervention: An Inquiry into Law and Morality* (Dobbs Ferry: Transnational Publishers, 1988); Oliver Ramsbotham and Tom Woodhouse, *Humanitarian Intervention in Contemporary Conflict* (Cambridge: Polity Press, 1996); Nicholas Wheeler, *Saving Strangers: Humanitarian Intervention in International Society* (Oxford: Oxford University Press, 2000).

[17] See Gareth Evans, "From Humanitarian Intervention to the Responsibility to Protect," *Wisconsin International Law Journal* 24, no. 3 (2006): 703–22; Gareth Evans and Mohamed Sahnoun, "The Responsibility to Protect," *Foreign Affairs* 81 (2002): 99–110; Alex J. Bellamy, "The Responsibility to Protect and the Problem of Military Intervention," *International Affairs* 84, no. 4 (2008): 615–39.

As Orford has argued, "by focusing upon the de facto authority, the responsibility to protect concept implicitly asserts not only that an international community exists, but that its authority to govern is, at least in situations of civil war and oppression, superior to that of the state."[18] Yet it was obvious that while humanitarian interventions undertaken in the name of this doctrine did not offer long-term solutions to violent conflicts, they must be understood as "an exercise in clearing away an obstacle so that a new political and social edifice can be built."[19] Thus, whereas humanitarian interventions could be expected to solve the most acute problems caused by the failure of states to protect their own populations from suffering, they were not designed to handle the sources of state failure that permitted humanitarian disasters to take place. To do this required failed states to be rebuilt more or less from scratch, as reflected in the many strategies of state-building and nation-building that subsequently emerged in response to the cataclysmic events of 9/11. As Rotberg now pointed out, "[b]ecause failed states are hospitable to and harbor non-state actors – warlords and terrorists – understanding the dynamics of nation-state failure is central to the war against terrorism."[20] Thus the grounds on which intervention in failed states could be justified had changed almost overnight to include the imperative of combating terrorism, all while the democratic peace thesis evolved from a relatively innocent academic exercise into a full-blown justification for intervening in nondemocratic states in the hope of thereby creating the preconditions for international peace.[21]

This is also the moment when the ontogenetic view of war reappeared and started to inform both academic and political discourse. Since a distinguishing mark of a failed state is the lack of effective control over its own territory and population, the paramount task of state builders is to create the conditions for state strength by means of

---

[18] Anne Orford, *International Authority and the Responsibility to Protect* (Cambridge: Cambridge University Press, 2011), 120.

[19] Seybolt, *Humanitarian Military Intervention*, 276.

[20] Robert I. Rotberg, "The New Nature of Nation-State Failure," *Washington Quarterly* 25, no. 3 (2002): 83–96, at 83.

[21] See the fascinating study by Piki Ish-Shalom, *Democratic Peace: A Political Biography* (Ann Arbor: University of Michigan Press, 2013). For one of the first attempts to dispute the viability of this strategy, see Karin von Hippel, *Democracy by Force: US Military Intervention in the Post–Cold War World* (Cambridge: Cambridge University Press, 2000).

strategic interventions in the political structures of such states.[22] What was subject to some disagreement, however, was the means most appropriate to this end. While some scholars and policymakers had been deterred by previous failures to achieve political order by military means and now placed their bet on softer measures, those disappointed by earlier attempts to democratize and liberalize failed states maintained that the creation of political order requires the prior establishment of a monopoly of violence in order to stand a chance of success.[23] From this it was a short step to argue that it takes military muscle to create order in states beset by inner discord and that the more the discord, the bigger the muscle needs to be. In the many templates for nation-building that soon were available off the shelf from think tanks, military intervention was regarded as the best available instrument to create political order out of the chaos of rivaling warlords and terrorist groups now thought to be the defining characteristic of failed states.[24]

In a widely circulated report with the revealing title "The Beginner's Guide to Nation-Building," we learn that nation-building "involves the use of armed force as part of a broader effort to promote political and economic reforms with the objective of transforming a society emerging from conflict into one at peace with itself and its neighbors."[25] Yet attempts at transformation must be encompassing in order to stand a chance of success. The measures the authors recommend largely fall under the heading of "deconstruction, under which the intervening authorities first dismantle an existing state apparatus and then build a new one, in the process consciously disempowering some element of society and empowering others."[26] The primary objective of this enterprise is "to make violent societies peaceful, not to make poor ones prosperous, or authoritarian ones democratic. Economic development

[22] Francis Fukuyama, *State-Building: Governance and World Order in the 21st Century* (Ithaca, NY: Cornell University Press, 2004); Francis Fukuyama, "The Imperative of State-Building," *Journal of Democracy* 15, no. 2 (2004): 17–31.

[23] See, for example, Roland Paris, *At War's End: Building Peace after Civil Conflict* (Cambridge: Cambridge University Press, 2004).

[24] See, for example, Paul Collier and Anke Hoeffler, *The Challenge of Reducing the Global Incidence of Civil War* (Oxford: Centre for the Study of African Economies, Department of Economics, Oxford University, 2004).

[25] James Dobbins, Seth G. Jones, Keith Crane, and Beth Cole Degrasse, *The Beginner's Guide to Nation-Building* (Santa Monica, CA: RAND Corporation 2007), xvii.

[26] *Ibid.*, xx.

and political reform are important instruments for effecting this transformation, but will not themselves ensure it."[27] Rather, what is more
important to the success of such missions is the provision of security.
"That security is sometimes imperiled by contending armies and is
always threatened by criminals, gangs, and violence-prone political
groups. International military forces are best suited for dealing with
the first sort of threat, police with the rest."[28]

This does not imply that democracy is unimportant, only that it
presupposes prior pacification in order to get off the ground because
"[o]nly when a modicum of security has been restored do prospects for
democracy and sustained economic growth brighten."[29] Hence
"[s]ocieties emerging from conflict may be able to wait for democracy,
but they need a government immediately to provide law enforcement,
education, and public health care."[30] So, although the authors professed to believe in the democratic peace thesis, they were quick to
caution their readers that "newly emerging democracies, on the other
hand, are often prone to external aggression and internal conflict."[31]
The same goes for governmental institutions, the rule of law, and civil
society in conflicted societies. "While there should be as much continuity as possible with preexisting constitutional traditions, many conflicts are partly caused by the weakness or failure of the preceding
institutional arrangements. Sometimes, significant innovation in institutional design is needed."[32]

Several things are striking about this report. First, the very practice of
nation-building presupposes an underlying claim to boundless sovereignty or empire that is taken for granted and hence left unwarranted.
The resort to military intervention for the purpose of nation-building is
never justified other than with the by then mandatory references to
the imperatives of protecting human rights and alleviating human
suffering. While the authors argue that "Western governments thus
increasingly accept that nation-building has become an inescapable
responsibility" and maintain that the practical responsibility for carrying such missions out must be divided roughly equally between actors
with sufficient military capability (NATO), on the one hand, and those
able to provide the civilian components required for success (UN), on
the other, no sustained attempt is being made to justify the claims to

---

[27] *Ibid.*, xxiii.   [28] *Ibid.*, xxvi.   [29] *Ibid.*, xxxvii.   [30] *Ibid.*, 135.
[31] *Ibid.*, 190.   [32] *Ibid.*, 198.

political authority implicit in the idea of nation-building beyond a broad reference to a Western responsibility to create order where there is chaos and human suffering. This is reminiscent of the justifications that invoked the barbarous warfare among uncivilized peoples as a sufficient ground for their conquest and subjugation. Second, and consequently, there is no mention of the fact that military interventions might compromise the territorial integrity and legal personality of the targeted states. Whereas previous justifications for intervention focused on restoring a modicum of domestic order while at least aspiring to preserve the territorial integrity and legal standing of targeted states, nation-building presupposes that since these latter dimensions of statehood already have been compromised by ongoing turmoil or previous interventions, military intervention does not require any justification beyond that provided by the de facto chaos and suffering present on the ground. In this we hear a distant echo from those writers of the early modern period who justified the use of force for the purpose of state-building with reference to the disorder that otherwise would ensue and possibly also spread to neighboring polities. Third, there is an insistence that public security has to be provided by an intervening military force before that security can be translated into the many blessings of a stable political order. Not only does this assume that the presence of an effective monopoly of violence is a necessary requirement of social and political order but that the absence of such an order is a default condition of targeted states that they cannot hope to escape by themselves. Here again we see the ontogenetic conception of war at work. Although some forms of war are believed to be productive of social and political order, others are merely destructive of the same ends and must therefore be suppressed by means of its productive forms whenever deemed necessary by the international community.

The fact that this guidebook did not offer any explicit justifications military intervention and nation-building does not imply that such justifications were in short supply: The war on terror had already made such justifications readily available. At least two main positions can be discerned here, one squarely imperialistic and the other vaguely cosmopolitan in outlook. The first and straightforward way of legitimizing military interventions in weak or failed states was by arguing that imperialism is legitimate to the extent that it creates and maintains peace and order and then conclude that the United States and its allies were most suited to fulfill this role by virtue of their superior military power. Weigel stated this point bluntly: "[T]he United States has a unique responsibility for leadership in the war against terrorism and the struggle for world order ... that responsibility may have to be exercised unilaterally on occasion."[33] Or, as Ferguson asked rhetorically, "[m]ight it not be that for some countries some form of imperial governance, meaning a partial or complete suspension of their national sovereignty, might be better than full independence, not just for a few months or years, but for decades?"[34] The conviction that American military action was necessary to combat terrorism and restore order to failed states was reinforced by the belief that while Europeans subscribe to a rosier view of international politics, "the United States remain mired in history, exercising power in an anarchic Hobbesian world where international laws and rules are unreliable, and where true security and the defense and promotion of a liberal order still depend on the possession and use of military might."[35] Thus the proponents of American empire were plugging into a rich tradition of imperial thought stretching back at least to Livy and Virgil, according to which the ultimate warrant of peace is imperial aggrandizement with military means.

A second set of justifications could be derived from an imagined community of all humankind and the universal values it was thought to embody.[36] Appeals to notions of humanity had already figured

---

[33] Georg Weigel, "The Just War Tradition and the World after September 11," *Logos* 5, no. 3 (2003): 13–44, at 32.

[34] Niall Ferguson, *Colossus: The Rise and Fall of the American Empire* (New York: Penguin, 2004), 170. For a penetrating critique, see Jeanne Morefield, *Empires without Imperialism: Anglo-American Decline and the Politics of Deflection* (Oxford: Oxford University Press, 2014), 133–68.

[35] Robert Kagan, *Paradise and Power: America and Europe in the New World Order* (New York, Knopf, 2003), 3. For illuminating discussions of American imperial ideology during this period, see Jef Huysmans, "International Politics of Exception: Competing Visions of International Political Order between Law and Politics," *Alternatives* 31, no. 2 (2006): 135–65; Andrew Hurrell, "Pax Americana or the Empire of Insecurity," *International Relations of the Asia-Pacific* 5, no. 2 (2005): 153–76; Michael Cox, "Empire, Imperialism, and the Bush Doctrine," *Review of International Studies* 30, no. 4 (2004): 585–608.

[36] See, for example, Mary Kaldor, "Cosmopolitanism and Organized Violence," in Steven Vertovec and Robin Cohen (eds.), *Conceiving Cosmopolitanism: Theory, Context, and Practice* (Oxford: Oxford University Press, 2002), pp. 268–78. For a critique, see Cécile Fabre, "Cosmopolitanism, Just War Theory and Legitimate Authority," *International Affairs* 84, no. 5 (2008): 963–76; Cécile Fabre, *Cosmopolitan War* (Oxford: Oxford University Press, 2012).

preeminently in earlier justifications for humanitarian interventions and had been incorporated into the core of the responsibility-to-protect doctrine. Military interventions in fragile or failed states – even if they amounted to stripping those states of whatever remained of their sovereignty – were now justified with reference to universal values such as the obligation of protecting human lives in the face of atrocities committed by governments or by groups challenging their right to rule. In such cases, the international community had a responsibility to assist and, if necessary, forcefully intervene, so quite aside from the obvious difficulty in determining who is entitled to act on its behalf, "this international community appears to date to be largely unlimited in terms of the actions it can take to achieve its universal mission."[37]

Yet it was obvious that attempts to legitimize war with reference to an imagined world community were profoundly problematic because the very same division of humankind into distinct communities that makes the idea of a world community look morally compelling is also the main obstacle to its realization. As Hedley Bull once described the Kantian view of international morality, "[t]he community of mankind ... is not only the central reality in international politics, in the sense that the forces able to bring it into being are present; it is also the end or object of the highest moral endeavour."[38] But at this point we encounter a paradox, since Bull was quick to add to this characterization that "[t]he rules that sustain coexistence and intercourse should be ignored if the imperatives of this higher morality require it."[39] This would imply that any successful attempt to legitimize war in the name of a world community must find a way to reconcile some set of universal values with the actual plurality of values present in the international system. But precisely because of its pluralistic makeup, every value can easily be recast as an expression of some particular identity or interest.[40] Thus, waging war in the name of some universal value is likely to generate more conflict rather than world peace.[41]

---

[37] Orford, *International Authority and the Responsibility to Protect*, 134.
[38] Hedley Bull, *The Anarchical Society: A Study of Order in World Politics* (London: Macmillan, 1977), 25.
[39] *Ibid.*
[40] See, for example, Thomas McCarthy, "On Reconciling Cosmopolitan Unity and National Diversity," *Public Culture* 11, no. 1 (1999): 175–208.
[41] For discussions of this problem, see Adda Bozeman, "The International Order in a Multicultural World," in Hedley Bull and Adam Watson (eds.), *The Expansion of International Society* (Oxford: Clarendon Press, 1984), 387–406;

But given assumptions about the ontogenetic capacities of war, imperialist and cosmopolitan justifications ultimately converged. Since implicit in appeals to a world community is a claim to possess rightful authority over humankind as a whole, cosmopolitan justifications of military intervention bear a striking resemblance to the early modern notion that those posing a threat to political order also were the enemies of humanity and therefore fair game for punishment or elimination in the interest of protecting humankind. So, despite their differences, both imperialist and cosmopolitan justifications entail claims to universal and boundless political authority and a corresponding obligation to provide the requirements of peace and order in times and places where these otherwise would be lacking or in short supply. Ultimately, the legitimacy of a world empire or a world community derives from its ability to protect the peoples brought under its sway from the enemies of empire or the enemies of humankind, but with no way left to distinguish clearly between different kinds of enemies. The legitimacy of any such endeavor would then have to depend on superior military capabilities alone; most advocates of military intervention in the context of nation-building have assumed that this is a Western prerogative that is bound to remain unchallenged in the foreseeable future. Yet, by tacitly accepting that what distinguishes legitimate from illegitimate interventions is their relative success in producing political order on the ground, those arguing in favor of military interventions in fragile or failed states had issued a generous license to other actors to embark on similar nation-building projects of their own, should they come to possess sufficient military capabilities.

Thus the ontogenetic view of war is likely to be as contagious in the present as it was in the past. Once it has taken hold among the powerful, it becomes an offer you cannot refuse but something that you have to emulate in order to survive. And, indeed, other states were already waiting on the sidelines. From a slightly paranoid perspective, efforts to create political order by military means are but the final stage of

Jens Bartelson, "The Trial of Judgment: A Note on Kant and the Paradoxes of Internationalism," *International Studies Quarterly* 39, no. 2 (1995): 255–72; Molly Cochran, *Normative Theory in International Relations: A Pragmatic Approach* (Cambridge: Cambridge University Press, 1999); Richard Shapcott, *Justice, Community and Dialogue in International Relations* (Cambridge: Cambridge University Press, 2001), 30–52; Beate Jahn, "Kant, Mill and Illiberal Legacies in International Affairs," *International Organization* 59, no. 1 (2005): 177–207.

carefully orchestrated campaigns to first destabilize states in order to create pretexts for military intervention. According to Gerasimov, "a perfectly thriving state can, in a matter of months and even days, be transformed into an arena of fierce armed conflict, become a victim of foreign intervention, and sink into a web of chaos, humanitarian catastrophe, and civil war."[42] State failure is the outcome of deliberate attempts to undermine existing governments by a wide range of non-military means, and "[t]he open use of forces – often under the guise of peacekeeping and crisis regulation – is resorted to only at a certain stage, primarily for the achievement of final success in the conflict."[43] In order to counteract such campaigns and regain the geopolitical initiative, Gerasimov proposes that the Russian military establishment should adopt its own version of such destabilizing tactics – tactics that have become known as "hybrid warfare" – to pave the way for the use of military force whenever necessary to produce the desired outcome.

War against War

While the above-mentioned justifications of intervention have continued to have rhetorical appeal among pundits and policymakers into the present day, they almost invariably failed to convince a more critical audience about the legitimacy of the use of force as a means to create political and social order out of its absence. Yet, curiously, some of those who have criticized the excesses of military intervention have done so from a perspective that presupposes that violence is constitutive of political and legal order. I have already touched on this line of reasoning in previous chapters, noting that it has informed many contemporary critical accounts of war. In this section, I will spell out some of its problematic implications for our ability to understand and pass moral judgment on contemporary forms of war and warfare. Doing this also raises some questions about my own approach to the study of war that need to be addressed.

The notion that violence and war are constitutive of politics and political order comes in two main versions, one by an international analogy and the other by a domestic analogy. To Schmitt – who has been

[42] Valery Gerasimov, "The Value of Science Is in the Foresight: New Challenges Demand Rethinking the Forms and Methods of Carrying Out Combat Operations," *Voyenno-Promyshlennyy Kurier*, February 27, 2013, trans. Robert Coalson, *Military Review*, January–February 2016: 24–9, at 24.
[43] *Ibid.*, 24.

a great source of inspiration for many contemporary critics – since war presupposes that a prior distinction between friends and enemies can be made, "a world in which the possibility of war is utterly eliminated, a completely pacified globe, would be a world without the distinction of friend and enemy, and hence a world without politics."[44] This implies that without war, the international system would cease to exist in its present shape and that states would slowly crumble in the absence of reciprocal enmity. To Agamben, by contrast, violence is constitutive of the domestic legal order. As he has argued, "if constituting power is, as the violence that posits law, certainly more noble than the violence that preserves it, constituting power still possesses no title that might legitimate something other than law-preserving violence and even maintains an ambiguous and ineradicable relation with constituted power."[45] This means that in the absence of foundational violence, law would lose its bite, and the state would lose its bearings, plunging us back to the primitive beginnings of things political.

But does this really help us to distinguish between legitimate and illegitimate uses of force? If we accept that violence is constitutive of political and legal order – whether internationally or domestically – it seems hard to resist the implication that no such order can claim to be legitimate on any ground uncontaminated by such violence. But then it becomes difficult to resist the conclusion that the imposition of political and legal order by means of force is legitimate whenever we succeed in counteracting its radical absence or its manifold negations, which is precisely what state-builders and imperialists of different stripes have always claimed in support of their schemes. Thus critical theorists who subscribe to an ontogenetic view of violence and war are not likely to offer much moral guidance in our present predicament and are instead unwittingly complicit in its perpetuation by debunking existing attempts to restrict the use of force.

This is no more evident than in the recent reappropriation of the works of Carl Schmitt by critical international theorists.[46] Following

---

[44] Carl Schmitt, *The Concept of The Political* (Chicago: University of Chicago Press, 2008), 35.

[45] Giorgio Agamben, *Homo Sacer: Sovereign Power and Bare Life* (Redwood City, CA: Stanford University Press, 1998), 40.

[46] For an excellent overview, see Benno Teschke, "Fatal Attraction: A Critique of Carl Schmitt's International Political and Legal Theory," *International Theory* 3, no. 2 (2011): 179–227.

him, one way of criticizing humanitarian interventions has been to point out that an appeal to humanity is but a fig leaf intended to conceal the real aspirations of the intervening powers.[47] Another way of debunking the imperial and cosmopolitan aspirations of the West has been to reject "every resurrection of eschatological desire, and to affirm conflict as the necessary and salutary basis of political life."[48] It would follow that all attempts to justify war on moral and legal grounds then are futile, since such justifications are but ideological expressions of state interests whose only real function is to demonize the opponent in times of war.[49] Hence no world unity beyond the current international system is possible other than as a contingent manifestation of Western imperial power.[50] It then becomes tempting to claim that politics cannot be but a continuation of war with other means, and what appears to be democratic consent only serves to mask underlying relations of hegemony and domination.[51] But since these accounts already presuppose that war is a priori productive of political and legal order, they cannot offer any ground for assessing the legitimacy of the domestic and international orders thus constituted.

Similar convictions about the constitutive function of war underwrite more sophisticated attempts to make sense of contemporary war and its role in world politics. Thus Jabri argues that in war, "[e]ven in its most instrumental articulation, therefore, violence has a constitutive manifestation and is hence seen as being formative of the subject."[52] This assumption is crucial to the rest of her argument, whose point is "to develop an understanding of the ways in which political violence and war are, in the late modern age, redefining politics and the sphere

---

[47] See, for example, Danilo Zolo, *Invoking Humanity: War, Law and Global Order* (New York: Bloomsbury Publishing, 2002).

[48] William Rasch, *Sovereignty and Its Discontents: On the Primacy of Conflict and the Structure of the Political* (London: Birkbeck Law Press, 2004), 3.

[49] See, for example, Gabriella Slomp, "Carl Schmitt's Five Arguments against the Idea of Just War," *Cambridge Review of International Affairs* 19, no. 3 (2006): 435–47.

[50] Fabio Petito, "Against World Unity: Carl Schmitt and the Western-Centric and Liberal Global Order," in Louiza Odysseos and Fabio Petito (eds.), *The International Political Thought of Carl Schmitt: Terror, Liberal War and the Crisis of Global Order* (London: Routledge, 2007), 166–84.

[51] See Chantal Mouffe, *The Return of the Political* (London: Verso, 1993); Chantal Mouffe, *The Democratic Paradox* (London: Verso, 2000).

[52] Vivienne Jabri, *War and the Transformation of Global Politics* (Basingstoke: Palgrave Macmillan, 2007), 12.

of the international."[53] As she goes on to explain, war is a constitutive force in the current transformation of world politics and the dissolution of modern boundaries and identities. "What we see in the late modern context of boundless and limitless warfare is the dismantling of traditional conceptions of state boundaries and their associated rules and the emergence of a global sovereign subjectivity that regards the global within its sphere of operations."[54] Wars waged for humanitarian purposes thus serve to domesticate the global arena in the name of such global sovereignty, thus having "a constitutive role in redefining, and potentially redesigning, the sphere of the international and its ordering in political and juridical terms."[55]

Unlike other critical theorists, however, Jabri makes a sustained effort to engage contemporary practices of war on critical cosmopolitan grounds. But since all universalistic claims are likely to be contested, such cosmopolitanism must incorporate the fact of irreducible antagonism into its core. A cosmopolitan ethics cannot therefore assume that a genuine world community is in existence or even that it is an attainable goal but must instead assume "an understanding of universality that is always in question, a universality that does not subsume conflict, but rather recognises the ever present condition of struggle and confrontation against all totalising practices, including those that seek cultural exclusion and domination."[56] With war and antagonism as inescapable characteristics of late modernity, the only remaining way to manage the use of force in world politics is by recognizing the primacy of antagonism in politics and to channel its productive force for more peaceful ends. In her view, a global politics of solidarity is the only remaining antidote to global war. Yet it could, of course, be objected that the process of getting there by means of antagonism equally well could result in a global politics of identity and further state failure.

Here the history of the ontogenetic conception of war seems to have come full circle. While contemporary war and warfare to a large extent are motivated by the conviction that war is necessary to create or restore order and peace where they are found lacking, many of those who criticize what they take to be illegitimate and excessive uses of force in the present start out from similar assumptions about the constitutive functions of violence and war that they thereby

[53] *Ibid.*, 7.   [54] *Ibid.*, 8.   [55] *Ibid.*, 187.   [56] *Ibid.*, 185.

unwittingly reaffirm. By attributing a range of constitutive functions to war and violence, those critics are not only relinquishing human responsibility for the phenomenon of war and the suffering this inevitably brings but also are perpetuating a conception of war whose looping effects have been and still remain both tragic and disastrous.

A more fruitful line of inquiry – one that I have attempted to pursue in this book – would be to historicize this view of war in the hope of lessening its grip on our political imagination and thereby increasing the scope of human responsibility in relation to its contemporary manifestations. Yet this historical and descriptive approach is vulnerable to the objection that it fails to distinguish between accounts that invoke the ontogenetic capacities of war for explanatory or critical purposes from those that actually celebrate the productive force of war in human affairs. But, although it seems very unfair to lump Tilly and Barkawi together with Montecuccoli and Bernhardi, the point of doing so derives from the precepts of historical ontology. What matters in the present context is not *why* ontogenetic capacities have been attributed to war but the cumulated consequences – the looping effects – of doing so across time and space regardless of the intentions of those who have done so. As I hope to have made plain, we should resist the temptation of passing moral judgments on the ontogenetic view of war because doing so would blind us to its looping effects and thus increase the risk of inadvertently perpetuating them even further into the future. What we as social scientists reasonably can aspire to, however, is to come up with new ways of understanding the emergence of political order that take the many disturbing historical functions of such violent imaginaries seriously enough without having to believe in them ourselves.

Bibliography

Abizadeh, Arash, "Hobbes on the Causes of War: A Disagreement Theory,"
American Political Science Review 105, no. 2 (2011): 298–315

Agamben, Giorgio, *Homo Sacer: Sovereign Power and Bare Life* (Redwood
City, CA: Stanford University Press, 1998)

State of Exception (Chicago: University of Chicago Press, 2005)

Agnew, John, "The Territorial Trap: The Geographical Assumptions of
International Relations Theory," *Review of International Political
Economy* 1, no. 1 (1994): 53–80

Akerman, James R., "The Structuring of Political Territory in Early Printed
Atlases," *Imago Mundi* 47, no. 1 (1995): 138–54

Anderson, Carolyn Jane, "State Imperatives: Military Mapping in Scotland,
1689–1770," *Scottish Geographical Journal* 125, no. 1 (2009): 4–24

Anghie, Antony, "Finding the Peripheries: Sovereignty and Colonialism in
Nineteenth-Century International Law," *Harvard International Law
Journal* 40, no. 1 (1999): 1–71

Imperialism, Sovereignty and the Making of International Law
(Cambridge: Cambridge University Press, 2007)

Anon., *Interests et Maximes des Princes et des États Souverains* (Cologne,
1666)

Aristotle, *Nicomachean Ethics*, trans. Roger Crisp (Cambridge: Cambridge
University Press, 2004)

Armitage, David, *The Ideological Origins of the British Empire* (Cambridge:
Cambridge University Press, 2002)

The Declaration of Independence: A Global History (Cambridge, MA:
Harvard University Press, 2007)

"What's the Big Idea? Intellectual History and the Longue Durée," *History
of European Ideas* 38, no. 4 (2012): 493–507

Foundations of Modern International Thought (Cambridge: Cambridge
University Press, 2013)

"The International Turn in Intellectual History," in Darrin M. McMahon
and Samuel Moyn (eds.), *Rethinking Modern European Intellectual
History* (Oxford: Oxford University Press, 2014), 232–52

Civil Wars: A History in Ideas (New York: Knopf, 2017)

Armitage, David, Guldi, Jo, and Baudry, Jérôme, "Le Retour de la Longue Durée: une perspective Anglo-Américaine," *Annales Histoire, Sciences Sociales* 70, no. 2 (2015): 289–318

Aron, Raymond, *Peace and War: A Theory of International Relations* (Cambridge: Cambridge University Press, 1966)

Penser La Guerre, Clausewitz, vol. I (Paris: Gallimard, 1976)

Asbach, Olaf, and Schröder, Peter (eds.), *War, The State, and International Law in the Seventeenth Century* (Farnham: Ashgate, 2010)

Ashworth, Lucian M., "Where Are the Idealists in Interwar International Relations?," *Review of International Studies* 32, no. 2 (2006): 291–308

Austin, John, *The Province of Jurisprudence Determined* (Cambridge: Cambridge University Press, 1995)

Avineri, Shlomo, "The Problem of War in Hegel's Thought," *Journal of the History of Ideas* 22, no. 4 (1961): 463–74

Ayoob, Mohammed, *The Third World Security Predicament: State Making, Regional Conflict, and the International System* (Boulder, CO: Lynne Rienner, 1995)

Baigent, Elizabeth, "Swedish Cadastral Mapping 1628–1700: A Neglected Legacy," *Geographical Journal* 156, no. 1 (1990): 62–9

Balázs, Péter, "Philosophie et Histoire dans l'œuvre du marquis d'Argenson," *Dix-Huitième Siècle* 1 (2010): 561–79

Balibar, Etienne, "What's in a War? (Politics as War, War as Politics)," *Ratio Juris* 21, no. 3 (2008): 365–86

Banai, Ayelet, Moore, Margaret, Miller, David, Nine, Cara, and Dietrich, Frank, "Symposium 'Theories of Territory beyond Westphalia,'" *International Theory* 6, no. 1 (2014): 98–104

Baracchi, Claudia, "The Πόλεμος That Gathers All: Heraclitus on War," *Research in Phenomenology* 45, no. 2 (2015): 267–87

Barber, Peter, "England I: Pageantry, Defense, and Government: Maps at Court to 1550," in David Buisseret (ed.), *Monarchs, Ministers, and Maps: The Emergence of Cartography as a Tool of Government in Early Modern Europe* (Chicago: University of Chicago Press, 1992), 26–56

"England II: Monarchs, Ministers, and Maps, 1550–1625," in David Buisseret (ed.), *Monarchs, Ministers, and Maps: The Emergence of Cartography as a Tool of Government in Early Modern Europe* (Chicago: University of Chicago Press, 1992), 57–98

Barkawi, Tarak, and Brighton, Shane, "Powers of War: Fighting, Knowledge, and Critique," *International Political Sociology* 5, no. 2 (2011): 126–43

Bar-le-Duc, Jean Errard de, *La Fortification Démontree et Reduicte en Art* [1600] (Paris, 1619)

Baronowski, Donald Walter, *Polybius and Roman Imperialism* (London: Bloomsbury Press, 2013)

Bartelson, Jens, *A Genealogy of Sovereignty* (Cambridge: Cambridge University Press, 1995)

"The Trial of Judgment: A Note on Kant and the Paradoxes of Internationalism," *International Studies Quarterly* 39, no. 2 (1995): 255–72

"Short Circuits: Society and Tradition in International Relations Theory," *Review of International Studies* 22, no. 4 (1996): 339–60

Visions of World Community (Cambridge: Cambridge University Press, 2009)

"Double Binds: Sovereignty and the Just War Tradition," in Hent Kalmo and Quentin Skinner (eds.), *Sovereignty in Fragments: The Past, Present, and Future of a Contested Concept* (Cambridge: Cambridge University Press, 2010), 81–95

"Recognition: A Short History," *Ethics & International Affairs* 30, no. 3 (2016): 303–21

"The Social Construction of Globality," *International Political Sociology* 4, no. 3 (2010): 219–35

"Sovereignty and the Personality of the State," in Robert Schuett and Peter M. R. Stirk (eds.), *The Concept of the State in International Relations: Philosophy, Sovereignty, and Cosmopolitanism* (Edinburgh: Edinburgh University Press, 2015), 81–107

Bassin, Mark, "Imperialism and the Nation State in Friedrich Ratzel's Political Geography," *Progress in Human Geography* 11, no. 4 (1987): 473–95

Bates, David William, *States of War: Enlightenment Origins of the Political* (New York: Columbia University Press, 2012)

Bayly, Christopher A., *The Birth of the Modern World 1780–1914* (Oxford: Blackwell, 2004)

Beaulac, Stéphane, "Emer de Vattel and the Externalization of Sovereignty," *Journal of the History of International Law* 5, no. 2 (2003): 237–92.

Behnke, Andreas, "Eternal Peace, Perpetual War? A Critical Investigation into Kant's Conceptualisations of War," *Journal of International Relations and Development* 15, no. 2 (2012): 250–71

Bell, Duncan, "Empire and International Relations in Victorian Political Thought," *The History Journal* 49 (2006): 281–98

(ed.), *Memory, Trauma and World Politics: Reflections on the Relationship between Past and Present* (Basingstoke: Palgrave Macmillan, 2006)

"Before the Democratic Peace: Racial Utopianism, Empire, and the Abolition of War," *European Journal of International Relations* 20, no. 3 (2014): 647–70

(ed.), *Victorian Visions of Global Order. Empire and International Relations in Nineteenth-Century Political Thought* (Cambridge: Cambridge University Press, 2007)

Bellamy, Alex J., "The Responsibility to Protect and the Problem of Military Intervention," *International Affairs* 84, no. 4 (2008): 615–39.

Benhabib, Seyla, *The Claims of Culture: Equality and Diversity in a Global Era* (Princeton, NJ: Princeton University Press, 2002)

Benjamin, Walter, "Critique of Violence," in Walter Benjamin, *Reflections: Essays, Aphorisms, Anthropological Writings*, ed. Peter Demetz (New York: Schocken Books, 1978), 277–300

Benton, Lauren, *Law and Colonial Cultures: Legal Regimes in World History, 1400–1900* (Cambridge: Cambridge University Press, 2002)

"From International Law to Imperial Constitutions: The Problem of Quasi-Sovereignty, 1870–1900," *Law and History Review* 26, no. 3 (2008): 595–620

A Search for Sovereignty: Law and Geography in European Empires, 1400–1900 (Cambridge: Cambridge University Press, 2010)

Berman, Harold J., "The Origins of Historical Jurisprudence: Coke, Selden, Hale," *Yale Law Journal* 103, no. 7 (1994): 1651–738

"The Historical Foundation of Law," *Emory Law Journal* 54, no. 1 (2005): 13–24

Berman, Nathaniel, "Privileging Combat? Contemporary Conflict and the Legal Construction of War," *Columbia Journal of Transnational Law* 43, no. 1 (2004): 1–71

Berthaut, Henri Marie Auguste, *Les Ingenieurs Geographes Militaires, 1624–1831*, vol. 1 (Paris: Imprimerie du Service Géographique, 1901)

Biggs, Michael, "Putting the State on the Map: Cartography, Territory, and European State Formation," *Comparative Studies in Society and History* 41, no. 2 (1999): 374–405

Bird, Wilkinson Dent, *The Direction of War: A Study and Illustration of Strategy* (Cambridge: Cambridge University Press, 1925)

Black, Jeremy, *War and the Cultural Turn* (Cambridge: Polity Press, 2012)

Bossuet, Jacques-Bénigne, *Discours sur l'Histoire Universelle* (Paris: S. Mabre-Cramoisy, 1681)

Botero, Giovanni, *Relazioni Universali* (Venice: Appresso Giorgio Angelieri, 1599)

Boucher, David, "Hobbes's Contribution to International Thought, and the Contribution of International Thought to Hobbes," *History of European Ideas* 41, no. 1 (2015): 29–48

Bowden, Brett, "The Colonial Origins of International Law: European Expansion and the Classical Standard of Civilization," *Journal of the History of International Law* 7, no. 1 (2005): 1–23

Bozeman, Adda, "The International Order in a Multicultural World," in Hedley Bull and Adam Watson (eds.), *The Expansion of International Society* (Oxford: Clarendon Press, 1984), 387–406

Branch, Jordan, *The Cartographic State: Maps, Territory, and the Origins of Sovereignty* (Cambridge: Cambridge University Press, 2014)

Brenner, Neil, and Elden, Stuart. "Henri Lefebvre on State, Space, Territory," *International Political Sociology* 3, no. 4 (2009): 353–77

Brett, Annabel S., *Changes of State: Nature and the Limits of the City in Early Modern Natural Law* (Princeton, NJ: Princeton University Press, 2011)

Brodie, Bernard (ed.), *The Absolute Weapon: Atomic Power and World Order* (New York: Harcourt, 1946)

"The Atom Bomb as Policy Maker," *Bulletin of the Atomic Scientists* 4, no. 12 (1948): 277–383

"The Development of Nuclear Strategy," *International Security* 2, no. 4 (1978): 65–83

Strategy in the Missile Age (Santa Monica, CA: RAND Corporation, 1959)

Brotton, Jerry, *Trading Territories: Mapping the Early Modern World* (Ithaca, NY: Cornell University Press, 1997)

Brown, Wendy, *Regulating Aversion: Tolerance in an Age of Identity and Empire* (Princeton, NJ: Princeton University Press, 2006)

Brunkhorst, Hauke, "The Right to War: Hegemonic Geopolitics or Civic Constitutionalism?," *Constellations* 11, no. 4 (2004): 512–26

Brunt, P. A., "Laus Imperii," in P. D. A. Garnsey and C. R. Whittaker (eds.), *Imperialism in the Ancient World* (Cambridge: Cambridge University Press, 1978), 160–92

Bryce, James, "The Relations of History and Geography," *Contemporary Review* 69 (1887), 426–43

Buchan, Bruce, "Enlightened Histories: Civilization, War and the Scottish Enlightenment," *European Legacy* 10, no. 2 (2005): 177–92

"Civilisation, Sovereignty and War: The Scottish Enlightenment and International Relations," *International Relations* 20, no. 2 (2006): 175–92

Bull, Hedley, "International Theory: The Case for a Classical Approach," *World Politics* 18, no. 3 (1966): 361–77

The Anarchical Society: A Study of Order in World Politics (London: Macmillan, 1977)

"The Emergence of a Universal International Society," in Hedley Bull and Adam Watson (eds.), *The Expansion of International Society* (Oxford: Clarendon Press, 1984), 117–26

"The Importance of Grotius and International Relations," in Hedley Bull, Benedict Kingsbury, and Adam Roberts (eds.), *Hugo Grotius and International Relations* (Oxford: Oxford University Press 1992), 65–93

Burckhardt, Jacob, *The Civilization of the Renaissance in Italy* [1860] (London: Phaidon Press, 1951)

Buisseret, David, "Monarchs, Ministers, and Maps in France before the Ascension of Louis XIV," in David Buisseret (ed.), *Monarchs, Ministers, and Maps: The Emergence of Cartography as a Tool of Government in Early Modern Europe* (Chicago: University of Chicago Press, 1992), 99–123

    "The Cartographic Definition of France's Eastern Boundary in the Early Seventeenth Century," *Imago Mundi* 36, no 1 (1984): 72–80

    The Mapmakers' Quest: Depicting New Worlds in Renaissance Europe (Oxford: Oxford University Press, 2003)

Burrow, John W., *Evolution and Society: A Study in Victorian Social Theory* (Cambridge: Cambridge University Press, 1966)

Butler, Judith, *Frames of War: When Is Life Grievable?* (London: Verso, 2009)

Buzan, Barry, *People, State and Fear: An Agenda for International Security Studies in the Post-Cold War Era* (Boulder, CO: Lynne Rienner, 1991)

Cadet, Félix, *Histoire de l'économie politique: les précurseurs Boisguilbert, Vauban, Quesnay, Turgot* (Paris: H. Gérard, 1869)

Carnegie, Andrew, "Letter to the Trustees," December 14, 1910

Cassini de Thury, César-François, *Description Géométrique de la France* (Paris: Desaint, 1783)

Church, William Farr, *Richelieu and Reason of State* (Princeton, NJ: Princeton University Press, 1972)

Clark, George, *War and Society in the 17th Century* (Cambridge: Cambridge University Press, 1958)

Cochran, Molly, *Normative Theory in International Relations: A Pragmatic Approach* (Cambridge: Cambridge University Press, 1999)

Coker, Christopher, *The Future of War: The Re-enchantment of War in the Twenty-First Century* (Oxford: Blackwell, 2004)

    Barbarous Philosophers: Reflections on the Nature of War from Heraclitus to Heisenberg (New York: Columbia University Press, 2010)

Collier, Paul, and Hoeffler, Anke, *The Challenge of Reducing the Global Incidence of Civil War* (Oxford: Centre for the Study of African Economies, Department of Economics, Oxford University, 2004)

Collingwood, Robin G, *An Autobiography* (Oxford: Oxford University Press, 1939)

Cosgrove, Denis, *Apollo's Eye: A Cartographic Genealogy of the Earth in the Western Imagination* (Baltimore: Johns Hopkins University Press, 2001)

"Globalism and Tolerance in Early Modern Geography," *Annals of the Association of American Geographers* 93, no. 4 (2003): 852–70

Costa Lopez, Julia, "Beyond Eurocentrism and Orientalism: Revisiting the Othering of Jews and Muslims through Medieval Canon Law," *Review of International Studies* 42, no. 3 (2016): 450–70

Courtilz de Sandras, Gatien, *Nouveaux Interets des Princes de L'Europe* (Cologne: Pierre Marteau, 1686)

Cox, Michael, "Empire, Imperialism, and the Bush Doctrine," *Review of International Studies* 30, no. 4 (2004): 585–608

Craig, Gordon A., "The Historian and the Study of International Relations," *American Historical Review* 88, no. 1 (1983): 1–11

Crawford, Neta, *Argument and Change in World Politics: Ethics, Decolonization, and Humanitarian Intervention* (Cambridge: Cambridge University Press, 2002)

Crook, Paul, *Darwinism, War and History: The Debate over the Biology of War from the "Origin of Species" to the First World War* (Cambridge: Cambridge University Press, 1994)

Croxton, Derek, "The Peace of Westphalia of 1648 and the Origins of Sovereignty," *International History Review* 21, no. 3 (1999): 569–91

da Mota, A. Teixeira, "Some Notes on the Organization of Hydrographical Services in Portugal before the Beginning of the Nineteenth Century," *Imago Mundi* 28 (1976): 51–60

Dann, Ernest W., *Historical Geography on a Regional Basis*, vol. II: *Europe* (London: Dent, 1908)

Darby, Henry Clifford, and Williams, Michael. *The Relations of History and Geography: Studies in England, France and the United States* (Exeter: University of Exeter Press, 2002)

D'Argenson, René Louis de Voyer de Paulmy, *Considérations sur le Gouvernement Ancient et Présent de la France* (Amsterdam: Reys, 1765)

Davidson, Donald, "Actions, Reasons, and Causes," *Journal of Philosophy* 60, no. 23 (1963): 685–700

Davidson, James, "The Gaze in Polybius' Histories," *Journal of Roman Studies* 81 (1991): 10–24

Davis, Kathleen, *Periodization and Sovereignty: How Ideas of Feudalism and Secularization Govern the Politics of Time* (Philadelphia: University of Pennsylvania Press, 2008)

D'Avity, Pierre, *Les Estats, Empires, Royaumes et Principautes du Monde* (Paris: Pierre Chevalier, 1625)

Debarbieux, Bernard, "La (M)montagne comme figure de la frontière: réflexions à partir de quelques cas," *Le Globe. Revue Genevoise de Géographie* 137 (1997): 145–66

de Bourcet, Pierre, *Principes de la Guerre de Montagnes* (Paris: Imprimerie Nationale, 1888)

de Cormontaigne, Louis, *Architecture Militaire, ou l'art de fortifier* (La Haye: Jean Neaulme & Adrien Moetjens, 1741)

de Fontenelle, Bernard Buyer, *Éloge de Monsieur le Maréchal de Vauban, Histoire de l'Académie Royale des Sciences* (Paris: Compagnie des Libraires, 1752)

de Jomini, Baron Antoine Henri, *The Art of War*, ed. and trans. G. H. Mendell and W. P. Craighill (Philadelphia: Lippincott, 1862)

Delbrück, Hans, *The Dawn of Modern Warfare*, trans. Walter Renfroe (Lincoln: University of Nebraska Press, 1990)

De la Croix, Horst, "Military Architecture and the Radial City Plan in Sixteenth Century Italy," *The Art Bulletin* 42, no. 4 (1960): 263–90

de Mably, Gabriel Bonnot, *Des Principes des Négociations, pour servir d'introduction au Droit Publique de l'europé, fondé sur les traités* (La Haye, 1757)

Derrida, Jacques, "Force of Law: The 'Mystical Foundation of Authority,'" in Drucilla Cornell, Michael Rosenfield, and David G. Carlson (eds.), *Deconstruction and the Possibility of Justice* (London: Routledge, 1992), 3–67

Devetak, Richard, "Law of Nations as Reason of State: Diplomacy and the Balance of Power in Vattel's Law of Nations," *Parergon* 28, no. 2 (2011): 105–28

"Historiographical Foundations of Modern International Thought: Histories of the European States-System from Florence to Göttingen," *History of European Ideas* 41, no. 1 (2015): 62–77

de Vattel, Emer, *The Law of Nations, or, Principles of the Law of Nature, Applied to the Conduct and Affairs of Nations and Sovereigns, with Three Early Essays on the Origin and Nature of Natural Law and on Luxury* [1758/1797], edited and with an introduction by Béla Kapossy and Richard Whatmore (Indianapolis: Liberty Fund, 2008)

de Vauban, Sebastién Prestre, "Observations a Faire sur la Reconnaissance des Places," in Eugène-Auguste-Albert de Rochas d'Aiglun, *Vauban. Sa famille et ses écrits: ses "Oisivetés" et sa Correspondance, analyse et extraits*, tome 1 (Paris: Berger-Levrault, 1910), 240–1

"Lettre sur la Manière de Faire les Statistiques," in Eugène-Auguste-Albert de Rochas d'Aiglun (ed.), *Vauban. Sa famille et ses écrits: ses "Oisivetés" et sa Correspondance, analyse et extraits*, tome 1 (Paris: Berger-Levrault, 1910), 590–5

"Relation du Voyage sur la Frontière Commence le 9 Avril 1698 et fini le 12 Fevrier 1699," in Eugène-Auguste-Albert de Rochas d'Aiglun (ed.),

Vauban. Sa famille et ses écrits: ses "Oisivetés" et sa Correspondance, analyse et extraits, tome 1 (Paris: Berger-Levrault, 1910), 603–12

Description Géographique de l'Élection de Vézelay, contenant ses revenus, sa qualité, les moeurs de ses habitants, leur pauvreté et richesse, la fertilité du pays et ce que l'on pourrait y faire pour en corriger la stérilité et procurer l'augmentation des peuples et l'accroissement des bestiaux, Janvier 1696, ed. Jean-Francois Pernot (Paris: Association des amis de la maison Vauban, 1986)

"de Vauban to Louvois, January 20, 1673," in Eugène-Auguste-Albert de Rochas d'Aiglun (ed.), *Vauban. Sa famille et ses écrits: ses "Oisivetés" et sa Correspondance, analyse et extraits*, tome 2 (Paris: Berger-Levrault, 1910)

Memorandum on the Places on the Flanders Frontier Which Must Be Fortified to Secure the Lands Owing Obedience to the King (November 1678), in Eugène-Auguste-Albert de Rochas d'Aiglun (ed.), *Vauban. Sa famille et ses écrits: ses "Oisivetés" et sa Correspondance, analyse et extraits* (Paris: Berger-Levrault, 1910), 189–92

"Places dont le Roi Pourrait se Défaire en Faveur d'un Traité de Paix Sans Faire Tort a l'État ni Affaiblir sa Frontière," in Eugène-Auguste-Albert de Rochas d'Aiglun (ed.), *Vauban. Sa famille et ses écrits: ses "Oisivetés" et sa Correspondance, analyse et extraits*, tome 1 (Paris: Berger-Levrault, 1910), 192–207

"Projet de Paix assez Raisonable Pour que Tous les Intéressez a La Guerre Présente, en deussent être contens, s'il avoit lieu et qu'il plut a Dieu d'y donner sa benediction" [1706], in Eugène-Auguste-Albert de Rochas d'Aiglun (ed.), *Vauban. Sa famille et ses écrits: ses "Oisivetés" et sa Correspondance, analyse et extraits*, tome 1 (Paris: Berger-Levrault, 1910), 496–532

"Intérets Present des États de la Chrétienté," in Eugène-Auguste-Albert de Rochas d'Aiglun (ed.), *Vauban. Sa famille et ses écrits: ses "Oisivetés" et sa Correspondance, analyse et extraits*, tome 1 (Paris: Berger-Levrault, 1910), 491–6

"Mémoire sur le Canal du Languedoc," in Eugène-Auguste-Albert de Rochas d'Aiglun (ed.), *Vauban. Sa famille et ses écrits: ses "Oisivetés" et sa Correspondance, analyse et extraits*, tome 1 (Paris: Berger-Levrault, 1910), 545–76

de Vitoria, Francisco, "On the Law of War," in Anthony Pagden and Jeremy Lawrance (eds.), *Vitoria: Political Writings* (Cambridge: Cambridge University Press, 1991)

de Vries, Kelly, "Warfare and the International System," in Frank Tallett and D. J. B. Trim (eds.), *European Warfare 1350–1750* (Cambridge: Cambridge University Press, 2010), 27–49

Dillon, Michael J., "Introduction: From Liberal Conscience to Liberal Rule," in Michael J. Dillon and Julian Reid (eds.), *The Liberal Way of War: Killing to Make Life Live* (London: Routledge, 2009), 1–13

Dobbins, James, Jones, Seth G., Crane, Keith, and Degrasse, Beth Cole, *The Beginner's Guide to Nation-Building* (Santa Monica, CA: RAND Corporation, 2007)

Doyle, Michael W., *Ways of War and Peace: Realism, Liberalism, and Socialism* (New York: Norton, 1997)

du Bellay, Martin, *Mémoires de messire Martin Du Bellay, in Choix de chroniques et mémoires sur l'histoire de France*, vol. 11, ed. J. A. C. Buchon (Paris: A. Desrez, 1836)

Duffy, Christopher, *The Fortress in the Age of Vauban and Frederick the Great: 1660–1789*, vol. 2 (London: Routledge Kegan Paul, 1985)

Edgerton, Samuel Y., *The Renaissance Rediscovery of Linear Perspective* (New York: Basic Books, 1975)

Edney, Matthew H., "Mathematical Cosmography and the Social Ideology of British Cartography, 1780–1820," *Imago Mundi* 46, no. 1 (1994): 101–16

"British Military Education, Mapmaking, and Military "Map-Mindedness" in the Later Enlightenment," *Cartographic Journal* 31, no. 1 (1994): 14–20

Mapping an Empire: The Geographical Construction of British India, 1765–1843 (Chicago: University of Chicago Press, 1997)

Ekstrand, Viktor, *Samlingar i Landtmäteri, första samlingen, instruktioner och bref, 1628–1699* (Stockholm: Isaac Marcus, 1901)

Elden, Stuart, *The Birth of Territory* (Chicago: University of Chicago Press, 2013)

"How Should We Do the History of Territory?," *Territory, Politics, Governance* 1, no. 1 (2013): 5–20

Engels, Friedrich, *Anti-Dühring* [1894], trans. Emile Burns (New York: International Publishers, 1966)

Ertman, Thomas, *Birth of the Leviathan: Building States and Regimes in Medieval and Early Modern Europe* (Cambridge: Cambridge University Press, 1997)

Escolar, Marcelo, "Exploration, Cartography and the Modernization of State Power," *International Social Science Journal* 49, no. 151 (1997): 55–75

Evans, Brad, "The Liberal War Thesis: Introducing the Ten Key Principles of Twenty-First-Century Biopolitical Warfare," *South Atlantic Quarterly* 110, no. 3 (2011): 747–56

Evans, Gareth, and Sahnoun, Mohamed, "The Responsibility to Protect," *Foreign Affairs* 81 (2002): 99–110

"From Humanitarian Intervention to the Responsibility to Protect," *Wisconsin International Law Journal* 24, no. 3 (2006): 703–22

Fabre, Cécile, *Cosmopolitan War* (Oxford: Oxford University Press, 2012)

"Cosmopolitanism, Just War Theory and Legitimate Authority," *International Affairs* 84, no. 5 (2008): 963–76

Fasolt, Constantin, *The Limits of History* (Chicago: University of Chicago Press, 2004)

Fearon, James D., and Laitin, David D., "Ethnicity, Insurgency, and Civil War," *American Political Science Review* 97, no. 1 (2003): 75–90

Ferguson, Adam, *An Essay on the History of Civil Society* (London: Millar & Cadell, 1767)

Ferguson, Michaele, "Unsocial Sociability: Perpetual Antagonism in Kant's Political Thought," in Elisabeth Ellis (ed.), *Kant's Political Theory: Interpretations and Applications* (University Park, PA: Pennsylvania State University Press, 2012), 150–69

Ferguson, Niall, *Colossus: The Rise and Fall of the American Empire* (New York: Penguin, 2004)

Finnemore, Martha, *The Purpose of Intervention: Changing Beliefs about the Use of Force* (Ithaca, NY: Cornell University Press, 2004)

Flint, Colin, "Introduction: Geography of War and Peace," in Colin Flint (ed.), *The Geography of War and Peace: From Death Camps to Diplomats* (Oxford: Oxford University Press, 2005), 1–15

Freeman, Edward A., *A Historical Geography of Europe*, vol. 1 (London: Longmans, Green, 1881)

Fogu, Claudio, and Kansteiner, Wulf, "The Politics of Memory and the Poetics of History," in Richard Ned Lebow, Wulf Kansteiner, and Claudio Fogu (eds.), *The Politics of Memory in Postwar Europe* (Durham, NC: Duke University Press, 2006), 284–310

Foucault, Michel, *Security, Territory, Population: Lectures at the Collège de France 1977–1978* (New York: Picador, 2007)

Society Must Be Defended (New York: Picador, 2003)

Fukuyama, Francis, *State-Building: Governance and World Order in the 21st Century* (Ithaca, NY: Cornell University Press, 2004)

Fukuyama, Francis, "The Imperative of State-Building," *Journal of Democracy* 15, no. 2 (2004): 17–31

Furet, Fraçois, and Ozouf, Mona, "Deux Légitimations Historiques de la Société Française au XVIIIe Siècle: Mably et Boulainvilliers," *Annales: Économies, Sociétés, Civilisations* 34, no. 3 (1979): 438–50

Gallie, W. B., *Philosophers of Peace and War: Kant, Clausewitz, Marx, Engles and Tolstoy* (Cambridge: Cambridge University Press, 1979)

Gat, Azar, *Military Thought in the Nineteenth Century* (Oxford: Oxford University Press, 1992)

A History of Military Thought: From the Enlightenment to the Cold War (Oxford: Oxford University Press, 2001)

War in Human Civilization (Oxford: Oxford University Press, 2006)

Gentili, Alberico, *De Jure Belli Libri Tres*, trans. John C. Rolfe (Oxford: Carnegie Endowment for International Peace, 1933)

George, Hereford B. *The Relations of Geography and History* (Oxford: Clarendon Press, 1901)

Gibbon, Edward, *The Decline and Fall of the Roman Empire*, vol. 1 (New York: Modern Library, n.d.)

Giddens, Anthony, *The Nation-State and Violence* (Berkeley: University of California Press, 1985)

Glanville, Luke, *Sovereignty and the Responsibility to Protect: A New History* (Chicago: University of Chicago Press, 2013)

Gobineau, Arthur de, *Essai sur l'Inegalité des Races Humaines* (Paris: Firmin Didot, 1853–5)

Godlewska, Anne, *Geography Unbound: French Geographic Science from Cassini to Humboldt* (Chicago: University of Chicago Press, 1999)

Goldsmith, Jack L., and Posner, Eric A., "Moral and Legal Rhetoric in International Relations: A Rational Choice Perspective," *Journal of Legal Studies* 31, no 1 (2002): 115–39

Goldsmith Jack L., and Posner, Eric A., *The Limits of International Law* (Oxford: Oxford University Press, 2005)

Gong Gerrit W., *The Standard of Civilization in International Society* (Oxford: Oxford University Press, 1984)

Goodman, Nelson, *Ways of Worldmaking* (Indianapolis: Hackett, 1978)

Greenfeld, Liah, *Nationalism: Five Roads to Modernity* (Cambridge, MA: Harvard University Press, 1992)

Greenwood, Christopher, "The Concept of War in Modern International Law," *International and Comparative Law Quarterly* 36, no. 2 (1987): 283–306

Greenwood, Ryan, "War and Sovereignty in Medieval Roman Law," *Law and History Review* 32, no. 1 (2014): 31–63

Grotius, Hugo, *Commentary on the Law of Prize and Booty*, trans. Gwladys L. Williams and W. H. Zeydel (Oxford: Clarendon Press, 1950)

The Rights of War and Peace, ed. Richard Tuck (Indianapolis: Liberty Fund, 2005)

Grove, Jairus Victor, "Becoming War: Ecology, Ethics, and the Globalization of Violence," Ph.D. dissertation, Johns Hopkins University, 2011

Gumplowicz, Ludwig, *Outlines of Sociology* [1885], trans. Frederick W. Moore (Philadelphia: American Academy of Political and Social Science, 1899)

Gunn, J. A. W., "'Interest Will Not Lie': A Seventeenth-Century Political Maxim," *Journal of the History of Ideas* 29, no. 4 (1968): 551–64

    Politics and the Public Interest in the Seventeenth Century (London: Routledge, 1969)

Gunn, Steven, "War and the Emergence of the State: Western Europe, 1350–1600," in Frank Tallett and D. J. B. Trim (eds.), *European Warfare 1350–1750* (Cambridge: Cambridge University Press, 2010), 50–73

Haakonssen, Knud, "Hugo Grotius and the History of Political Thought," *Political Theory* 13, no. 2 (1985): 239–65

Hacking, Ian, "The Looping Effects of Human Kinds," in Dan Sperber, David Premack, and Ann James Premack (eds.), *Causal Cognition: A Multi-Disciplinary Approach* (Oxford: Clarendon Press, 1995), 351–94

    Historical Ontology (Cambridge, MA: Harvard University Press, 2002)

Halas, Matus, "Searching for the Perfect Footnote: Friedrich Ratzel and the Others at the Roots of Lebensraum," *Geopolitics* 19, no. 1 (2014): 1–18

Hale, John, "Warfare and Cartography, ca. 1450 to ca. 1640," in David Woodward (ed.), *The History of Cartography*, vol. 3 (Chicago: University of Chicago Press, 2007), 719–37

Hall, W. E., *Treatise on International Law* (Oxford: Clarendon Press, 1890)

Hampton, Jean, "Hobbes's State of War," *Topoi* 4, no. 1 (1985): 47–60

Hardt, Michael, and Negri, Antonio, *Multitude: War and Democracy in the End of Empire* (New York: Penguin, 2004)

Harley, Brian J., "Silences and Secrecy: The Hidden Agenda of Cartography in Early Modern Europe," *Imago Mundi* 40, no. 1 (1988): 57–76

Harley, John, and Laxton, Paul, *The New Nature of Maps: Essays in the History of Cartography* (Baltimore: Johns Hopkins University Press, 2002)

Hassner, Pierre, "Beyond the Three Traditions: The Philosophy of War and Peace in Historical Perspective," *International Affairs* 70, no. 4 (1994): 737–56

Hatton, R. M., *Charles XII of Sweden* (London: Weidenfeld & Nicolson, 1968)

Havercroft, Jonathan, *Captives of Sovereignty* (Cambridge: Cambridge University Press, 2011)

Hawkins, Mike, *Social Darwinism in European and American Thought 1860–1945* (Cambridge: Cambridge University Press, 1997)

Headley, John, "The Sixteenth-Century Venetian Celebration of the Earth's Total Habitability: The Issue of the Fully Habitable World for Renaissance Europe," *Journal of World History* 8, no. 1 (1997): 1–27

    "Geography and Empire in the Late Renaissance: Botero's Assignment, Western Universalism, and the Civilizing Process," *Renaissance Quarterly* 53, no. 4 (2000): 1119–55

Heeren, Arnold, and Hermann, Ludwig, *A Manual of the History of the Political System of Europe and Its Colonies from Its Formation at the Close of the Fifteenth Century, to Its Reestablishment upon the Fall of Napoleon* (London: Henry G. Bohn, 1834)

Heffernan, Michael, "On Geography and Progress: Turgot's plan d'un ouvrage sur la géographie politique (1751) and the Origins of Modern Progressive Thought," *Political Geography* 13, no. 4 (1994): 328–43

Hegel, Georg, and Wilhelm, Friedrich, *Elements of the Philosophy of Right*, trans. H. B. Nisbet (Cambridge: Cambridge University Press, 1991)

Heidegger, Martin, "On the Grammar and Etymology of the Word 'Being,'" in *Introduction to Metaphysics*, trans. Ralph Mannheim (New Haven, CT: Yale University Press, 1959)

Helman, Gerald B., and Ratner, Steven R., "Saving Failed States," *Foreign Policy* 89 (1992): 3–20

Helmfrid, Staffan, "De geometriska jordeböckerna – 'skattläggningskartor,'" *YMER* 79, no. 3 (1959): 224–31

Herz, John H "Rise and Demise of the Territorial State," *World Politics* 9, no. 4 (1957): 473–93

Heuser, Beatrice, *The Evolution of Strategy: Thinking War from Antiquity to the Present* (Cambridge: Cambridge University Press, 2010)

Hill, Lisa, "Eighteenth-Century Anticipations of the Sociology of Conflict: The Case of Adam Ferguson," *Journal of the History of Ideas* 62, no. 2 (2001): 281–99

Hinsley, Francis Harry, *Power and the Pursuit of Peace: Theory and Practice in the History of Relations between States* (Cambridge: Cambridge University Press, 1967)

Hirschi, Caspar, *The Origins of Nationalism: An Alternative History from Ancient Rome to Early Modern Germany* (Cambridge: Cambridge University Press, 2012)

Hirschman, Albert O., *The Passions and the Interests: Political Arguments for Capitalism before Its Triumph* (Princeton, NJ: Princeton University Press, 1977)

Hobbes, Thomas, *De Cive or the Citizen* (New York: Appleton-Century -Crofts, 1949)

    The Elements of Law Natural and Politic, ed. Maurice Goldsmith (London: Frank Cass, 1969)

    Leviathan, ed. Richard Tuck (Cambridge: Cambridge University Press, 1991)

Hoffmann, Stanley, "Rousseau on War and Peace," in ed. Stanley Hoffmann, *The State of War: Essays on the Theory and Practice of International Politics* (New York: Praeger, 1965), 54–87

"An American Social Science: International Relations," *Daedalus* 106, no. 3 (1977): 41–60

Hofstadter, Richard, *Social Darwinism in American Thought* (Boston: Beacon Press, 1992)

Holland, Ben, *The Moral Person of the State: Pufendorf, Sovereignty and Composite Polities* (Cambridge: Cambridge University Press, 2017)

Holland, Thomas Erskine, *The Elements of Jurisprudence* [1880] (Oxford: Clarendon Press, 1916)

Holsti, Kalevi J., *The State, War, and the State of War* (Cambridge: Cambridge University Press, 1996)

Hont, Istvan, *Jealousy of Trade: International Competition and the Nation-State in Historical Perspective* (Cambridge, MA: Harvard University Press, 2005)

Howard, Michael (ed.), *Restraints on War: Studies in the Limitation of Armed Conflict* (Oxford: Oxford University Press, 1979)

   The Invention of Peace: Reflections on War and International Order (New Haven, CT: Yale University Press, 2000)

Hume, David, "On the Origin of Government," in *Essays* (Indianapolis: Liberty Fund, 1987)

   "Jealousy of Trade" [1742], in *Essays* (Indianapolis: Liberty Fund, 1987)

Hunt, Lynn, "The French Revolution in Global Context," in David Armitage and Sanjay Subrahmanyam (eds.), *The Age of Revolutions in a Global Context, c. 1760–1840* (Basingstoke: Palgrave Macmillan, 2010), 20–36

Hunter, Ian, "Vattel's Law of Nations: Diplomatic Casuistry for the Protestant Nation," *Grotiana* 31, no. 1 (2010): 108–40

Hurrell, Andrew, "Pax Americana or the Empire of Insecurity," *International Relations of the Asia-Pacific* 5, no. 2 (2005): 153–76

Huysmans, Jef, "International Politics of Exception: Competing Visions of International Political Order between Law and Politics," *Alternatives* 31, no. 2 (2006): 135–65

Höpfl, Harro, and Thompson, Martyn P., "The History of Contract as a Motif in Political Thought," *American Historical Review* 84, no. 4 (1979): 919–44

Hörnqvist, Mikael, "Machiavelli's Three Desires: Florentine Republicans on Liberty, Empire, and Justice," in Sankar Muthu (ed.), *Empire and Modern Political Thought* (Cambridge: Cambridge University Press, 2012), 7–29.

Ish-Shalom, Piki, *Democratic Peace: A Political Biography* (Ann Arbor: University of Michigan Press, 2013)

Jabri, Vivienne, "War, Security and the Liberal State," *Security Dialogue* 37, no. 1 (2006): 47–64

War and the Transformation of Global Politics (Basingstoke: Palgrave Macmillan, 2007)

Jackson, Robert H., "Quasi-States, Dual Regimes, and Neoclassical Theory: International Jurisprudence and the Third World," *International Organization* 41, no. 4 (1987): 519–49

Jackson, Robert H., and Rosberg, Carl G., "Why Africa's Weak States Persist: The Empirical and the Juridical in Statehood," *World Politics* 35, no. 1 (1982): 1–24

Jacob, Christian, *The Sovereign Map: Theoretical Approaches in Cartography throughout History* (Chicago: University of Chicago Press, 2006)

Jahn, Beate, "IR and the State of Nature: The Cultural Origins of a Ruling Ideology," *Review of International Studies* 25, no. 3 (1999): 411–34

"Kant, Mill and Illiberal Legacies in International Affairs," *International Organization* 59, no. 1 (2005): 177–207

Janssen, Wilhelm, "Krieg," in *Geschichtliche Grundbegriffe: Historisches Lexikon zur politisch-sozialen Sprache in Deutschland*, vol. III (Stuttgart: Klett-Cotta, 1982), 567–615

Jennings, Ronald C., "Sovereignty and Political Modernity: A Genealogy of Agamben's Critique of Sovereignty," *Anthropological Theory* 11, no. 1 (2011): 23–61

Joas, Hans, and Knöbl, Wolfgang, *War in Social Thought: Hobbes to the Present* (Princeton, NJ: Princeton University Press, 2013)

Johannesson, Kurt, *Saxo Grammaticus: Komposition och världsbild i Gesta Danorum* (Stockholm: Almqvist & Wiksell International, 1978)

Johnson, James Turner, *Just War Tradition and the Restraint of War: A Moral and Historical Inquiry* (Princeton, NJ: Princeton University Press, 1981)

Johnston, David, *The Rhetoric of Leviathan: Thomas Hobbes and the Politics of Cultural Transformation* (Princeton, NJ: Princeton University Press, 1986)

Kagan, Robert, *Paradise and Power: America and Europe in the New World Order* (New York, Knopf, 2003)

Kahn, Charles H., *The Art and Thought of Heraclitus: A New Arrangement and Translation of the Fragments with Literary and Philosophical Commentary* (Cambridge: Cambridge University Press, 1981)

Kain, Roger J. P., and Baigent, Elizabeth, *The Cadastral Map in the Service of the State: A History of Property Mapping* (Chicago: University of Chicago Press, 1992)

Kaldor, Mary, *New and Old Wars: Organized Violence in a Global Era* (Oxford: Polity Press, 1999).

"Cosmopolitanism and Organized Violence," in Steven Vertovec and Robin Cohen (eds.), *Conceiving Cosmopolitanism: Theory, Context, and Practice* (Oxford: Oxford University Press, 2002), 268–78

Kalyvas, Andreas, and Katznelson, Ira, "Adam Ferguson Returns: Liberalism through a Glass, Darkly," *Political Theory* 26, no. 2 (1998): 173–97

Kalyvas, Stathis, "New and Old Civil Wars," *World Politics* 54, no. 1 (2001): 99–118

"The Ontology of 'Political Violence': Action and Identity in Civil Wars," *Perspectives on Politics* 1, no. 3 (2003): 475–94

Kant, Immanuel, "Idea for a Universal History with a Cosmopolitan Purpose," in Hans Reiss (ed.), *Kant: Political Writings* (Cambridge: Cambridge University Press, 1991), 41–53

Kavka, Gregory S., "Hobbes's War of All against All," *Ethics* 93, no. 2 (1983): 291–310

Keene, Edward, *Beyond the Anarchical Society: Grotius, Colonialism, and Order in World Politics* (Cambridge: Cambridge University Press, 2002)

Kelley, Donald R., *Foundations of Modern Historical Scholarship: Language, Law, and History in the French Renaissance* (New York: Columbia University Press, 1970)

"The Old Cultural History," *History of the Human Sciences* 9, no. 3 (1996): 101–26

Kennedy, David, "Primitive Legal Scholarship," *Harvard Journal of International Law* 27, no. 1 (1986): 1–98

Of Law and War (Princeton, NJ: Princeton University Press, 2006)

A World of Struggle: How Power, Law and Expertise Shape the Global Political Economy (Princeton, NJ: Princeton University Press, 2016)

Keohane, Robert O., "Political Authority after Interventions: Gradations in Sovereignty," in Jeff L. Holzgrefe and Robert O. Keohane (eds.), *Humanitarian Intervention: Ethical, Legal and Political Dilemmas* (Cambridge: Cambridge University Press, 2003), 275–98

Kessler, Oliver, and Werner, Wouter G., "Extrajudicial Killing as Risk Management," *Security Dialogue* 39, nos. 2–3 (2008): 289–308

Kingsbury, Benedict, "Grotian Tradition of Theory and Practice: Grotius, Law, and Moral Skepticism in the Thought of Hedley Bull," *Quinnipiac Law Review* 17, no. 3 (1997): 3–33

"Confronting Difference: The Puzzling Durability of Gentili's Combination of Pragmatic Pluralism and Normative Judgment," *American Journal of International Law* 92, no. 1 (1998): 713–23

Kingsbury, Benedict, and Straumann, Benjamin, "The State of Nature and Commercial Sociability in Early Modern International Legal Thought," *Grotiana* 31, no. 1 (2010): 22–43

Kirk, Geoffrey Stephen, "Natural Change in Heraclitus," *Mind* 60, no. 237 (1951): 35–42

Koeman, Cornelis, and van Egmond, Marco, "Surveying and Official Mapping in the Low Countries, 1500–ca. 1670," in David Woodward (ed.), The History of Cartography, vol. 3, part II (Chicago: University of Chicago Press, 1996), 1246–94

Konvitz, Josef W., *Cartography in France, 1660–1848: Science, Engineering, and Statecraft* (Chicago: University of Chicago Press, 1987)

"The Nation-State, Paris and Cartography in Eighteenth- and Nineteenth-Century France," *Journal of Historical Geography* 16, no. 1 (1990): 3–16

Koselleck, Reinhart, *Futures Past: On the Semantics of Historical Time* (Cambridge, MA: MIT Press, 1985)

The Practice of Conceptual History: Timing History, Spacing Concepts (Redwood City, CA: Stanford University Press, 2002)

Koskenniemi, Martti, "International Law as Political Theology: How to Read *Nomos der Erde?*," *Constellations* 11 (2004): 492–511

"Into Positivism: Georg Friedrich von Martens (1756–1821) and Modern International Law," *Constellations* 15, no. 2 (2008): 189–207

"International Law and Raison d'État: Rethinking the Prehistory of International Law," in Benedict Kingsbury and Benjamin Straumann (eds.), *The Roman Foundations of the Law of Nations: Alberico Gentili and the Justice of Empire* (Oxford: Oxford University Press, 2010), 297–339

"Empire and International Law: The Real Spanish Contribution," *University of Toronto Law Journal* 61, no. 1 (2011): 1–36

The Gentle Civilizer of Nations: The Rise and Fall of International Law 1870–1960 (Cambridge: Cambridge University Press, 2001)

Knox, Robert, *Races of Men: A Fragment* (Philadelphia: Lea & Blanchard, 1850)

Krasner, Stephen D., "Sharing Sovereignty: New Institutions for Collapsed and Failing States," *International Security* 29, no. 2 (2004): 85–120

Krieger, Leonard, "History and Law in the Seventeenth Century: Pufendorf," *Journal of the History of Ideas* 21, no. 2 (1960): 198–210

Langins, Janis, *Conserving the Enlightenment: French Military Engineering from Vauban to the Revolution* (Cambridge, MA: MIT Press, 2004)

Lasson, Adolf, *Princip und Zukunft des Völkerrechts* (Berlin: Wilhelm Hertz, 1871)

Lauterpacht, Hersch, "The Grotian Tradition in International Law," *British Yearbook of International Law* 23, no. 1 (1946): 1–53

Lawrence, Thomas Joseph, "The Evolution of Peace," in *Essays on Some Disputed Questions of International Law* (Cambridge: Deighton, Bel & Co., 1885), 234–77

The Principles of International Law [1894] (Boston: D.C. Heath, 1900)
Le Bon, Gustave, *L'Homme et les Sociétés: leurs orgines at leur histoire*, vol. II (Paris: Rotschild, 1881)
The Psychology of Socialism (New York: Macmillan, 1899)
Lebow, Richard Ned, "Constitutive Causality: Imagined Spaces and Political Practices," *Millennium* 38, no. 2 (2009): 211–39
Lefebvre, Henri, *The Production the Space* (Oxford: Blackwell, 1991)
Lesaffer, Randall, "The Grotian Tradition Revisited: Change and Continuity in the History of International Law," *British Yearbook of International Law* 73, no. 1 (2003), 103–39
"Defensive Warfare, Prevention and Hegemony: The Justifications for the Franco-Spanish War of 1635," parts I and II, *Journal of the History of International Law* 8, nos. 1 and 2 (2006): 91–123, 141–79
"The Classical Law of Nations (1500–1800)," in Alexander Orakhelashvili (ed.), *Research Handbook on the Theory and History of International Law* (Cheltenham: Elgar, 2011), 408–40
Lestringant, Frank, *Mapping the Renaissance World: The Geographical Imagination in the Age of Discovery* (Cambridge: Polity Press, 1994)
Lieber, Francis, *Fragments on Political Science on Nationalism and Inter-Nationalism* (New York: Schribner, 1868)
Livy, Titus, *History of Rome*, vol. I, trans. Rev. Canon Roberts (New York: E.P. Dutton, 1912)
Lloyd, Henry, "Reflections on the General Principles of War; and on the Composition and Characters of the Different Armies in Europe," in *Continuation of the History of the Late War in Germany between the King of Prussia and the Empress of Germany and Her Allies* (London: Hooper, 1781)
Lorimer, James, "La doctrine de la reconnaissance, fondement du droit international," *Revue de Droit International et de Législation Comparée* 16 (1884): 335–59
Luke, Tim, and Tuathail, Gearóid Ó, "The Spatiality of War, Speed and Vision in the Work of Paul Virilio," in Mike Crang and Nigel Thrift (eds.), *Thinking Space* (London: Routledge, 2000), 360–79
Machiavelli, Niccolò, *The Art of War*, trans. Christopher Lynch (Chicago: University of Chicago Press, 2003)
Mackinder, Halford J., "On the Scope and Methods of Geography," *Proceedings of the Royal Geographical Society*, no. 3 (1887), 141–74
"The Geographical Pivot of History," *Geographical Journal* 23, no. 4 (1904): 421–44
Maguire, T. Miller, *Outlines of Military Geography* (Cambridge: Cambridge University Press, 1899)

Maier, Charles S., *Once within Borders: Territories of Power, Wealth, and Belonging since 1500* (Cambridge, MA: Harvard University Press, 2016)

Maine, Henry Sumner, *International Law: A Series of Lectures Delivered before the University of Cambridge* (London: John Murray, 1888)

Malcolm, Noel, *Reason of State, Propaganda, and the Thirty Years' War. An Unknown Translation by Thomas Hobbes* (Oxford: Clarendon Press, 2007)

"Alberico Gentili and the Ottomans," in Benedict Kingsbury and Benjamin Straumann (eds.), *The Roman Foundations of the Law of Nations: Alberico Gentili and the Justice of Empire* (Oxford: Oxford University Press, 2010), 127–45

Malmvig, Helle, *State Sovereignty and Intervention: A Discourse Analysis of Interventionary and Non-interventionary Practices in Kosovo and Algeria* (London: Routledge, 2006)

Mantena, Karuna, *Alibis of Empire: Henry Maine and the Ends of Liberal Imperialism* (Princeton, NJ: Princeton University Press, 2010)

Manual of Military Law (London: War Office, 1914)

Marx, Karl, "The Revolt in the Indian Army," *New York Daily Tribune*, July 15, 1857

Grundrisse: Foundations of the Critique of Political Economy [1859], trans. S. W. Ryazanskaya (Moscow: Progress Publishers, 1964)

Massumi, Brian, *Ontopower: War, Powers, and the State of Perception* (Durham, NC: Duke University Press, 2015)

Mastnak, Tomaz, *Crusading Peace: Christendom, The Muslim World, and Western Political Order* (Berkeley: University of California Press, 2002)

May, Larry (ed.), *War: Essays in Political Philosophy* (Cambridge: Cambridge University Press, 2008)

McCarthy, Thomas, "On Reconciling Cosmopolitan Unity and National Diversity," *Public Culture* 11, no. 1 (1999): 175–208

McCormick, Ted, *William Petty and the Ambitions of Political Arithmetic* (Oxford: Oxford University Press, 2009)

McDaniel, Iain, *Adam Ferguson in the Scottish Enlightenment: The Roman Past and Europe's Future* (Cambridge, MA: Harvard University Press, 2013)

McMahan, Jeff, *Killing in War* (Oxford: Oxford University Press, 2009)

Mégret, Frédéric, "From 'Savages' to 'Unlawful Combatants': A Postcolonial Look at International Humanitarian Law's 'Other,'" in Anne Orford (ed.), *International Law and Its Others* (Cambridge: Cambridge University Press, 2006), 265–317

Mehta, Uday Singh, *Liberalism and Empire: A Study in Nineteenth-Century British Liberal Thought* (Chicago: University of Chicago Press, 1999)

Meinecke, Friedrich, *Machiavellism: The Doctrine of Raison d'État and Its Place in Modern History*, trans. Douglas Scott (New Haven, CT: Yale University Press 1962)

Migdal, Joel S., *Strong Societies and Weak States: State-Society Relations and State Capabilities in the Third World* (Princeton, NJ: Princeton University Press, 1988)

Milliken, Jennifer, and Krause, Keith, "State Failure, State Collapse, and State Reconstruction: Concepts, Lessons and Strategies," *Development and Change* 33, no. 5 (2002): 753–74

Moloney, Pat, "Hobbes, Savagery, and International Anarchy," *American Political Science Review* 105, no. 1 (2011): 189–204

Montecuccoli, Raimundo, *Mémoires* (Paris: Muzier, 1712)

Morefield, Jeanne, *Covenants without Swords: Liberal Idealism and the Spirit of Empire* (Princeton, NJ: Princeton University Press, 2005)

  Empires without Imperialism: Anglo-American Decline and the Politics of Deflection (Oxford: Oxford University Press, 2014)

Morgenthau, Hans J., "Public Affairs: Death in the Nuclear Age," *Commentary* 32, no. 3 (1961), 233

  Politics among Nations: The Struggle for Power and Peace (New York: Knopf, 1985)

Mouffe, Chantal, *The Return of the Political* (London: Verso, 1993)

  The Democratic Paradox (London: Verso: 2000).

Mueller, John, *Retreat from Doomsday: The Obsolescence of Major War* (New York: Basic Books, 1990)

  "Changing Attitudes towards War: The Impact of the First World War," *British Journal of Political Science* 21, no. 1 (1991): 1–28

Mukerji, Chandra, *Impossible Engineering: Technology and Territoriality on the Canal du Midi* (Princeton, NJ: Princeton University Press, 2009)

  "The Territorial State as a Figured World of Power: Strategics, Logistics, and Impersonal Rule," *Sociological Theory* 28, no. 4 (2010): 402–24

Muldoon, James, *Popes, Lawyers, and Infidels: The Church and the Non-Christian World 1250–1550* (Liverpool: Liverpool University Press, 1979)

Müller, Jan-Werner (ed.), *Memory and Power in Post-War Europe* (Cambridge: Cambridge University Press, 2002)

  "On Conceptual History," in Darrin M. McMahon and Samuel Moyn (eds.), *Rethinking Modern European Intellectual History* (Oxford: Oxford University Press, 2014), 74–93.

Murphy, Alexander B., "The Sovereign State System as Political-Territorial Idea: Historical and Contemporary Considerations," in Thomas J. Biersteker and Cynthia Weber (eds.), *State Sovereignty as Social Construct* (Cambridge: Cambridge University Press), 81–120

Muthu, Sankar, *Enlightenment against Empire* (Princeton, NJ: Princeton University Press, 2003)

Nabulsi, Karma *Traditions of War: Occupation, Resistance, and the Law* (Oxford: Oxford University Press, 1999)

Nakhimovsky, Isaac, "Vattel's Theory of the International Order: Commerce and the Balance of Power in the Law of Nations," *History of European Ideas* 33, no. 2 (2007): 157–73

Napoleoni, Loretta, *The Islamist Phoenix* (New York: Seven Stories Press, 2014)

Neff, Stephen C., *War and the Law of Nations: A General History* (Cambridge: Cambridge University Press, 2005)

   Justice among Nations (Cambridge, MA: Harvard University Press, 2014)

Neocleous, Mark, "Off the Map: On Violence and Cartography," *European Journal of Social Theory* 6, no. 4 (2003): 409–25

Nichols, Robert Lee, "Realizing the Social Contract: The Case of Colonialism and Indigenous Peoples," *Contemporary Political Theory* 4, no. 1 (2005): 42–62

Nietzsche, Friedrich, *On the Genealogy of Morality*, trans. Carol Diethe (Cambridge: Cambridge University Press, 2006)

Nordin, Astrid H. M., and Öberg, Dan, "Targeting the Ontology of War: From Clausewitz to Baudrillard," *Millennium: Journal of International Studies* 43, no. 2 (2015): 392–410

Nordman, Daniel, "Des Limites d'État aux Frontières Nationales," in Pierre Nora (ed.), *Les Lieux de Memoire*, vol. II, *La Nation* (Paris: Gallimard, 1997), 1125–46

Normand, Roger, and af Jochnick, Chris, "The Legitimation of Violence: A Critical History of the Laws of War," *Harvard International Law Journal* 35, no. 1 (1994): 49–95

Ogilby, John, *Britannia, or, an Illustration of the Kingdom of England and Dominion of Wales* (London: author, 1675)

Onuf, Nicholas Greenwood, *The Republican Legacy in International Thought* (Cambridge: Cambridge University Press, 1998)

Onuf, Peter S., and Onuf, Nicholas Greenwood, *Federal Union, Modern World: The Law of Nations in an Age of Revolutions, 1776–1814* (Madison, WI: Madison House, 1993)

Orford, Anne, *International Law and Its Others* (Cambridge: Cambridge University Press, 2006)

   International Authority and the Responsibility to Protect (Cambridge: Cambridge University Press, 2011)

   "Scientific Reason and the Discipline of International Law," *European Journal of International Law* 25, no. 2 (2014): 369–85

Osiander, Andreas, "Rereading Early Twentieth-Century IR Theory: Idealism Revisited," *International Studies Quarterly* 42, no. 3 (1998): 409–32

"Sovereignty, International Relations, and the Westphalian Myth," *International Organization* 55, no. 2 (2001): 251–87

Pagden, Anthony, *Lords of All the World: Ideologies of Empire in Spain, Britain and France c. 1500–c. 1850* (New Haven, CT: Yale University Press, 1995)

Palladini, Fiammetta, "Pufendorf Disciple of Hobbes: The Nature of Man and the State of Nature – The Doctrine of Socialitas," *History of European Ideas* 34, no. 1 (2008): 26–60

Panizza, Diego, "Political Theory and Jurisprudence in Gentili's *De Iure Belli*: The Great Debate between 'Theological' and 'Humanist' Perspectives from Vitoria to Grotius," *International Law and Justice Working Papers* 15/5 (2005)

Paris, Roland, *At War's End: Building Peace after Civil Conflict* (Cambridge: Cambridge University Press, 2004)

Parker, Geoffrey, "Maps and Ministers: The Spanish Habsburgs," in David Buisseret (ed.), *Monarchs, Ministers, and Maps: The Emergence of Cartography as a Tool of Government in Early Modern Europe* (Chicago: University of Chicago Press, 1992), 124–52

Parry, John T., "What Is the Grotian Tradition in International Law?," *University of Pennsylvania Journal of International Law* 35, no. 2 (2014): 299–377

Patterson, David S., "Andrew Carnegie's Quest for World Peace," *Proceedings of the American Philosophical Society* (1970): 371–83

Pearson, Karl, *National Life from the Standpoint of Science* [1900] (London: Adam & Charles Black, 1901)

Pedley, Mary, "Map Wars: The Role of Maps in the Nova Scotia/Acadia Boundary Disputes of 1750," *Imago Mundi* 50, no. 1 (1998): 96–104

Pelletier, Monique, "Cartography and Power in France during the Seventeenth and Eighteenth Centuries," *Cartographica: The International Journal for Geographic Information and Geovisualization* 35, nos. 3–4 (1998): 41–53

Petito, Fabio, "Against World Unity: Carl Schmitt and the Western-Centric and Liberal Global Order," in Louiza Odysseos and Fabio Petito (eds.), *The International Political Thought of Carl Schmitt: Terror, Liberal War and the Crisis of Global Order* (London: Routledge, 2007), 166–84

Petto, Christine, *Mapping and Charting in Early Modern England and France: Power, Patronage, and Production* (Lanham, MD: Lexington Books, 2015)

Piirimäe, Pärtel, "Politics and History: An Unholy Alliance? Samuel Pufendorf as Official Historiographer," in M. Engelbrecht, U. Hanssen-Decker, and D. Höffker (eds.), *Rund um die Meere des Nordens. Festschrift für Hain Rebas* (Heyde: Boyens Buchverlag, 2008), 237–52

"Alberico Gentili's Doctrine of Defensive War and Its Impact on Seventeenth-Century Normative Views," in Benedict Kingsbury and Benjamin Straumann (eds.), *The Roman Foundations of the Law of Nations: Alberico Gentili and the Justice of Empire* (Oxford: Oxford University Press, 2010), 187–209

Pitts, Jennifer, *A Turn to Empire: The Rise of Imperial Liberalism in Britain and France* (Princeton, NJ: Princeton University Press, 2005)

Pocock, J. G. A., *The Machiavellian Moment: Florentine Political Thought and the Atlantic Republican Tradition* (Princeton, NJ: Princeton University Press, 1975)

The Ancient Constitution and the Feudal Law: A Study of English Historical Thought in the Seventeenth Century (Cambridge: Cambridge University Press, 1987)

Barbarism and Religion, Vol. II. *Narratives of Civil Government* (Cambridge: Cambridge University Press, 1999)

Polsybius, *Histories*, vol. I, trans. W. R. Paton (Cambridge, MA: LOEB Classical Library, 2010)

Rahmatian, Andreas, "Friedrich Carl von Savigny's *Beruf and Volksgeistlehre*," *Journal of Legal History* 28, no. 1 (2007): 1–29

Ramsay, W. M., *The Historical Geography of Asia Minor* (London: John Murray, 1890)

Ramsbotham, Oliver, and Woodhouse, Tom, *Humanitarian Intervention in Contemporary Conflict* (Cambridge: Polity Press, 1996)

Rapoport, Anatol, "Introduction," in Carl von Clausewitz, *On War* (Harmondsworth: Penguin, 1984), 11–80

Rasch, William, *Sovereignty and Its Discontents: On the Primacy of Conflict and the Structure of the Political* (London: Birkbeck Law Press, 2004)

Rasmussen, Mikkel Vedby, *Risk Society at War* (Cambridge: Cambridge University Press, 2006)

Ratzel, Friedrich, *The History of Mankind*, vol. 1 [1885], trans. A. J. Butler (London: Macmillan 1896)

"Studies in Political Areas. I. The Political Territory in Relation to Earth and Continent," *American Journal of Sociology* 3, no. 3 (1897): 297–313

"Studies in Political Areas. II. Intellectual, Political, and Economic Effects of Large Areas," *American Journal of Sociology* 3, no. 4 (1898): 449–63

Reichberg, Gregory M., "Preventive War in Classical Just War Theory," *Journal of the History of International Law* 9, no. 1 (2007): 5–34

"Just War and Regular War: Competing Paradigms," in David Rodin and Henry Shue (eds.), *Just and Unjust Warriors: Moral Equality on the Battlefield* (Oxford: Oxford University Press, 2008), 193–213

Rengger, Nicholas, *Just War and International Order: The Uncivil Condition in World Politics* (Cambridge: Cambridge University Press, 2013)

Rennell, James, "Letter to the Court of Directors, March 30, 1767," in *The Journals of Major James Rennell, First Surveyor-General of India, Written for the Information of the Governors of Bengal during His Surveys of the Ganges and Brahmaputra Rivers 1764 to 1767* (Calcutta: The Asiatic Society, 1910)

Memoir of a Map of Hindoostan or the Mogul Empire (London, 1788)

Rich, John, and Shipley, Graham (eds.), *War and Society in the Roman World* (London: Routledge, 1993)

Robertson, William, *The History of the Reign of the Emperor Charles V, with a View of the Progress of Society in Europe, from the Subversion of the Roman Empire to the Beginning of the Sixteenth Century*, vol. I [1769] (London: Routledge, 1857)

Rohan, Henri Duc de, *De l'Interest des Princes et Estats de la Chrestienté* (Paris: Augustin Courbé, 1643)

Ross, Dorothy, *The Origins of American Social Science* (Cambridge: Cambridge University Press, 1992)

Rotberg, Robert I., "The New Nature of Nation-State Failure," *Washington Quarterly* 25, no. 3 (2002): 83–96

Rousseau, Jean-Jacques, "L'État de Guerre," in Jean Jacques Rousseau, *The Political Writings of Jean Jacques Rousseau*, vol. I, ed. by C. E. Vaughan (Cambridge: Cambridge University Press, 1915), 293–307

"Discourse on the Origin of Inequality," in Jean-Jacques Rousseau, *The Social Contract and Discourses*, trans. G. D. H. Cole (London: Dent, 1990)

Rousset, Jean, *Les Interets Presens des Puissances de l'Europe* (La Haye, 1734)

Rubiés, Joan-Pau, "Hugo Grotius's Dissertation on the Origin of the American Peoples and the Use of Comparative Methods," *Journal of the History of Ideas* 52, no. 2 (1991): 221–44

"Oriental Despotism and European Orientalism: Botero to Montesquieu," *Journal of Early Modern History* 9, nos. 1–2 (2005): 109–80

Ruggie, John Gerard, "Territoriality and Beyond: Problematizing Modernity in International Relations," *International Organization* 47, no. 1 (1993): 139–74

Sahlins, Peter, "Natural Frontiers Revisited: France's Boundaries since the Seventeenth Century," *American Historical Review* 95, no. 5 (1990): 1423–51

Sassen, Saskia, *Territory, Authority, Rights: From Medieval to Global Assemblages* (Princeton, NJ: Princeton University Press, 2006)

Schiffman, Zachary Sayre, "An Anatomy of the Historical Revolution in Renaissance France," *Renaissance Quarterly* 42, no. 3 (1989): 507–33

Schmidt, Brian C, *The Political Discourse of Anarchy: A Disciplinary History of International Relations* (Albany, NY: SUNY Press, 1998)

"On the History and Historiography of International Relations," in Walter Calsnaes, Thomas Risse, and Beth Simmons (eds.), *Handbook of International Relations* (London: SAGE, 2002), 3–22

Schmitt, Carl, *The Nomos of the Earth in the International Law of the Jus Publicum Europaeum* (New York: Telos Press, 2006)

The Concept of the Political [1927] (Chicago: University of Chicago Press, 2008)

"The Turn to the Discriminating Concept of War" [1937], in Carl Schmitt, *Writings on War*, trans. Timothy Nunan (Cambridge: Polity Press, 2011), 30–74

Schröder, Peter, "Taming the Fox and the Lion: Some Aspects of the Sixteenth Century's Debate on Inter-State Relations," in Olaf Asbach and Peter Schröder (eds.), *War: The State, and International Law in the Seventeenth Century* (Farnham: Ashgate, 2010), 83–102

"Vitoria, Gentili, Bodin: Sovereignty and the Law of Nations," in Benedict Kingsbury and Benjamin Straumann (eds.), *The Roman Foundations of the Law of Nations: Alberico Gentili and the Justice of Empire* (Oxford: Oxford University Press, 2010), 163–86

Seaberg, R. B., "The Norman Conquest and the Common Law: The Levellers and the Argument from Continuity," *Historical Journal* 24, no. 4 (1981): 791–806

Seybolt, Taylor B., *Humanitarian Military Intervention: The Conditions of Success and Failure* (Oxford: Oxford University Press, 2008)

Shah, Nisha, "The Territorial Trap of the Territorial Trap: Global Transformation and the Problem of the State's Two Territories," *International Political Sociology* 6, no. 1 (2012): 57–76

Shapcott, Richard, *Justice, Community and Dialogue in International Relations* (Cambridge: Cambridge University Press, 2001)

Silvestrini, Gabriella, "Justice, War and Inequality: The Unjust Aggressor and the Enemy of the Human Race in Vattel's Theory of the Law of Nations," *Grotiana* 31, no. 1 (2010): 44–68

Skinner, Quentin, *The Foundations of Modern Political Thought* (Cambridge: Cambridge University Press, 1978)

Reason and Rhetoric in the Philosophy of Hobbes (Cambridge: Cambridge University Press, 1996)

"A Genealogy of the Modern State," in *Proceedings of the British Academy* 162 (2009): 325–70

Slomp, Gabriella, "Carl Schmitt's Five Arguments against the Idea of Just War," *Cambridge Review of International Affairs* 19, no. 3 (2006): 435–47

Sloterdijk, Peter, "Geometry in the Colossal: The Project of Metaphysical Globalization," *Environment and Planning D: Society and Space* 27 (2009): 29–40

Globes, Spheres, vol. II: *Macrospherology* (Los Angeles: Semiotext(e), 2014)

Smith, Adam, *An Inquiry into the Nature and Causes of the Wealth of Nations* [1776], ed. Edwin Cannan (London: Methuen & Co., 1904)

Smith, Craig, "We Have Mingled Politeness with the 'Use of the Sword': Nature and Civilisation in Adam Ferguson's Philosophy of War," *The European Legacy*, 19, no. 1 (2014): 1–15

Smith, Richard H. P., "Peninsular War Cartography: A New Look at the Military Mapping of General Sir George Murray and the Quartermaster General's Department," *Imago Mundi* 65, no. 2 (2013): 234–52

Smith, Steven B., "Hegel's Views on War, the State, and International Relations," *American Political Science Review* 77, no. 3 (1983): 624–32

Smith, Woodruff D., "Friedrich Ratzel and the Origins of Lebensraum," *German Studies Review* 3, no. 1 (1980): 51–68

Spruyt, Hendrik, *The Sovereign State and Its Competitors* (Princeton, NJ: Princeton University Press, 1994)

Strandsbjerg, Jeppe, *Territory, Globalization and International Relations: The Cartographic Reality of Space* (Houndsmills: Palgrave Macmillan, 2010)

Stoddart, David R. "Darwin's Impact on Geography," *Annals of the Association of American Geographers* 56, no. 4 (1966): 683–98

Suganami, Hidemi, "Understanding Sovereignty through Kelsen/Schmitt," *Review of International Studies* 33, no. 3 (2007): 511–30

Sumner, William Graham, "War" [1903], in *War and Other Essays* (New Haven, CT: Yale University Press, 1919), 3–40

Sylvest, Casper, "Interwar Internationalism, the British Labour Party, and the Historiography of International Relations," *International Studies Quarterly* 48, no. 2 (2004): 409–32

"International Law in Nineteenth-Century Britain," *British Yearbook of International Law* 75, no. 1 (2005): 9–70

British Liberal Internationalism, 1880–1930: Making Progress? (Manchester: Manchester University Press, 2009)

Tallett, Frank, and Trim, D. J. B., "'Then Was Then and Now Is Now': An Overview of Change and Continuity in Late-Medieval and Early Modern

Warfare," in Frank Tallett and D. J. B. Trim (eds.), *European Warfare 1350–1750* (Cambridge: Cambridge University Press, 2010), 1–26

Tammita-Delgoda, Asoka SinhaRaja "Nabob, Historian and Orientalist: The Life and Writings of Robert Orme (1728–1801)," Ph.D. dissertation, King's College, London, 1991

Teschke, Benno, "Fatal Attraction: A Critique of Carl Schmitt's International Political and Legal Theory," *International Theory* 3, no. 2 (2011): 179–227

Tesón, Fernando, *Humanitarian Intervention: An Inquiry into Law and Morality* (Dobbs Ferry: Transnational Publishers, 1988)

Thompson, Martyn P., "The History of Fundamental Law in Political Thought from the French Wars of Religion to the American Revolution," *American Historical Review* 91, no. 5 (1986): 1103–28

Thucydides, *The Peloponnesian War* (London: J. M. Dent, 1910)

Tilly, Charles, "Reflections on the History of European State-Making," in Charles Tilly (ed.), *The Formation of National States in Western Europe* (Princeton, NJ: Princeton University Press, 1975), 3–83

"War Making and State Making as Organized Crime," in Peter B. Evans, Dietrich Rueschemeyer, and Theda Skocpol (eds.), *Bringing the State Back In* (Cambridge: Cambridge University Press, 1985), 169–87

Coercion, Capital, and European States AD 990–1990 (Oxford: Blackwell, 1990)

Toews, John E., "The Immanent Genesis and Transcendent Goal of Law: Savigny, Stahl, and the Ideology of the Christian German State," *American Journal of Comparative Law* 37, no. 1 (1989): 139–69

Toft, Monica Duffy, "Territory and War," *Journal of Peace Research* 51, no. 2 (2014): 185–98.

Traité de Paix entre La France et La Savoye conclu à Utrecht le 11 April 1713 (Paris: Fournier, 1713)

Traité entre le Roi et le Roi de Sardaigne, conclu à Turin le 24 Mars 1760 (Paris: Imprimerie Royale, 1762)

Tuck, Richard, *Hobbes* (Oxford: Oxford University Press, 1989)

Rights of War and Peace: Political Thought and International Order from Grotius to Kant (Oxford: Oxford University Press, 1999)

Philosophy and Government 1572–1651 (Cambridge: Cambridge University Press, 1993)

Turgot, Anne-Robert-Jacques, "Plan d'un Ouvrage sur la Géographie Politique" [1751], in Gustave Schelle (ed.), *Oeuvres de Turgot* (Paris: Félix Alcan, 1913), 255–74

Turnbull, David, "Cartography and Science in Early Modern Europe: Mapping the Construction of Knowledge Spaces," *Imago Mundi* 48, no. 1 (1996): 5–24

Tyler, Colin, "Hegel, War and the Tragedy of Imperialism," *History of European Ideas* 30, no. 4 (2004): 403–31

van Creveld, Martin, *Transformation of War* (New York: Free Press, 1991)

van Munster, Rens, "The War on Terrorism: When the Exception Becomes the Rule," *International Journal for the Semiotics of Law* 17, no. 2 (2004): 141–53

Vasquez, John, *The War Puzzle* (Cambridge: Cambridge University Press, 1993)

Ventura, Comino, *Trésor Politique* (Paris: Nicolas de Fossé, 1608)

Viroli, Maurizio, *From Politics to Reason of State: The Acquisition and Transformation of the Language of Politics 1250–1600* (Cambridge: Cambridge University Press, 1992)

Virilio, Paul, *Speed and Politics* (New York: Semiotext(e), 1986)

L'Insecurité du Territoire (Paris: Galilée, 1993)

Vitruve, *Les Dix Livres d'Architecture* [reprint of the 1673 translation by Claude Perrault] (Paris: Balland, 1979)

Voltaire, *The Age of Louis XIV* [1751], vol. 12, in *The Works of Voltaire: A Contemporary Version* (New York: E.R. Dumont, 1901)

von Bernhardi, Friedrich, *Germany and the Next War*, trans. Allen H. Powles (New York: Longmans, Green, 1914)

von Clausewitz, Carl, *On War*, trans. Michael Howard and Peter Paret (Oxford: Oxford University Press, 2007)

von Hippel, Karin, *Democracy by Force: US Military Intervention in the Post–Cold War World* (Cambridge: Cambridge University Press, 2000)

von Martens, Georg Friedrich, *A Compendium of the Law of Nations Founded on the Treatises and Customs of the Modern Nations of Europe*, trans. William Cobbett (London: Cobbett & Morgan, 1802)

Nouveaux Supplémens au Receuil de Traités (Göttingen: Dietrich, 1839)

von Pufendorf, Samuel, *The Compleat History of Sweden from Its Origin to This Time* (London: Wild, 1702)

Introduction to the History of the Principal Kingdoms and States in Europe (London: Peele, 1719)

Of the Law of Nature and Nations, trans. Basil Kennet (London, 1749)

von Ranke, Leopold, "The Great Powers," trans. Theodore von Laue, in Theodore von Laue (ed.), *Leopold Ranke: The Formative Years* (Princeton, NJ: Princeton University Press, 1950), 181–218

von Savigny, Freidrich Karl, *Vom Beruf unserer Zeit für Gesetzgebung und Rechtswissenschaft [1814]*, *Of the Vocation of Our Age for Legislation and Jurisprudence*, trans. Abraham Hayward (London: Littlewood & Co, 1831)

Wagner, Andreas, "Francisco de Vitoria and Alberico Gentili on the Legal Character of the Global Commonwealth," *Oxford Journal of Legal Studies* 31, no. 3 (2011): 565–82

Wagner, Moritz, *The Darwinian Theory and the Law of the Migration of Organisms*, trans. James L. Laird (London: Edward Stanford, 1873)

Wagner, R. Harrison, *War and the State: The Theory of International Politics* (Ann Arbor: University of Michigan Press, 2007)

Waldron, Jeremy, "Hobbes and the Principle of Publicity," *Pacific Philosophical Quarterly* 82, nos. 3–4 (2001): 447–74

Walter, Ryan, "The Analysis of Interest and the History of Economic Thought," *Parergon* 28, no. 2 (2011): 129–47

Waltz, Kenneth N., *Man, the State, and War: A Theoretical Analysis* (New York: Columbia University Press, 1959)

   Theory of International Politics (Reading, MA: Addison Wesley, 1979)

Walzer, Michael, *The Revolution of the Saints: A Study in the Origins of Radical Politics* (Cambridge, MA: Harvard University Press, 1965)

   Just and Unjust Wars: A Moral Argument with Historical Illustrations (New York: Basic Books, 1977)

Ward, Lester F., *Pure Sociology: A Treatise on the Origin and Spontaneous Development of Society* [1903] (New York: Macmillan, 1916)

Weber, Cynthia, *Simulating Sovereignty: Intervention, the State and Symbolic Exchange* (Cambridge: Cambridge University Press, 1994)

Weber, Max, "The Profession and Vocation of Politics," in Peter Lassman and Ronald Spiers (eds.), *Max Weber: Political Writings* (Cambridge: Cambridge University Press, 1994), 309–69

Weigel, Georg, "The Just War Tradition and the World after September 11," *Logos* 5, no. 3 (2003): 13–44

Weikart, Richard, "Progress through Racial Extermination: Social Darwinism, Eugenics, and Pacifism in Germany, 1860–1918," *German Studies Review* 26, no. 2 (2003): 273–94

   From Darwin to Hitler: Evolutionary Ethics, Eugenics, and Racism in Germany (New York: Palgrave Macmillan, 2004)

Werner, Wouter G, "From Justus Hostis to Rogue State the Concept of the Enemy in International Legal Thinking," *International Journal for the Semiotics of Law* 17, no. 2 (2004): 155–68

Westlake, John, *Chapters on the Principles of International Law* (Cambridge: Cambridge University Press, 1894)

Whatmore, Richard, *Against War and Empire: Geneva, Britain and France in the Eighteenth Century* (New Haven, CT: Yale University Press, 2012)

Wheaton, Henry, *Elements of International Law* (London: Sampson Low, Son & Co, 1864)

Wheeler, Nicholas, *Saving Strangers: Humanitarian Intervention in International Society* (Oxford: Oxford University Press, 2000).

Whelan, Frederick G., "Robertson, Hume, and the Balance of Power," *Hume Studies* 21, no. 2 (1995): 315–32.

Whewell, William, *The Elements of Morality, Including Polity* (London: John W. Parker, 1845)

White, Lynn, "Jacopo Aconcio as an Engineer," *American Historical Review* 72, no. 2 (1967): 425–44

Wicquefort, Abraham de, *Histoire de Provinces-Unies des Pais-Bas* (La Haye: Johnson 1719)

Widmalm, Sven, "Accuracy, Rhetoric, and Technology: The Paris-Greenwich Triangulation, 1784–88," in Tore Frängsmyr and John L. Heilbron (eds.), *The Quantifying Spirit in the 18th Century* (Berkeley: University of California Press, 1990), 179–206

Wight, Martin, "Why Is There No International Theory?," *International Relations* 2, no. 1 (1960): 35–48

International Theory: The Three Traditions, ed. Gabriele Wight and Brian Porter (Leicester: Leicester University Press, 1991)

Wildman, Richard, *Institutes of International Law* (London: William Benning & Co, 1849)

Winch, Peter, *The Idea of a Social Science and Its Relation to Philosophy* (London: Routledge, 1958)

Withers, Charles W. J., *Placing the Enlightenment: Thinking Geographically about the Age of Reason* (Chicago: University of Chicago Press, 2007)

Yack, Bernhard, "Popular Sovereignty and Nationalism," *Political Theory*, 29 no. 4 (2001): 517–36

Zacher, Mark W., "The Territorial Integrity Norm: International Boundaries and the Use of Force," *International Organization* 55, no. 2 (2001): 215–50

Zarakol, Ayşe, "What Makes Terrorism Modern? Terrorism, Legitimacy, and the International System," *Review of International Studies* 37, no. 5 (2011): 2311–36

Zeller, Gaston, *L'organisation défensive des frontières du Nord et de l'Est au XVIIe siècle: avec une carte hors texte* (Paris: Berger-Levrault, 1928)

Zimmern, Alfred, "German Culture and the British Commonwealth," in *Nationality and Government with Other War-Time Essays* (London: Chatto & Windus, 1918), 1–31

Zolo, Danilo, *Invoking Humanity: War, Law and Global Order* (New York: Bloomsbury Publishing, 2002).

Zouche, Richard, *An Exposition of Fecial Law and Procedure, or of Law between Nations, and Questions Concerning the Same*, trans. J. L. Brierly (Washington, DC: Carnegie Endowment for International Peace, 1911)

Index